Attacking Faulty Reasoning

A Practical Guide to Fallacy-Free Arguments

Third Edition

OTHER CRITICAL THINKING TITLES FROM WADSWORTH

Cederblom/Paulsen, *Critical Reasoning: Understanding and Criticizing Arguments and Theories,* Third Edition

Conway/Munson, *The Elements of Reasoning*

Dowden, *Logical Reasoning*

Govier, *A Practical Study of Argument,* Third Edition

Govier, *Selected Issues in Logic and Communication*

Gray, *Thinking Critically About New Age Ideas*

Hinderer, *Building Arguments*

Kahane, *Logic and Contemporary Rhetoric,* Seventh Edition

Mayfield, *Thinking For Yourself,* Third Edition

Seech, *Open Minds and Everyday Reasoning*

Attacking Faulty Reasoning

A Practical Guide to Fallacy-Free Arguments

Third Edition

T. Edward Damer
EMORY & HENRY COLLEGE

Wadsworth Publishing Company
Belmont, California
A Division of Wadsworth, Inc.

Consulting Editor: Joel Feinberg
Philosophy Editor: Tammy Goldfeld
Editorial Assistant: Kelly Zavislak
Production Editors: Julie Davis and Cathy Linberg
Managing Designer: Cloyce Wall
Print Buyer: Karen Hunt
Designer: Janet Wood
Copy Editor: Melissa Andrews
Cover: Craig Hanson
Compositor: Steven Bolinger, Wadsworth Digital Productions
Printer: Malloy Lithographing, Inc.

International Thomson Publishing
The trademark ITP is used under license.

Printed in the United States of America

1 2 3 4 5 6 7 8 9 10—99 98 97 96 95

Library of Congress Cataloging-in-Publication Data
Damer, T. Edward
    Attacking faulty reasoning: a practical guide to fallacy-free arguments /
T. Edward Damer.—3rd ed.
        p.   cm.
    Includes bibliographical references and index.
    ISBN 0-534-21750-8
    1. Fallacies (Logic)   2. Reasoning.   I. Title.
BC175.D35   1994
165–dc20   94-15081

For Nancy Jean

Contents

PREFACE   xi

INTRODUCTION   1

I. WHAT IS AN ARGUMENT?   4

An Argument Is a Claim Supported by Other Claims   4
Distinguishing Argument from Opinion   5
The Standard Form of an Argument   5
The Principle of Charity   6
The Burden of Proof   7
Deductive Versus Inductive Strength of Arguments   8
Moral Arguments   9

II. WHAT IS A GOOD ARGUMENT?   12

A Good Argument Must Meet Four Criteria   12
The Relevance Criterion   12
The Acceptability Criterion   13
The Sufficient Grounds Criterion   15
The Rebuttal Criterion   16
Making Arguments Stronger   17
Applying the Criteria to Arguments   17
Constructing Good Arguments   22

III. WHAT IS A FALLACY? 24

A Fallacy Violates a Criterion of a Good Argument 24
Named Versus Unnamed Fallacies 25
Organization of the Fallacies 26
Attacking the Fallacy 26
Rules of the Game 29

IV. FALLACIES THAT VIOLATE THE RELEVANCE CRITERION 31

Fallacies of Irrelevance 31
  Irrelevant or Questionable Authority 31
  Appeal to Common Opinion 34
  Genetic Fallacy 36
  Rationalization 37
  Drawing the Wrong Conclusion 38
  Using the Wrong Reasons 40
  Exercises 43
Irrelevant Emotional Appeals 44
  Appeal to Pity 44
  Appeal to Force or Threat 47
  Appeal to Tradition 48
  Appeal to Personal Circumstances or Motives 50
  Exploitation of Strong Feelings and Attitudes 51
  Use of Flattery 53
  Assigning Guilt by Association 54
  Exercises 56
  Additional Exercises 58

V. FALLACIES THAT VIOLATE THE ACCEPTABILITY CRITERION 61

Fallacies of Linguistic Confusion 62
  Equivocation 62
  Ambiguity 64
  Improper Accent 67
  Illicit Contrast 69
  Argument by Innuendo 70
  Misuse of a Vague Expression 72
  Distinction Without a Difference 74
  Exercises 76
Begging-the-Question Fallacies 77
  Arguing in a Circle 77
  Question-Begging Language 80
  Loaded or Complex Question 81
  Leading Question 83
  Question-Begging Definition 84
  Exercises 86

Unwarranted Assumption Fallacies   88
    Fallacy of the Continuum   88
    Fallacy of Composition   90
    Fallacy of Division   92
    False Alternatives   93
    Is-Ought Fallacy   95
    Wishful Thinking   96
    Misuse of a General Principle   98
    Fallacy of the Golden Mean   99
    Faulty Analogy   101
    Fallacy of Novelty   103
    Exercises   104
    Additional Exercises   106

VI. FALLACIES THAT VIOLATE THE
    SUFFICIENT GROUNDS CRITERION   109

Fallacies of Missing Evidence   109
    Insufficient Sample   109
    Unrepresentative Data   111
    Arguing from Ignorance   113
    Contrary-to-Fact Hypothesis   116
    Improper Use of a Cliché   118
    Inference from a Label   119
    Fallacy of Fake Precision   120
    Special Pleading   122
    Omission of Key Evidence   124
    Exercises   126
Causal Fallacies   128
    Confusion of a Necessary with a Sufficient Condition   128
    Causal Oversimplification   129
    Post Hoc Fallacy   131
    Confusion of Cause and Effect   132
    Neglect of a Common Cause   134
    Domino Fallacy   135
    Gambler's Fallacy   137
    Exercises   138
    Additional Exercises   140

VII. FALLACIES THAT VIOLATE THE REBUTTAL CRITERION   144

Fallacies of Counterevidence   145
    Denying the Counterevidence   145
    Ignoring the Counterevidence   147
    Exercises   149
Ad Hominem Fallacies   150
    Abusive *Ad Hominem*   150

Poisoning the Well   153
"You Do It, Too" Argument   154
Exercises   156
Fallacies of Diversion   157
Attacking a Straw Man   157
Trivial Objections   159
Red Herring   161
Resort to Humor or Ridicule   163
Exercises   164
Additional Exercises   166

VIII. A CODE OF CONDUCT FOR EFFECTIVE RATIONAL DISCUSSION   172

The Fallibility Principle   173
The Truth-Seeking Principle   175
The Burden of Proof Principle   176
The Principle of Charity   177
The Clarity Principle   178
The Relevance Principle   179
The Acceptability Principle   180
The Sufficient Grounds Principle   181
The Rebuttal Principle   182
The Resolution Principle   183
The Suspension of Judgment Principle   185
The Reconsideration Principle   185

GLOSSARY OF FALLACIES   187

ANSWERS TO EXERCISES   193

INDEX   197

Preface

This text is single-minded in its focus. It is designed to help students construct and evaluate arguments. More specifically, its purpose is to help students recognize when they have constructed or encountered a good or successful argument for a particular action or belief. This skill is reinforced in every section, beginning with the first three chapters that focus on the criteria for a good argument, through each of the four major chapters on specific fallacies.

One of the most difficult things to learn in critical thinking courses is how to determine when one should conclude a debate or discussion and make a decision about what to do or believe. This is a matter of recognizing when an argument is good enough for a reasonable person to embrace its conclusion. This book outlines a simple and effective method for doing that by means of the four basic criteria of a good argument. These criteria also provide the basis for a theory of fallacy.

A fallacy is defined as a violation of one or more of the four criteria of a good argument. While most treatments of fallacies simply list fallacies as things not to do, with no theory of fallacy provided or understood, this approach is different. Fallacies are categorized by the criterion they violate. The four criteria are: (1) Relevance of the argument's premises, (2) acceptability of the argument's premises, (3) sufficiency of the premises to support the conclusion of the argument, and (4) an effective rebuttal of the strongest arguments against one's argument or the position it represents.

By its careful treatment of the criteria of a good argument, this book helps the reader to recognize when the argument is a successful one. The approach is so clear and uncomplicated, that the reader should come away from th study of the text with a well-developed, life-long skill in assessing and formulating arguments.

NEW FEATURES IN THE THIRD EDITION

1. The first chapter from the second edition is divided into three chapters and organized to explain the following: What is an argument? (Chapter I), What is a good argument? (Chapter II), and What is a fallacy? (Chapter III).

2. The second chapter now has a major "application" section in which the four criteria of a good argument are applied to the arguments in four sample letters to the editor.

3. The material on specific fallacies in Chapters IV–VII is now organized in terms of the four criteria of a good argument.

4. The number of exercises in Chapters IV–VII has increased from 160 to 350.

5. The examples are updated, and most of them deal with current controversial issues.

6. A new chapter, Chapter VIII, summarizes the material of the text into a "Code of Conduct" specifying twelve basic principles to guide the student to become an effective and fair participant in rational discussion.

7. The chapter in earlier editions dealing with syllogistic and other deductive fallacies is omitted.

8. A much expanded section on moral arguments is added to Chapter I, and a new section on strengthening arguments is included in Chapter III.

9. Virtually all commentaries and Attacking the Fallacy sections are expanded or altered in some way. A number of definitions of fallacies are revised or renamed.

10. The Glossary of Fallacies now includes page references to allow the student to easily find and review the commentaries on and examples of particular fallacies.

ORGANIZATION OF THE TEXT

The 60 fallacies treated in the book are organized in Chapters IV, V, VI, and VII by the criterion violated, with one chapter for each criterion. The specific fallacies treated in each chapter are ways that criterion is commonly violated. Commentary on each fallacy shows exactly how the fallacy violates the criterion.

Each fallacy is well-defined—in most cases with a single sentence—followed by extensive commentary. At the end of the text, the Glossary of Fallacies brings all the definitions together in one place for easy reference. The Glossary is one of the most valuable features of the book.

Several examples follow the commentary on each fallacy. Unlike many other textbooks, these examples are realistic and practical. All of them are about real issues or common situations. The subject matter is usually as current as the most recent newspaper editorial or letter to the editor.

Following the treatment of each fallacy, is a unique Attacking the Fallacy section, which makes specific suggestions for dealing constructively with particular fallacious arguments when we encounter them. Here, as is the case throughout the book, the emphasis is more on resolving issues than on pointing out flaws in arguments.

There are usually 20 exercises at the end of each section in the chapter. These give the student considerable practice in identifying fallacious pieces of reasoning. At the end of each of the four main chapters on fallacies are additional cumulative exercises. These cumulative exercises provide a systematic review of all previously covered material. In each exercise, the reader is asked not only to identify the fallacy by name, but also to explain how the specific piece of reasoning commits that fallacy.

The last chapter summarizes the insights and suggestions scattered throughout the text into 12 distinct principles or guides for participants in rational discussion. This is another very valuable feature of the text for it represents everything a person needs to know to engage responsibly in the evaluation and construction of arguments and to participate fairly and effectively in a rational discussion of controversial issues.

USE OF THE TEXT

Students will be able to read and absorb the material on the specific fallacies in Chapters IV–VII with very little assistance. The material in the first three chapters and in Chapter VIII may require more discussion.

I have found that the material in this text is most effective when used in critical thinking or informal logic courses. The students in my own course are asked to bring examples of reasoning from current magazines, newspaper editorials, letters to the editor in newspapers and magazines, speeches, lectures, conversations, and advertisements. Class time is spent assessing the merit of these student-submitted arguments by applying the four criteria discussed in the first three chapters and identifying specific argument flaws discussed in the other chapters. We also spend a considerable amount of time attempting either to strengthen the argument or to devise a better argument for an alternative view. Students also construct their own arguments to support a position on a current controversial issue. These are also evaluated by all class members according to the four criteria.

ACKNOWLEDGMENTS

Several people have been especially helpful in the preparation of this third edition. My colleague in philosophy at Emory & Henry College, Ben Letson, read parts of the manuscript and made many good suggestions. Lawrence Habermehl, of American International College, read the entire manuscript, as he did for the first two editions, and discovered a number of confusions, which he was most willing to help me resolve. My wife, Nancy Jean Bradford, again assisted me in the refinement of many of the ideas in this new edition.

I also wish to thank the following prerevision reviewers who provided very helpful comments and suggestions: Ronald G. Aichele, University of Southern Colorado, David Benfield, Montclair State College, Cynthia D. Gobatie, Riverside Community College, Robert G. Pielke, El Camino College, and David Rhea, Bakersfield College.

I am very thankful to the staff at Wadsworth Publishing Company for their friendly and highly professional guidance with this project. The philosophy editor, Tammy Goldfeld, and production editors Cathy Linberg and Julie Davis, were especially helpful.

Finally, I wish to thank my students for contributing many of the examples found in the text. Two of my students, David Graybeal and Clint Vranian, who had used the second edition of this book read the manuscript for this edition and suggested a number of ways to make some of the ideas clearer. I am also grateful to Emory & Henry College for granting me the sabbatical that provided the time to work on this new edition.

T. Edward Damer

Introduction

It has been my experience that few people are really interested in the study of logic, because, as Charles Peirce suggested, "Everybody conceives himself to be proficient enough in the art of reasoning already."[1] It is interesting to note, however, that those who are "proficient" rarely recognize in others a similar proficiency. Few arguments other than one's own are regarded as genuinely good ones, and it is sincerely believed that what the rest of the world needs is "to study a little logic."

Those who make the effort to study "a little logic" will no doubt improve their ability to think correctly and to express that thinking more clearly. One of the current terms for such activity is *critical thinking*. One philosopher has defined critical thinking as "reasonable reflective thinking that is focused on deciding what to believe or do."[2] To do such reflective thinking, students of logic need to learn not only the techniques of distinguishing bad arguments from good ones, but also how to *construct* good arguments.

There are a number of practical reasons why it is important to formulate quality arguments and to expect others to do the same. First, and most important, good arguments help us to make better personal decisions. Indeed, there is reason to believe that those who use rational criteria in all aspects of their lives have a better chance of success in achieving their goals or completing their projects.

---

[1] Charles Sanders Peirce, "The Fixation of Belief," in *Collected Papers of Charles Sanders Peirce*, (ed.) Charles Hartshorne and Paul Weiss (Cambridge, MA: The Belknap Press of Harvard University Press, 1934), Vol. 223.

[2] Robert H. Ennis, "Goals for a Critical Thinking/Reasoning Curriculum," working paper, February 5, 1985, University of Illinois, Urbana/Champaign.

Second, good arguments promote our general interest in holding only those views that we have reason to believe are true or defensible ones. If we demand good arguments of ourselves, that demand will lead us to new and better ideas, reinforce the strength of our present beliefs, and expose weaknesses that might lead to qualification or abandonment of those beliefs.

Third, the use of arguments raises the level of thinking and discussion in social, business, and personal contexts. Good arguments are usually more effective in trying to convince others of a point of view than are methods such as fear, intimidation, social pressure, or emotional bribery. At least they have a more permanent effect.

Fourth, the method of argument is a nonviolent way to resolve personal disputes or to settle conflicts.

Fifth, by examining an opponent's arguments, one is better able to understand his or her ideas and thinking processes and to discover weaknesses that make that arguer's position more vulnerable to attack.

Finally, good arguments play an important role in helping us to make difficult moral deciscions. Not only do they help us to decide what positive action to take but also to avoid actions with harmful results. False beliefs, to which fallacious arguments sometimes lead, blur our moral vision and often issue actions that cause considerable harm to others. Since each of us is responsible for the consequences of our actions, it is important that we base our beliefs and decisions on the conclusions of *good* arguments.

If good or fallacy-free arguments are so important, then why should one spend time studying *fallacious* reasoning, or, more specifically, the fallacies in this book? One should study these fallacies because the ability to discriminate between fallacious and nonfallacious patterns of reasoning is a necessary condition for good reasoning. A person cannot construct good arguments if he or she does not know the difference between a good one and a bad one.

The primary purpose of this book, then, is to assist students in becoming better thinkers by giving attention to some of the most common errors in our ordinary ways of thinking. However, because little constructive purpose is served by simply learning to identify errors, it is my hope that the skills that may be developed in recognizing *bad* reasoning may help to generate habits of *good* reasoning. In other words, focusing attention on errors should help others to construct good or fallacy-free arguments.

A second purpose of this book is to suggest some concrete ways of challenging the faulty reasoning of others. If one is conscientious in this task, it is usually possible to confront one's verbal opponents with their faulty reasoning without creating any ill feeling. It can even be done in a way that will move a debate beyond the question of who has committed the worst fallacy to the question of what can be reasonably concluded or believed. The strategies that are suggested for each fallacy in the "Attacking the Fallacy" sections are designed to get reasoning back on the right track, that is, to turn faulty reasoning into good reasoning. Indeed, they are designed to assist faulty arguers in doing what they allegedly wish to do—to effectively demonstrate the truth of a claim or the rightness of an action.

The strategies found in this book may also help to alleviate another problem often created by faulty reasoning—the feeling of helplessness often experienced when one is the *target* of fallacious reasoning. This experience often results from simply not knowing any effective way to deal with the error in question. Familiarity with some of the most common errors in reasoning is a defense against being misled or victimized by others. Moreover, the suggestions accompanying the treatment of each fallacy will assist one in gaining control of such situations by not only exposing the error, but also redirecting the line of reasoning toward more constructive ends.

One of the main goals of an education is to develop the ability to discover and to defend reliable ideas about ourselves and our world. A careful study of this practical guide to fallacy-free arguments should be of help in accomplishing that aim. And because it is likely that the book will expose some of the careless and defective ways that you yourself have examined and/or defended ideas in the past, you may soon come to believe that not only the rest of the world, but you too, may need "to study a little logic."

I
What Is an Argument?

AN ARGUMENT IS A CLAIM SUPPORTED BY OTHER CLAIMS

The kind of faulty reasoning that we will be concerned about in this book is that which is found in arguments. By *argument*, of course, I am not referring to a bitter controversy or heated disagreement. I have in mind the use of statements that one already believes to be true as reasons for the truth or acceptability of another statement. An *argument*, then, is a group of statements, one or more of which (the *premises*) support or provide evidence for another (the *conclusion*). If a claim or position is being set forth and no other explicit or implicit statement is used to support it, then the spoken or written material in question is not an argument. It may express an opinion or take a position on an issue, but it is not an argument unless that opinion or position is defended with at least one reason, a piece of evidence, or some statement of support. An argument, by definition, is aimed at the goal of *demonstrating* the truth or falsity of a particular claim, by presenting evidence that may convince the hearer or reader to accept it.

One of the most difficult tasks in evaluating arguments is the first one—that of identifying which of several statements in a piece of writing or discourse is the conclusion. *The conclusion of an argument should be the statement or claim that has at least one other statement in support of it.* The conclusion of an argument should not be confused with the main point in the material being examined. Many editorials and letters to the editor, for example, have a point to make, but frequently are not arguments at all. No reasons are given for the position taken, so there is no conclusion. The letter or editorial is simply a series of unsupported claims or points. If you are uncertain about whether there is a conclusion lurking about, look for a statement that is supported by at least one other statement. That claim is likely to be the conclusion.

In a long argument, there may be more than one such supported statement. If so, it may be that some support is being given to one or more of the argument's premises. To find the conclusion of the *argument*, it will be necessary to determine which supported statement also seems to be the primary thesis being defended in the passage. It is possible, of course, that there is more than one argument being presented. If that is the case, you should treat each argument separately.

DISTINGUISHING ARGUMENT FROM OPINION

The expression of personal opinion is one of the most common forms of verbal exchange; and since reasons for our opinions are often not requested, we become unaccustomed to defending them and are even lulled into thinking that reasons are not required. Everyone is entitled to his or her own opinion, we say. That is true, but if an opinion is not accompanied by reasons in support of it, it is difficult to determine whether it deserves our acceptance.

Most people usually have difficulty understanding the difference between an argument and the expression of a personal belief or opinion. They often use the words *argument* and *opinion* interchangeably. If I ask students for an argument that shows how the evidence leads them to a particular position on an issue, they often set forth their *opinion* about that issue rather than an argument. Even when they do formulate an argument, they sometimes also express their *opinion* about the issue—an opinion that is often at odds with the conclusion of their own argument. But the very word *conclusion* suggests that it is an opinion or judgment resulting from some process of rational reflection on the evidence. The only opinion (belief, claim, thesis, position) that deserves acceptance is one that can be defended by a good argument.

Even though most people listen to the authority of their own opinions, *the only good authority is the authority of a good argument*. Most of us enjoy exchanging our opinions with others, but rarely do our opinions change unless arguments are presented. And since some of our opinions are in conflict with each other and with the opinions of others, it is obvious that there are some opinions that need to be changed. For example, if there are two opposing opinions about some matter, probably only one of those opinions merits acceptance. If the views happen to *contradict* each other, only one of them can be true, for we know that contradictory claims cannot both be true. But *which* one is true? That question can be answered only by looking at the quality of the argument presented in behalf of each view.

THE STANDARD FORM OF AN ARGUMENT

After the conclusion of an argument has been identified, the next step is to reconstruct the argument into what is called a *standard form*. Whether this is done mentally or in writing, it is a crucial step in the process of evaluating effectively the quality of the argument.

When extracting an argument from written or spoken material, a standard format that will exhibit the logical structure of the argument is as follows:

Since (premise),

and (premise),

and (premise),

Therefore, (conclusion).

One will seldom encounter an argument in so clear a form, but any argument can be reconstructed in this manner by an orderly separation of the premises from the conclusion. Argument indicator words like *since* and *therefore* may vary, of course, from argument to argument. Moreover, the number of premises may vary from one to as many as is thought to be necessary to establish the truth of the conclusion. One will also find that a statement of support, and sometimes even the conclusion, is often unstated but understood from the context. These missing parts should be carefully "spelled out" when the argument is put into standard form.

The premises of an argument are those statements that together constitute the grounds for affirming the conclusion. They are of many types. Some premises are conclusions of previous arguments, while others may be definitions, principles, or rules that are supportive of or relevant to the truth of the conclusion. Statements of fact, personal observation, expert testimony, or common knowledge may also be used to support a particular conclusion.

If the premises of an argument are adequate to establish the argument's conclusion, we are logically required to accept it. If they do not adequately support the conclusion, we should not accept it, or we should at least suspend judgment about it. Our refusal to accept the conclusion of a particular argument does not necessarily mean that we think it false. It might simply mean that we do not think that we are *justified* in believing it to be true, based on the argument presented. If we could find a better argument to support it, it might very well be a justifiable conclusion.

THE PRINCIPLE OF CHARITY

In reconstructing an argument into standard form, one should supply any missing parts, if they are implicitly present. The so-called *Principle of Charity* requires that an opponent's argument always be formulated in its strongest possible version. This includes supplying any missing elements—but only those that are regarded as part of the original intention of the arguer. One should not try to improve the argument by supplying premises that are neither explicitly nor implicitly present.

One may and should improve the argument by eliminating any obviously irrelevant clutter and messy language found in the original argument. Cleaning up the argument by restating it in its most economical form can also save time in the evaluation process. Where there is some question about whether an argument should be construed in what is probably a stronger version, the Principle of Charity suggests that the arguer be given the benefit of any doubt.

Using this principle will also probably prevent haggling with an opponent over what he or she was really saying. Besides, if the argument is attacked in a weaker form, it can always be subsequently amended by an opponent to conform to the stronger version. Ultimately, then, one will still have to address the stronger form.

Once the strongest version of an opponent's argument has been put into standard form, with all extraneous material cleared away, its faulty character may be quite transparent. Indeed, the defects may be so obvious that the opponent might even accuse you of distorting his or her argument. To help avoid such a charge, it is very important that you be as careful as possible in the reconstruction. You might even ask the arguer to confirm the correctness of your work before you call attention to any flaw.

If the argument's defects are clearly exposed by putting it into standard form, your opponent may be inclined to start amending it right away in order to turn it into a better argument. If you are feeling especially charitable, you might even want to lend a helpful hand to the process. After all, any improvement in the general quality of human reasoning must be regarded as a positive step forward.

THE BURDEN OF PROOF

Who has the responsibility to provide an argument for a disputed claim? Since a person is generally held accountable for his or her own actions, one who makes a positive or negative claim about something has what is called the *burden of proof*. In many cases, of course, one does not have to supply such proof, for we are not always called on to defend our claims. But if the claimant is asked "Why?" or "How do you know that is true?" he or she is logically obligated to produce reasons in behalf of the claim. An exception to this rule is a situation in which the claim in question is well established or noncontroversial. In such a case, the burden of proof might rest on the one who wishes to challenge that claim.

If one had to defend not only the basic claim but also each of the premises, each of the statements in support of the premises, and each of the statements in support of the statements of support, there would be an infinite chain of proofs—an obviously impractical task. But one at least has the responsibility to provide evidence for the main thesis and for any questionable premise, if asked to do so.

This is as it should be. Indeed, we follow this procedure in our basic social institutions. If a pharmaceutical firm wishes to market a new drug, it has the burden of proving to the Food and Drug Administration that the drug is safe and effective. Our legal system places the burden of proof in a criminal case on the one who does the accusing, the prosecutor. We would not permit either the drug manufacturer or the prosecutor to get by with simply expressing an opinion on the matter at issue. Neither should we allow others to get by without defending their opinions, especially about important or controversial issues.

DEDUCTIVE VERSUS INDUCTIVE STRENGTH OF ARGUMENTS

Arguments have traditionally been divided into two categories: deductive arguments and inductive arguments. Although we do not find it especially useful to call attention to this distinction throughout the text, it should at least be pointed out that the category to which an argument may belong suggests something important about its relative strength. An understanding of what gives deductive arguments their greater power should also provide an additional tool to use as part of our argument-strengthening strategy.

A correctly formed deductive argument is one whose form is such that the conclusion follows with logical necessity or certainty from the premises. In other words, if the premises are true, the conclusion must also be true.[3] For example:

Since all senators in the U.S. Senate are at least 35 years old,

and Joseph Winters is a U.S. senator,

Therefore, Joseph Winters is 35 years or older.

The conclusion of this or any deductive argument simply spells out what is already implicit in the premises. If one can get the reader or hearer to accept the crucial premises, which already include the conclusion, then the arguer's work is done. The argument is indeed so strong that its conclusion cannot be denied.

A very effective strategy that is sometimes employed in argumentation is that of constructing an argument in such a way that the conclusion is, in effect, accepted when the crucial premise is accepted. One would then have a foolproof argument for one's claim. Moral arguments are often presented in this deductive form. Consider the following example:

Since sexist practices are wrong,

and the use of male-dominated language is a sexist practice or tradition,

Therefore, the use of male-dominated language is wrong.

If the arguer can get his or her opponent to accept the first premise, there is little likelihood that the conclusion can be denied. This is not to say that there cannot be any disagreement about the factual claim made in the second premise, or even that there cannot be any confusion about the meaning of *sexism*. The point is that the crucial and most controversial premise here is most likely to be the first one, and if it is accepted, the deal, in effect, is closed.

An *inductive* argument is one in which the premises provide *some* evidence for the truth of the conclusion. However, the conclusion of an inductive argument does not follow with logical necessity or certainty from the premises, even if all the

---

[3] Another way of describing the relationship between the premises and the conclusion of a valid (or correctly formed) deductive argument would be to say that it is impossible for such an argument to have true premises and a false conclusion. One could not accept the premises and deny the conclusion without contradicting oneself.

premises are true, because the conclusion is not already contained in any of its premises. Therefore, in contrast to a deductive argument, the truth or acceptance of relevant premises in an inductive argument does not force or guarantee the truth of its conclusion. For example:

> Since Joseph Winters is the most popular Democrat in the Senate,
>
> and he is personally very charming and articulate,
>
> and he has moved to a politically moderate position on most issues,
>
> and he always easily wins re-election to his Senate seat,
>
> and he is in great demand on the speaking circuit,
>
> and he is often mentioned by prominent journalists and other Democrats as a possible presidential candidate,
>
> ---
>
> Therefore, Senator Joseph Winters will be chosen by the Democrats as their next presidential candidate.

The conclusion of this or any inductive argument is at best only probable, not certain, because the conclusion makes a claim that *goes beyond* the evidence provided in the premises. It is quite possible that an inductive argument might fail to take into account crucial information that would be relevant to the truth of the conclusion. For example, if Senator Winters is uncertain or even negative about running for the presidency, that fact could obviously affect the truth of the argument's conclusion.

Most of the arguments that we encounter in our everyday world will be inductive arguments. For that reason, most of them will not exhibit the force of deductive arguments. Nevertheless, it is sometimes possible to reformulate an inductive argument in such a way that it takes on the form and the power of a deductive one. If one uses a premise that is likely to be accepted that implicitly contains the conclusion, acceptance of the conclusion is virtually guaranteed.

Since we are interested in learning to evaluate and construct arguments in ordinary situations, most of the arguments treated in this book are of the inductive type. However, many of the same argumentative errors found in these arguments can also be found in deductive arguments.

MORAL ARGUMENTS

Moral issues are sometimes thought to present a special problem for critical thinkers and other logicians, since many participants in moral discussion assume that disputes involving moral issues cannot be settled by argument. Moral views are mere personal opinions, they contend, and there is no way to say that one opinion is any better than another. We reject this assumption, for we believe that moral and even aesthetic claims should be treated like any other kind of claim. Indeed, if this were not so, there would be very little for many of us to discuss, for moral issues engage our most serious intellectual interest and activity.

Some moral claims are indeed rightly categorized as mere opinions—those not defended with any relevant evidence. But this feature of discourse is not unique to moral discussion. We also hear mere opinions expressed, for example, about historical or scientific matters. However, an opinion ceases to be a mere opinion, whatever the subject matter, whenever it is the conclusion of an argument.

A moral argument can be reconstructed into standard form like any other kind of argument, and then the relevant question becomes that of determining whether the conclusion is worthy of our acceptance. That question, as we have said, can be answered only by looking at the quality of the argument in support of it.

The parts of a moral argument are very much like those of any other kind of argument. For example, factual and definitional premises, which form a part of most arguments in other areas, are important features of moral arguments as well. A properly constructed moral argument, however, has at least one essential feature not found in nonmoral arguments. A moral argument has a *moral premise*. A moral premise is usually expressed with the help of moral words like *ought, should, right, wrong, good, bad, moral,* or *immoral*. Examples of moral premises would be "One *should* treat other people with respect" and "It is *wrong* to discriminate against a person on the basis of gender."

A moral premise provides a general principle, rule, or standard for behavior from which a particular moral conclusion can be drawn. In other words, it provides a warrant to move the argument forward to a particular moral judgment. Without such a moral principle, no moral conclusion can be drawn; for it is not logically sound to move in an argument from a factual claim, a so-called "is," to a moral claim, a so-called "ought." To do so is to commit the well-known "is-ought" fallacy. The only possible moves are from factual claims to factual claims, a feature of most arguments, or from moral claims to moral claims, the unique feature of moral arguments.

A moral argument, then, moves from a moral premise, along with other premises, to a moral judgment or conclusion. This means that when constructing or evaluating moral arguments, one should always keep in mind that a moral claim about a particular action or policy that is part of an argument's conclusion must be based on a more general moral principle that is one of the argument's premises. If the principle is a controversial one or one not likely to be accepted by those to whom the argument is addressed, the arguer will need to supply good reasons in support of it. The arguer will also probably need to show why the principle or rule would apply in the present case. For example, if someone argued that it would be *wrong* for a student to study from an "advance" copy of a logic exam, one of the premises would have to be some more general moral claim like "cheating is wrong." To make that premise a relevant one, the argument should also include a premise that would show the connection between cheating and studying from an "advance" copy of the exam. The argument might be standardized as follows:

Since cheating is wrong (general moral principle),

and studying from an "advance" copy of a logic exam is a form of cheating (connection between the principle and the act in question),

---

Therefore, studying from an "advance" copy of a logic exam is wrong.

Notice that this argument has the form and strength of a deductive argument. If one accepts the premises, one cannot rationally deny the conclusion.

Many people think that moral arguments are by their very nature weak and unconvincing to those to whom they are directed. While it is true that moral arguments are often among the worst that we encounter, that does not have to be the case. If an argument's moral premise is adequately defended and clearly expressed, and especially if the argument is presented in the more powerful deductive form illustrated previously, moral arguments can be among the very strongest of arguments.

Unfortunately, in our own moral arguments and in those of others, the crucial moral premise is usually not clearly or explicitly stated. If we follow the principle of charity in our reconstruction of moral arguments, we should, of course, acknowledge any implicit moral premise and then attempt to spell it out clearly as part of the argument.

Making implicit premises explicit serves several important purposes in moral argumentation. Seeing exactly what principles are being employed will perhaps help us to explain and understand the precise nature of our moral disagreements. It is also more likely that the moral premise, once articulated, will trigger reflection about possible exceptions to and conflicts with other relevant moral principles, which may go a long way toward helping us to resolve our moral controversies.

But the most important purpose served by making the moral premise explicit is that it puts us in a position to evaluate it as the most important feature of a moral argument. If we cannot clearly focus our attention on the crucially important moral premise, it is not likely that we are going to be able to evaluate effectively the merit of the argument.

Because so many of the matters of real concern to us center on controversial moral issues, it is important to know how to construct and evaluate moral arguments effectively. Indeed, you will soon discover that moral arguments will command the greatest portion of your time and energy in the world of arguments. Therefore, you should not shy away from using your whole arsenal of argumentative skills when dealing with them.

II
What Is a Good Argument?

A GOOD ARGUMENT MUST MEET FOUR CRITERIA

There are four general criteria of a good argument. A good argument must have premises that are *relevant* to the truth of the conclusion, premises that are *acceptable*, premises that together constitute *sufficient grounds* for the truth of the conclusion, and premises that anticipate and provide an *effective rebuttal* to all reasonable challenges to the argument or to the position supported by it. An argument that meets all of these conditions is a good one, and its conclusion should be accepted. If an argument fails to satisfy these conditions, it is probably a flawed one.

Some faulty arguments, of course, are less flawed than others, just as some good arguments are better than others. Every assessment of an argument is to some extent a judgment call, for the criteria lend themselves to a wide range of application. There are degrees of relevance, just as there are degrees of acceptability, sufficiency of grounds, and effectiveness of rebuttal. However, there are a number of specific guidelines available for applying these criteria that may be helpful in assessing the relative quality of arguments.

THE RELEVANCE CRITERION

The premises of a good argument must be *relevant* to the truth of the conclusion. We begin with this criterion because there is no reason to waste time assessing the acceptability of a premise if it is not even relevant to the truth of the conclusion.

A premise is relevant if its acceptance provides some reason to believe, counts in favor of, or makes a difference to the truth or falsity of the conclusion. A premise is irrelevant if its acceptance has no bearing on, provides no evidence for, or makes no difference to the truth or falsity of the conclusion.

In most cases, the relevance of a premise is also determined by its relation to other premises. Indeed, in some cases, additional premises may be needed to make the relevance of another premise apparent. Most of us are familiar with the case of the television attorney who convinces an initially skeptical judge that a seemingly irrelevant question or piece of testimony is relevant by introducing other evidence or testimony.

It is sometimes difficult to know whether an arguer intends a particular claim to be a relevant reason for believing the conclusion to be true or whether the claim is simply important and/or colorful background information for understanding the context of the issue under review. If the latter is true, it is not a part of the argument and should obviously not be included as part of its reconstruction. If the former is true, it should definitely be included, even though you may at the time believe it to be irrelevant.

In the terms of traditional logic, the premises are relevant if the conclusion *follows from* the premises. If the argument is a deductive one, the conclusion follows from the premises if the argument is patterned after a logically correct or valid form. A validly formed deductive argument is one in which the acceptance of its premises forces or guarantees the truth of its conclusion. In such cases, the premises are obviously relevant to the conclusion, because the conclusion of a correctly formed deductive argument simply spells out what is already implicit in the premises.

If the argument is an inductive one, the conclusion follows from the premises if those premises are used to support or confirm the truth of that conclusion. A *good* inductive argument is one in which the premises *strongly* support or confirm the truth of the conclusion. However, determining whether the premises of an inductive argument strongly or adequately support the truth of its conclusion depends on how well those premises meet the other criteria of a good argument.

THE ACCEPTABILITY CRITERION

The premises of a good argument must also be *acceptable*. The term *acceptable* is preferable to the more traditional term *true* for several reasons.

First, the notion of acceptability stems from the very nature of argumentative interchange. One who presents an argument is usually trying to get a skeptic or an opponent to *accept* a particular conclusion. The arguer typically starts with premises that the skeptic is likely to accept or that a rational person *ought to* accept. On acceptance of the premises (assuming that other criteria of a good argument are satisfied), the opponent is logically led to the acceptance of the conclusion. In most argumentative situations, then, the key to achieving agreement on the conclusion is gaining *acceptance* of the premises.

Second, since it is notoriously difficult to establish the absolute truth of any statement, it would be an impractical requirement of a good argument that its premises be true in any absolute or strict sense. If such a condition were enforced, there would obviously be very few *good* arguments.

Third, it seems obvious that as a matter of practice, we don't actually use the notion of truth in our arguments. Consider, for example, the contradictory testimony from courtroom witnesses, each of whom is telling "the truth, the whole truth, and nothing but the truth." If we assume that each of the witnesses sincerely believes what he or she is saying is the truth, the best that can be said of the situation is that each is telling what he or she *accepts* as true—not what *is* true.

Fourth, even if a premise were true in the absolute sense, it may be unacceptable to a particular audience, because that audience may not be in a position to *determine* its truth. For example, the evidence for a premise may be inaccessible to them or too technical for them to understand. The truth of the premise would therefore not add anything to the practical force of the argument; the argument can be a good one in a particular context only if the premises are *accepted* or *recognized* as true.

Finally, there are many somewhat minor claims that we encounter as premises in arguments, about which we have no evidence either for or against. But most of us are probably willing to accept them, because they seem to be a reasonable assumption in the context. We cannot say they are true, but we find it a practical matter to accept them as true in the absence of contrary evidence. To treat them as acceptable moves the discussion along.

For all these reasons, the notion of *acceptability* rather than *truth* seems to be the most appropriate way of understanding this second criterion of a good argument. It is very important, however, that we not give the impression that a premise is acceptable simply because one accepts it or can get an audience or reader to accept it. Acceptability does not mean whatever is accepted. It has to do with what a reasonable person *should* accept. Indeed, it is very much akin to the criminal court standard of "beyond reasonable doubt." It certainly does not refer to what one finds is comfortable or easy to believe.

The task of assessing the acceptability of premises is a process that will probably benefit from more specific guidelines, just as in criminal cases, lawyers and judges are guided by rules of evidence and juries by specific jury instructions. Whether one is evaluating arguments or constructing arguments, one should find the following conditions of acceptability helpful.

A premise should be acceptable if it expresses any of the following:

1. A claim that is a matter of undisputed common knowledge or of one's own personal knowledge or evidence.

2. A claim that is adequately defended in the same discussion or at least capable of being adequately defended on request or further inquiry.

3. A conclusion of another good argument.

4. An uncontroverted eyewitness testimony.

5. An uncontroverted report from an expert in the field.

An alternative way of employing the acceptability criterion is to apply what might be called the conditions of *unacceptability*. A premise should be an unacceptable one if it expresses any of the following:

1. A claim that contradicts the evidence, a well-established claim, a credible source, one's own personal knowledge, or other premises in the same argument.

2. A questionable claim that is not adequately defended in the context of the discussion or in some other accessible source.

3. A claim that is self-contradictory, linguistically confusing, or otherwise unintelligible.

4. A claim that is no different from, or that is as questionable as, the conclusion that it is used to support.

5. A claim that is based on a usually unstated but highly questionable assumption.

The premises of an argument, then, should be regarded as acceptable if each of them conforms to at least one of the conditions of acceptability and if none of them conforms to a condition of unacceptability.

THE SUFFICIENT GROUNDS CRITERION

The premises of a good argument must also provide *sufficient grounds* for the truth of its conclusion. If the premises are not sufficient in number, kind, and weight, they may not be strong enough to establish the truth of the conclusion, even though they may be both relevant and acceptable. Additional relevant and acceptable premises may be needed to make the case.

This is perhaps the most difficult criterion to apply, because we have available to us no clear guidelines to help us to determine what constitutes sufficient grounds for the truth of a claim or the rightness of an action. Each argumentative context seems to be different and thus creates different sufficiency demands. For example, what constitutes sufficient grounds for voting for one of the two opposing candidates for political office is very different from what are sufficient grounds for buying rather than renting a house. It is therefore quite difficult sometimes to determine at what point the grounds in an argument for one of the alternatives are sufficient for us to feel confident in endorsing it.

Such a situation requires at least two things: experience and honesty. The more experience we have in evaluating arguments, the more likely we will have a feel for what constitutes sufficient evidence in a particular context. A small child thinks that a sufficient reason for granting his or her every wish is that he or she wants it granted. But parents and most college students, I assume, are usually experienced enough to know that such an argument does not provide sufficient grounds for giving the child everything that he or she desires.

Experience teaches us that certain kinds of evidence do provide sufficient grounds for conclusions in some arenas. For example, polling data taken by objective polling services do provide sufficient grounds for drawing conclusions about which political candidate is likely to win, what television shows are being watched, and what current attitudes are toward college professors. But as critical thinkers, we must be honest about this information and thus not discount it simply because it comes into conflict with our own opinions about a particular political candidate, television show, or college professor.

There are many specific ways that arguments may fail to satisfy the sufficiency criterion. For example, the premises may provide evidence that is based on too small a sample or on unrepresentative data. The evidence may be simply anecdotal, that is, evidence that is based entirely on the personal experience of the arguer or a few people of his or her acquaintance. Moreover, the evidence might be based on a faulty causal analysis of a situation. Perhaps the most common way of violating this criterion is found in arguments in which crucial evidence is simply missing.

THE REBUTTAL CRITERION

A good argument should also provide an *effective rebuttal* to the strongest arguments against one's conclusion and also perhaps to the strongest arguments in support of the alternative position. An argument is usually being presented against the background that there is another side to the issue, and a good argument must meet that other side head-on.

Most reasonably clever people can devise what *appears* to be a good argument for whatever it is that they want to believe or want us to believe. This may partly explain why so many people are skeptical about the ability of good arguments to settle controversies. It all seems to come out even. There appear to be good arguments on both sides of controversial issues—the typical context for the deliverance of opposing arguments. But the fact is that there cannot be good arguments in support of both sides of opposing or contradictory positions, because at least half of the arguments presented will not be able to satisfy the rebuttal criterion. If we have two plausible-sounding but opposing positions being defended, only one will be able to effectively answer the challenges of the other. Otherwise, we could find ourselves in a situation where each of two contradictory positions would merit our acceptance. But we cannot logically or practically tolerate such a situation. It is simply not the case, for example, that abortion is both wrong and not wrong.

The ultimate key to distinguishing between a good and a not-so-good argument is how well the rebuttal criterion has been met. But, unfortunately, rebuttal is also the most frequently neglected feature of arguments. There are perhaps several reasons why this factor is missing from otherwise good arguments. First, we can't think of any good answers to the challenges to our position, so we just keep quiet about them. Second, we don't want to mention the contrary evidence for fear that our position will be weakened by bringing it to the attention of our opponents. Finally, we are so convinced by our own position that we really don't believe that there *is* another side to the issue. Whatever might be the reason, an argument that lacks this feature cannot be a good one; for in order for us to be properly convinced of anything, we must first look at all the evidence. And we have not looked at all the evidence until we have looked at the contrary evidence.

An argument that violates any one of the four criteria of a good argument is a flawed one. Yet, the fact that it is flawed does not mean that it could not be turned into at least a better argument by amending it.

MAKING ARGUMENTS STRONGER

There are a number of general suggestions that we have for making our arguments stronger and for helping others to do the same with their arguments. You will notice that almost all of our advice for improving the quality of arguments comes directly from explicit or implicit standards embodied in the four criteria. More specific recommendations for strengthening arguments are made in the treatment of individual fallacies throughout the text.

1. Find ways to give additional support to weak or questionable premises.

2. Substitute less controversial premises if they will do the job required.

3. Add additional or missing premises if needed to give sufficient grounds for the conclusion.

4. Soften, if necessary, any absolute claims made in the premises in a way that might make them more acceptable.

5. Take out irrelevant matters that tend to clutter up the argument.

6. Recast the argument in a more orderly form, so that the direction of the argument is clear.

7. Restate premises in their clearest and most economical form.

8. Declare which are the weakest points in the argument, not only to demonstrate your objectivity, but also to blunt the force of your opponent's counterfire.

9. Clear up any vague or confusing language used.

10. Spell out any implicit premises important to the argument, so that there will be no question about their role.

11. Introduce as much deductive character to the argument as the subject matter will allow.

12. Be as exhaustive in your rebuttal as the context calls for.

Some arguments, of course, cannot be improved on, not because they are good enough already, but because they defend views for which no good arguments are likely to be found. Our commitment to the search for truth demands that we not spend time and energy trying to make a hopelessly weak or bad argument a trifle less weak—unless, of course, we are in the unique position of being attorneys who are required by our profession to give the best defense possible in the service of our clients.

APPLYING THE CRITERIA TO ARGUMENTS

The attention we have given to the four criteria of a good argument and the general suggestions for improving not-so-good arguments should give us a pretty clear picture of what a good argument looks like. We should, then, be ready to apply these criteria to some sample arguments to see if they measure up to the standards we have set.

The first step in evaluating arguments is to become mentally prepared. We must remember that the issue is not whether one is inclined to believe the conclusion. The primary question in evaluating arguments is whether one should believe the conclusion on the grounds *provided by the argument*. Even if the conclusion is true, the argument presented might not authorize our acceptance of it.

Let us put the criteria of a good argument to work in evaluating arguments that might be found in some of the following "Letters to the Editor."

Letter A

Dear Editor,

I think that Governor Morgan is doing a great job, in spite of all his Republican critics. Just last week, Nancy Stone said in a news conference that she thought Governor Morgan was one of the best governors in the South and that he was doing an excellent job dealing with the complex problems of the state. And she should know! She's the state chair of the Democratic party.

Let us first put this argument into standard form. This means that we must first identify the conclusion and then find the premises that are used to support that conclusion, along with any supporting statements for those premises. The other or extraneous material can then be ignored. The reconstructed argument about Governor Morgan would look something like this:

Since Nancy Stone, the chair of the Democratic party, says that the Democratic governor is doing a good job,

---

Therefore, Governor Morgan is doing a good job.

Our next step is to test the reformulated argument against the four criteria of a good argument—beginning with the criterion of relevance; for, as we have indicated previously, there is no reason to waste time assessing the acceptability of a premise if it is not even relevant to the truth of the conclusion.

Stated in its most economical form, the argument before us gives only one reason for the positive assessment of the governor's performance in office. That premise fails to meet the very first requirement—relevance. Since the chair of the governor's party is likely to be less than objective in her assessment of his effectiveness, her statement must be seen as irrelevant, for the testimony of a biased authority cannot "count in favor of" the truth of a claim. Perhaps an excellent argument *could* be constructed for the conclusion in question, but that is not the issue at this point. The issue is whether the argument being examined is a good one; and our evaluation says that it is not, since its only premise is irrelevant.

Letter B

Dear Editor,

The seat-belt law is unfair and a clear abuse of governmental authority. By not wearing a belt we are not endangering anyone but perhaps ourselves. In some cases, wearing seat belts can actually endanger your life. Recently, in an accident in Jackson County, the vehicle hit a tree and was crushed except for a small space. Since the driver broke the seat-belt law, his life was saved when he was thrown to the floor of the car.

Reconstructing this argument will take a little more effort than the first one. The clear impression is given that the writer wants to argue that seat-belt laws are unfair or that the government has no right to require us to use them, but no reasons are given in support of either of those claims. Hence, neither of them can be the conclusion of this argument—unless we want to be more than charitable. The only claim that is supported within the argument is the one that wearing a seat belt can be dangerous and should not be required. The reconstructed argument would probably look like this:

(Since laws should not require things that endanger our lives)

and wearing seat belts can endanger our lives because one man's life was saved because he was not wearing his seat belt,

---

(Therefore, we should not be required by law to wear seat belts.)

The Principle of Charity requires us to grant that the first premise and the conclusion are implicit. For that reason, we have enclosed them in parentheses to indicate that they were not explicitly stated but are understood as part of our reconstruction of the argument. We believe the argument exhibited in this form actually looks better than the original one, but that does not mean that it is a good argument.

How well does it meet the criteria of a good argument? The premises seem clearly relevant to the truth of the conclusion. There is therefore no problem with regard to the relevance criterion. The first premise also seems to be acceptable, for it is a commonly accepted view by reasonable people that the government should not pass laws that endanger our lives. But the second premise clearly fails to meet the acceptability criterion, because it is a questionable claim that is not adequately supported in the context and also conflicts with credible evidence to the contrary.

The second premise is also a kind of subargument with its own problems. The anecdotal evidence given in support of the conclusion that seat belts endanger our lives is hardly sufficient grounds for such a claim. The argument also fails to meet the rebuttal criterion, for it makes no attempt to effectively answer the arguments on the other side of this issue. The seat-belt argument fails at least three criteria of a good argument; therefore, it is not a good argument.

Letter C

Dear Editor,

I am a resident of the Monroe District in Washington County. I am very thankful to have someone of Supervisor Althea Morton's intellect, dedication, and experience who not only is willing to serve, but also has the time to devote to all the citizens of this county.

I called Mrs. Morton at home the other night and learned that she had been out of town for two days on Washington County business. On other occasions when I wanted to speak with her, I found her working in the county offices.

My understanding is that someone is running against her for the Monroe district seat. I don't want to trade Mrs. Morton, who has proven ability and experience, for someone who could not possibly bring to the office of supervisor the expertise and devotion that we citizens now enjoy.

Most of us would probably agree that the unstated conclusion of this argument is that we should all vote for the incumbent in the upcoming election. The rest of the reconstruction would be as follows:

Since Mrs. Morton is experienced,

and she is devoted to the citizens of the county,

and she is willing and has time to serve,

and she works hard,

and she is intelligent,

and no other person in the Monroe district could do a better job in the office of supervisor,

---

(Therefore, district residents should vote for Mrs. Morton.)

All of the premises presented in this argument seem to be relevant to the issue of choosing county representatives. Moreover, since the first five premises are fairly standard descriptions of persons running for local office, there is probably no good reason not to find them acceptable. Even though some of these premises may be questioned with regard to the adequacy of supporting evidence, these are probably not crucial issues in the argument. The sixth or last premise, however, is highly questionable. Indeed, it is so overstated that it is unlikely that any support for it could be found. This would perhaps not matter, if the premise were not so crucial. But the question of the merits of rival political candidates is one of the crucial issues in an argument about choosing between them. The sixth premise, then, is one that is not adequately defended and is therefore unacceptable.

To the arguer's credit, the sixth premise is probably an attempt to rebut the argument against the election of Mrs. Morton, but it is hardly an effective one. The argument therefore fails the rebuttal criterion as well.

Perhaps the most serious problem with the argument, however, is its violation of the sufficient grounds criterion. When discussing that criterion earlier, it was mentioned that the context of an argument often determines what constitutes sufficient grounds for a claim. In this case, sufficient grounds for taking the action of voting for a particular political candidate would at least include information about the goals, ideas, and perspective of the person whose candidacy is being supported. In this argument, however, such matters are totally absent. For this and for the other reasons given, this argument is not a good one.

Letter D
Dear Editor,

The American Heart Association is debating whether to fund a proposed study that would involve drowning 42 dogs at the State University. The University's College of Medicine received permission to use stray dogs from the local pound to determine whether the Heimlich maneuver could be used to save drowning victims.

Dr. Heimlich himself has denounced the proposed study as a "needless experiment" and as one that "must be classified as cruelty." Others have stated that a dog's windpipe and diaphragm are not comparable to humans and therefore cannot be used in determining whether mouth-to-mouth resuscitation or the Heimlich maneuver would be preferable.

Concerned readers should urge the American Heart Association to reject the study.

Although the arguer wants readers to contact the American Heart Association with their concerns, no specific reasons are given for that action, so we can infer that it is not the argument's conclusion, even though one might take that action if convinced of the actual conclusion. The substantive conclusion is that the American Heart Association should not approve the study. The reformulated argument might look like this:

Since some people have said that a dog's breathing apparatus is different from that of humans and therefore an experiment involving dogs would not help to determine whether the Heimlich maneuver could be used effectively for drowning victims,

and Dr. Heimlich himself has said that such an experiment would be needless and cruel,

(And experiments that are cruel and not useful in any way should not be performed)

(Therefore, the American Heart Association should not fund the experiment with the Heimlich maneuver involving dogs.)

The conclusion is clear, although it is not explicitly stated. The first premise does not pass the relevance criterion, because the testimony is from an unidentified source. Since we don't know whether the "others" are experts in physiology, we don't know whether their testimony about a dog's breathing apparatus should "count in favor of" the conclusion or even be taken seriously. Even if the testimony were relevant, it would probably not be acceptable; for it is difficult to believe that personnel from the College of Medicine, who submitted the grant proposal, would not know whether there is a crucially relevant physiological difference between dogs and humans that might make the proposed experiment worthless.

The third premise is an acceptable self-evident principle. The second premise may be acceptable as well, but it probably carries very little real weight in the argument; for we are not told *why* Dr. Heimlich thinks the experiment is "needless."

We have, then, one relevant and acceptable self-evident premise and one premise with very little weight in the argument. Together they do not constitute sufficient grounds for embracing the conclusion. The argument could possibly have been saved from being totally flawed if it had tried to rebut the argument of the College of Medicine that the experiment was a worthwhile one. But it contains no such rebuttal. The argument, as presented, is not a good one.

CONSTRUCTING GOOD ARGUMENTS

The process of argument evaluation encourages the construction of good arguments by constantly reminding us of the criteria of a good argument. Just as a prosecutor or defense attorney gets a clear picture of what the law requires by participating in the process of dealing with those who violate it, one can come to understand what is required of good arguments by becoming sensitive to the great number of ways that they can go wrong. Moreover, in many cases, a criticism or evaluation of an argument is actually a construction of an implicit counterargument. If one does not accept the conclusion presented, one is often, in effect, thinking that there are good reasons for an alternative view. The very process of evaluating is therefore constructive.

The first step in the construction of an argument is to make very clear just what claim is being defended. Don't let your audience become confused about your stand on the issue. Moreover, don't confuse your arguments. If you have more than one argument for your position, don't mix them together into one big argument. Separate the arguments so that if one of them turns out to be a weak one, it will not affect the strength of the others.

Set forth the strongest evidence you have in support of your conclusion and articulate all premises that may not be obvious. It would also be a good idea to put your premises in some order of importance, so that your audience knows which are your strongest supports. You might even mention which are your weaker or less important premises, thus disarming a critic's likely attack on those more vulnerable points.

Ask the same questions of your own arguments that you might ask of an opponent's argument, and make whatever adjustments are necessary to render your arguments invulnerable to attack. You should be sure that all of your premises are *relevant* to the conclusion; you should be especially careful to use only *acceptable* premises; you should be acquainted enough with the context to know what constitutes *sufficient grounds* to support your conclusion; and you should be prepared to provide an *effective rebuttal* to the strongest challenges to your position. You might even specify the kind of evidence that would weaken or possibly falsify your position. This device would have the effect of *strengthening* your position if no such evidence could be produced by your critics. Do not neglect to qualify, or at least admit possible exceptions to, your claims—failure to qualify claims is a fault of many otherwise good arguments. Finally, if your self-criticism exposes a serious flaw or fallacy in your argument, and corrective surgery does not seem to eliminate the problem, you should be willing to abandon the claim gracefully.

III
What Is a Fallacy?

A FALLACY VIOLATES A CRITERION OF A GOOD ARGUMENT

In ordinary language, the term *fallacy* is often used broadly to refer not only to an error in logic but also to a mistaken or false belief. This book restricts the term exclusively to the context of reasoning. A fallacy is a mistake in reasoning, and a fallacious argument is one that contains such an error.

More specifically, *a fallacy is a violation of one of the criteria of a good argument.* Any argument that fails to satisfy one or more of the four criteria is a fallacious one. Fallacies, then, stem from the irrelevance of a premise, from the unacceptability of a premise, from the insufficiency of the grounds (the combined premises) of an argument to establish its conclusion, or from the failure of an argument to give an effective rebuttal to the most serious challenges to its conclusion or to the argument itself.

The concept of fallacy is the key to the evaluation and construction of good arguments. Understanding the notion of fallacy helps one not only to recognize a poor argument but also to know what a good argument should look like. A fallacy, then, is much more than something to avoid in argumentation—it is not just one of those things on a list of things that you shouldn't do. The theory of fallacy functions at the very heart of good argumentation. A fallacy is so conceived that if an argument exhibits a fallacy (a violation of one of the criteria of a good argument), the argument is probably a bad one; if the argument exhibits no such violation, it is a good one.

Fallacies are mistakes in reasoning that typically do not seem to be mistakes at all. Indeed, part of the etymology of the word *fallacy* comes from the notion of deception. Fallacious arguments usually have the deceptive *appearance* of being good arguments. That perhaps explains why we are so often misled by them. Such deceptiveness, of course, may be unintentional on the part of the arguer. But it really doesn't matter whether the mistake was intended or not; a mistake is a mistake, regardless of the arguer's intention.

In most cases, fallacies are mistakes made by those who construct or present arguments for our consideration. However, those to whom arguments are addressed may also be guilty of faulty reasoning if they accept the conclusions of a faulty argument. If they accept the argument as a good one, they are, in effect, making the same argument and thus bear the same responsibility for its problems.

NAMED VERSUS UNNAMED FALLACIES

Many patterns of faulty reasoning have been exhibited in arguments so frequently that they have been assigned specific names. To be able to identify these particular patterns of fallacious reasoning by name serves an important function. If a mistake in reasoning is so common that even a name has been assigned to it, we should be considerably more confident about our assessment of its faulty character when we encounter it in an argument. It is intellectually reassuring to discover that particular kinds of reasoning have been specifically identified by experts in argumentation as fallacious, even to the point of having been assigned a name.

To say of an argument simply that it is "illogical" or that "something seems wrong with it" is not very helpful in eliminating its problems. It is analogous to the situation of one who does not feel well, goes to a physician and is told "You're sick!" If a medical problem is to be treated effectively, one must first diagnose the problem. If the physician is well acquainted with the symptoms of particular diseases, he or she is more likely to identify the patient's problem correctly and to respond to it appropriately.

If a problem in reasoning is to be treated effectively, we must first diagnose the problem. This diagnosis entails specifying precisely what makes the argument fallacious. If we are well acquainted with the features of particular faulty patterns of reasoning, we are more likely to identify the mistake correctly and to respond to it effectively.

It should be clear, however, that a fallacy does not have to have a name in order to be a fallacy. Indeed, our evaluations of the four "Letters to the Editor" in the previous chapter were done without reference to any particular or named fallacy— although some of the mistakes found there *do* have names. It has thus been demonstrated that it is not necessary to know or to remember all the names of particular fallacies in order to engage in the evaluation of an argument. It is entirely sufficient to be able to recognize features of the argument that may violate one or more of the four criteria of a good argument. Recognizing the mistakes by name or by identifiable pattern, however, will make the task easier.

ORGANIZATION OF THE FALLACIES

Various systems of classifying defects in reasoning have been used by text-book writers on reasoning. The organization of the fallacies in this book, however, is dictated by the criteria of a good argument. Each type of fallacy treated here is a species of an irrelevant premise, an unacceptable premise, insufficient grounds, or a failure to provide an effective rebuttal. Some of these fallacies, however, share some common features and can be grouped into subclasses. For example, there are a number of begging-the-question fallacies, all of which commit the same basic error, even though each does so in a distinguishable way.

Each of the commonly committed fallacies is assigned to one of ten different subclasses or categories. Generally, the fallacies of irrelevance and irrelevant emotional appeals belong to the class of *irrelevant premise*; the fallacies of linguistic confusion, begging-the-question fallacies, and unwarranted assumption fallacies fall into the general class of *unacceptable premise*; the fallacies of missing evidence and causal fallacies are categorized in the class of *insufficient grounds*, and *ad hominem* fallacies, fallacies of diversion, and fallacies of counterevidence are placed in the category of those that fail the *rebuttal criterion*.

Just as any argument may violate more than one criterion of a good argument, particular fallacies may fail to meet more than one of the criteria as well. In such cases, the mistake in reasoning could be construed as properly belonging either to several categories or subclasses or to the category that seems to describe best the error's most serious infraction of the rules of good reasoning.

Each of the next four chapters is devoted entirely to one of the four ways arguments can go wrong. Even though the fallacies are grouped in terms of some common features among them, careful attention is focused on each individual fallacy. Each one is given a precise definition. In most cases, this definition is restricted to one or two sentences. Although the definition could be memorized, it is more important that readers understand and translate it into their own words—as long as they include each of the important features of the fallacy. Several examples are given for each fallacy, along with some suggestions for how one might respond to those who use such faulty patterns of reasoning.

No special effort is made to preserve the traditional names for the fallacies studied. For example, traditional Latin names are maintained in only two cases, the *post hoc* fallacy and the *ad hominem* fallacy, because of the relative familiarity of these terms in ordinary discourse. In general, I have tried to assign names that give some indication of the actual character of the argument error, and for that reason, I have abandoned some of the traditional nomenclature.

ATTACKING THE FALLACY

A number of strategies may be used effectively to attack faulty reasoning. Specific strategies for particular fallacies are offered throughout the book. However, three principal lines of attack deserve special attention.

The first of these three ways of attacking arguments has already been discussed—the method of allowing the argument to destroy itself. Sometimes the easiest way of attacking an argument is to reconstruct the argument into standard form and then let the argument destroy itself by having its flawed character exposed more clearly. Consider the following argument expressed in a recent conversation:

Jason: I think that the college orchestra's performance of Mahler's symphony was terrible.
Dave: Why do you say that?
Jason: Because the way they played it was not the way the composer intended it at all.

A simple reconstruction of this argument will immediately expose its flawed character—almost without further comment.

(Since orchestral performances of a composer's work that are not in line with the composer's original intention cannot be good ones)

and this orchestra's performance was not in line with composer Mahler's intention,

---

Therefore, this was not a good performance.

Even though the arguer was clearly using the principle found in the first premise to justify his conclusion, once it is stated as starkly as it is here, it will probably seem so clearly false that even the arguer may want to withdraw it. Very few people would regard it as a justifiable or acceptable principle, because most of us have come to expect and appreciate a performing artist's own unique interpretation of a created work. Since the conclusion is based exclusively on that questionable principle, the argument cannot be a good one.

A second way of attacking faulty reasoning is the counterexample method, which challenges an unacceptable premise by a counterexample. For instance, if someone claims that a particular product is good or better because it is new or different, the claim is based on an implicit premise that whatever is new or different is better. You could attack that premise by pointing to an obvious counterexample to the claim, such as the fiasco experienced by Coca-Cola when it came out with the "New Coke." Although the counterexample approach is risky, since every claim usually has some legitimate exceptions, it is typically very effective.

A third way of attacking faulty reasoning is perhaps the most imaginative and effective of the strategies. It is called the "absurd example method" and shares some of the features of the other two. This method is a way of demonstrating faulty patterns of reasoning without appealing to technical jargon or rules. It is particularly effective with people unfamiliar with or unimpressed by the special names and distinctions logicians use.

If you wish to demonstrate the flaw in your opponent's argument by using the absurd example method, you should construct an argument of your own that has the same form or pattern as the faulty argument of your opponent. Construct your argument, however, so that it leads to an obviously false conclusion. Since a *good* argument cannot yield an obviously false conclusion, your opponent should be able to easily understand, maybe with your help, exactly what is wrong with the pattern of your argument.

Once you point out that there is no essential difference in the pattern of reasoning exhibited in your argument and that of your opponent, he or she will be compelled logically to acknowledge the faulty nature of that argument as well. If further convincing is required, it will probably be best not to identify a particular fallacy by name, but to try to explain in your own words what it is about the premises or the structure of the two arguments that makes them both flawed.

This method can be used with almost any kind of fallacy. Suppose that an antiabortionist argued in the following manner: "Because the fetus at birth is regarded as a human being, and because it would be arbitrary to insist that at some point in the term of pregnancy the allegedly nonhuman fetus suddenly becomes a human being, it could be concluded that the fetus at conception is no less a human being than it is at delivery."

This kind of faulty reasoning exhibits what is called the "fallacy of the continuum." To demonstrate the faulty character of this kind of reasoning, you might construct another argument of the same form as that of the antiabortionist argument, but with an obviously false conclusion. For example, "Because an atmospheric temperature of 100°F is regarded as hot, and because it would appear to be arbitrary to insist that at some particular point during a period in which the temperature rises from 40°F to 100°F the temperature suddenly becomes hot, one could conclude that 40°F is really no less hot than 100°F."

The similarity of the two arguments could be shown in the following reconstructions:

Opponent's Argument

Since contraries or extremes, connected by small intermediate differences, are very much the same,

and it would be arbitrary to insist that at some particular point between the extremes they become different,

and conception and delivery are extremes connected by small intermediate differences,

and a fetus is a human being at delivery,

Therefore, a fetus is a human being at conception.

Absurd Example

Since contraries or extremes, connected by small intermediate differences, are very much the same,

and it would be arbitrary to insist that at some particular point between the extremes they become different, and the temperatures of 40°F and 100°F are extremes connected by small intermediate differences,

and a temperature of 100°F is hot,

Therefore, a temperature of 40°F is hot.

The patterns of the two arguments are exactly the same, but the conclusion in the second is obviously false.

The most serious problem with the temperature argument is that the conclusion comes directly from the highly questionable assumptions expressed in the first two premises. Yet those same premises appear in both arguments. If they lead to such an absurd conclusion in one context, it is rational to infer that they cannot be used to reach an acceptable conclusion in another. Hence, the opponent's argument is also fatally flawed, although his or her conclusion does not appear as ridiculous as the conclusion in the absurd example.

This method serves as a graphic demonstration of the faulty character of the opponent's argument. I am not saying that the antiabortionist's conclusion is false. I am simply saying that this particular argument should not lead one to the antiabortionist's conclusion, because it follows a pattern of reasoning that has been shown to be faulty.

It is often difficult to produce an example of an absurd argument spontaneously, so it might be wise to keep examples in mind for most of the named fallacies. In many of the "Attacking the Fallacy" sections following the discussion of each fallacy, particular examples are supplied for such a purpose. The absurd example method of confronting others with their mistakes in reasoning is not easy to master. It requires considerable practice, imagination, and a thorough understanding of the most common patterns of faulty reasoning. You will find, however, that this method is sometimes easier and more effective than trying to explain to your opponent the terminology and sometimes complex nature of the particular fallacy that he or she has committed.

RULES OF THE GAME

Argumentation, like sports and many other activities, must be conducted in accordance with certain ground rules. In this case, however, the rules I have in mind are not the rules of correct reasoning. Detecting violations of or encouraging conformity to those rules is part of the game itself. The ground rules I am referring to here are the rules of good sportsmanship. If you wish to maintain friendly relationships with your verbal opponents, and if you hope ultimately to win your point with the least amount of embarrassment and bitterness, I suggest you use the following guidelines.

First, don't be a fallacymonger. Some people, with a little knowledge of fallacious reasoning, develop a kind of obsession with identifying fallacies in the utterances of others. They sniff suspiciously at every argument and point of debate. Such pouncing on others creates more alienation than clarification. Several students have reported to me that while taking my course in logic, they experienced considerably more difficulty in relating to their friends, parents, and other professors. Perhaps these difficulties stem from a kind of fallacymongering, wherein one attempts to point out, in a pedantic fashion, all the fallacies in even the most casual comments of friends and acquaintances.

Second, confront verbal opponents with their fallacious reasoning only when you are convinced that a false conclusion has been reached as a result of a particular error in reasoning or in order to explain why you find the conclusion of the argument unacceptable. To point out errors that have no significant bearing on the basic thrust of the argument may only delay the progress of the debate and divert attention away from the point at issue.

Third, when you yourself are caught committing a fallacy, admit the mistake and make the appropriate adjustments in your thinking. Don't try to deny the charge or explain it away by making excuses or by claiming you were misunderstood. Don't be a sore loser.

Finally, avoid the word *fallacy* altogether, if possible. There are subtle ways of informing verbal opponents that they have committed an error in reasoning without having to shout, "Aha! That's a fallacy!" Because names assigned to fallacies vary from list to list and because people are often "turned off" by technical jargon, the wisest course of action would be to find ways of focusing attention on the pattern of faulty reasoning itself. Be imaginative. Find ways of challenging the reasoning processes of others without alienating them or causing them unnecessary embarrassment. After all, our purpose is to assist people in thinking more clearly, not to catch them in a fallacy.

IV
Fallacies That Violate the Relevance Criterion

The patterns of faulty reasoning discussed in this chapter are fallacies that violate the relevance criterion of a good argument; they employ premises that are logically irrelevant to their conclusions. A good argument must have premises that are relevant to the truth of its conclusion. A premise is relevant if its acceptance provides some reason to believe, counts in favor of, or makes a difference to the truth or falsity of the conclusion. A premise is irrelevant if its acceptance has no bearing on, provides no evidence for, or makes no difference to the truth or falsity of the conclusion.

Arguments with irrelevant premises are often called *non sequiturs*, which means that the conclusion does not seem to follow from the premises. They are also sometimes called *argumentative leaps*, which suggests that since no connection is seen between the premises and the conclusion, a huge leap would be required to move from one to the other.

The 13 fallacies treated in this chapter display irrelevance in a variety of ways. For example, some faulty arguments make an appeal to public opinion or to inappropriate authorities, while others employ reasons that appeal to us on an emotional level. These fallacies are divided into two basic categories: (1) fallacies of irrelevance and (2) irrelevant emotional appeals.

FALLACIES OF IRRELEVANCE

Irrelevant or Questionable Authority

Definition This fallacy consists in attempting to support a claim by quoting the judgment of one who is not an authority in the field, the judgment of an unidentified authority, or the judgment of an authority who is likely to be biased in some way.

An authority in a given field is one who has access to the knowledge that he or she claims to have, is qualified by training or ability to draw appropriate inferences from that knowledge, and is free from any prejudices or conflicts of interest that would prevent him or her from formulating sound judgments or communicating them honestly.

Such authorities may be found in virtually every field of interest. Authorities in very controversial areas, such as religion, politics, or ethics, are no different in kind from authorities in other fields. Ethicists, for example, are often called on as expert witnesses in court cases involving euthanasia, and the media regularly enlists political analysts and theologians to provide us with insight about complicated political and religious matters.

While it is true that disagreement among authorities in these controversial fields is more likely to occur than in many other areas, such disagreement would not be a sufficient reason to deny them their status as authorities, just as the fact that there is disagreement among economic experts would not be considered a good reason to deny economists their status as authorities. Ethicists, political analysts, and religious scholars are in a position not only to inform us about the history and literature of their fields, but to share with us their analyses of many important matters.

There is nothing at all inappropriate about appealing to the judgment of qualified authorities in a field of knowledge as a means of supporting some particular claim related to that field. When the "authority" on whose judgment the argument rests fails to meet the stated criteria, however, the argument should be regarded as fallacious.

The fallacious appeal to authority occurs most frequently in the form of a transfer of an authority's competence from one field to another. An entertainer or athlete, for example, is appealed to as an authority on automobile mufflers or panty hose; a biologist is called on to support some religious claim; or a politician is treated as an expert on marriage and the family. Indeed, the judgment of a famous and highly respected person is likely to be indiscriminately invoked on almost any subject.

An unidentified authority is questionable because there is no way for the listener to determine whether the unnamed authority is in fact a qualified one. If we do not know who the authority is, we are not in a position to know whether his or her testimony should count in favor of the claim being defended.

Another type of improper authority is a biased one. Some people may be qualified in a particular field by training, ability, and position, yet they are so vitally affected by or "interested" in an arguer's conclusion that there would be good reason to treat their testimony with suspicion.

If an arguer uses an unqualified, unidentified, or biased authority to support a particular thesis, then he or she has used a premise that is irrelevant to the conclusion. The testimony of an unqualified or biased authority has no bearing on the truth or falsity of the conclusion. The testimony of an unidentified authority may have some bearing on the truth of the conclusion, but since it is unidentified, there is no way to know whether it does so. It must therefore be treated as if it is coming from an irrelevant or questionable authority. The same thing must be said of a case involving contradictory testimony from what appear to be equally qualified and unbiased authorities. In this case, the proper response would be to accept the testimony of neither authority, unless you have some independent evidence for accepting the testimony of one and not the other.

Example "It's not true that the government is innocent of any wrongdoing with regard to pollution. I read the other day that the government itself is responsible for over 50 percent of the country's water pollution."

Although it may be true that the U.S. government is in some sense responsible for much of our water pollution, there is no reason to believe such a claim because the source of the claim is as yet unidentified. It should be clear that it is not the speaker's honesty that is being questioned, although his or her memory could possibly be faulty. The appeal is fallacious because the listener is not in a position to evaluate the qualifications of the source.

Example

Ben: Did you know that interference from in-laws is the number one cause of divorce in this country?
Valerie: Really? How do you know?
Ben: I heard it on "Oprah" yesterday.

It is not clear from this exchange whether the authority is Oprah herself, one of her recently divorced guests, an audience member, a writer plugging a new book, or an unidentified invited "expert." But if the "authority" fits any one of these categories, his or her testimony should not be treated as relevant to the claim.

Example "Senator, if you think that the FBI has been engaging in unauthorized or illegal activities, why don't we ask the director and his staff to testify at this hearing so that we can get to the bottom of this matter? Who is in a better position to testify about FBI operations than the director and his division heads?"

The appeal to authority here would be proper in most inquiries concerning FBI operations; yet such testimony might be questionable if the inquiry were intended to evaluate claims of wrongdoing within the Bureau that might even in some way involve the director himself.

Attacking the Fallacy If an argument in support of a claim invokes an unidentified authority, a first step in attacking the argument may be to ask for the authority to be identified. If the arguer is able to do this, then you are in a position to evaluate that authority by the standard criteria. If the arguer is not able to identify the authority, and especially if the claim at issue is a dubious one, you should not treat the testimony as supportive of it.

In determining whether an authority is a biased one, you should be careful not to disqualify a source too quickly by claiming that he or she is prejudiced. Unfortunately, it is all too common a practice to find or to fabricate some reason why the judgment of almost *any* authority might be biased. Such a charge should be registered against an authority, who is otherwise qualified, only when the possibility of bias is clear and might impede the discovery of the truth. If you suspect that an authority may have a conflict of interest, you might point out the presence of that possible conflict, without in any way accusing the authority of either bias or dishonesty. You might also explain why the sheer possibility of a conflict of interest is usually sufficient reason to make the testimony at least doubtful in some way.

If an argument uses an authority in one field to support a claim in another, you might use an absurd example like this: "That would be like using Michael Jordan, the former Chicago Bulls star, to support a claim about Chevrolet trucks." That should convince the arguer about the inappropriateness of his or her own move. If the response is "That's different!" ask him or her to explain just where the difference lies.

Finally, do not be intimidated when great names and respected professions are used in support of various claims. Shakespeare, Socrates, Jesus, Mark Twain, Abraham Lincoln, Will Rogers, Dwight Eisenhower, John Kennedy, Walter Cronkite, and many other "famous" and well-respected people were or are experts, if at all, in very limited ranges of subject matter, and they are not at all qualified to speak authoritatively in most other areas of human concern.

Appeal to Common Opinion

Definition   This fallacy consists in urging the acceptance of a position simply on the grounds that most or at least great numbers of people accept it or in urging the rejection of a position on the grounds that very few people accept it.

Two other names sometimes given to this fallacy are *bandwagon fallacy* and *consensus gentium*. The bandwagon notion suggests that an idea or action must be true or good because "everyone" is accepting it or jumping on it as if it were a wagon full of musicians in a circus parade. *Consensus gentium* is literally translated "consent of the people." If a claim or idea is accepted by a majority, we are often led to believe that it is true or worthy. However, the truth or merit of an idea is in no way dependent on the number of people who support it.

Nevertheless, we commonly infer that a film is a good one if there are long lines of people waiting to see it; or we infer that a restaurant serves good food if there are a great number of cars outside it. Remember, however, that crowds are not usually noted for sound judgments and that a number of other factors could account for the long lines and the large number of cars.

An argument that uses the number of people that accept or reject an idea as a premise for determining its merit uses an irrelevant premise. An argument that employs such a premise as its principal and perhaps only support cannot qualify as a good one, because the criteria of a good argument require that the premises have a bearing on the truth or falsity of the argument's conclusion.

Example   "Marijuana can't be *all* wrong. According to a recent Gallup survey published in yesterday's *Wall Street Journal*, more than 70 percent of all college students see nothing wrong with it."

The benefits or dangers of smoking marijuana cannot be ascertained by taking a poll. Polls may indicate what people are thinking, doing, or anticipate doing, but very little regarding the truth or merit of an idea, claim, or action can be inferred from such surveys.

Example "If tanning beds were really unsafe, then millions of Americans would not be using them every week. Neither can the sun be all that harmful to your skin. Virtually everyone I know goes to the beach every year for one primary purpose—the sun. Do you know anyone who goes to the beach and then sits inside the hotel or beach house?"

What large numbers of beachgoers and tanning salon users *think* is the truth is irrelevant to what is actually the case. Neither should anything be inferred about the issue from what large numbers of tan-seekers actually do.

Example "I'm going to buy Garth Brooks's new album. It's been on the top of the country charts for over a month. It must be a good one."

Large numbers of people may believe, accept, buy, vote for, or reject any number of different things. What large numbers of people do or believe, however, tells us nothing more than what large numbers of people do or believe. It tells nothing about the quality of the thing. Indeed, the same faulty argument made for Brooks's music could be made for the music of a very different group: "How can you say that the music of the Grateful Dead is awful, when so many people love them? Their concerts are always sold out, and fans follow them around the country on their tours." If the same argument can be made in support of the merit of the music of both Garth Brooks and the Grateful Dead—namely, that it is good because large numbers of people like it—there must be some flaw in the argument.

Attacking the Fallacy Since this fallacy is so tempting to commit, we perhaps should remind ourselves daily to infer *nothing* about *anything* on the basis of what large groups or even the majority of people believe. The weight of public opinion is simply not relevant to the matter of whether a claim is true.

Maybe we should also keep in mind that public opinion is fickle. With regard to the Clarence Thomas–Anita Hill conflict in testimony at the Senate confirmation hearings, the majority of public opinion about who was telling the truth has shifted more than once since the debate. But because your verbal opponent regards public opinion as representing the truth, you might ask if a true claim would become a false one if public opinion were to shift to the other side. Although it is unlikely that anyone would answer "yes" to such a question, you should be prepared to point out that such thinking could lead to the absurd conclusion that a claim is both true *and* false, depending on when the people are surveyed, and that such thinking surely must be faulty in some way.

If your opponent is unconvinced, you could remind him or her about beliefs from both science and history that were at one time held to be true by large numbers of people, yet turned out to be false. Or you could cite examples of claims that at one time no one believed to be true but that turned out to be true. Probably the best strategy would be to use examples from your opponent's own experience. You might refer, for example, to a claim that the arguer had recently and correctly assessed as false, even in the face of it being believed to be true by large numbers of people.

Genetic Fallacy

Definition   This fallacy consists in evaluating a thing in terms of its earlier context and then carrying over that evaluation to the thing in the present.

The genetic fallacy occurs when one attempts to reduce the significance of an idea, person, practice, or institution merely to an account of its origin (genesis) or its earlier forms, thereby overlooking the development, regression, or difference to be found in it in the present situation. One who commits this fallacy typically transfers the positive or negative esteem that he or she has for the thing in its original context or earlier forms to the thing in its present form.

The genetic fallacy exhibits a pattern of reasoning that fails to meet the first criterion of a good argument—that the premises must have a bearing on the truth or falsity of the claim in question. Since the origin of a thing rarely has any relevance to its merit, an argument that uses such a premise for accepting or rejecting a claim about the thing in question should be regarded as a flawed one.

Example   "You're not going to wear a wedding ring, are you? Don't you know that the wedding ring originally symbolized the ankle chains worn by women to prevent them from running away from their husbands? I would not have thought you would be a party to such a sexist practice."

There may be reasons why people may not wish to wear wedding rings, but it would be logically inappropriate for a couple to reject the notion of exchanging wedding rings on the sole grounds of its alleged sexist origins.

Example   The genetic fallacy is sometimes committed by religious leaders and others who forbid certain practices on the basis of their supposed origins. For example, it is sometimes asserted that "a good Christian" should not dance, because dancing was originally used in pagan mystery cults as a way of worshiping pagan gods. Although there could be good reasons to argue against some forms of dance, the alleged genesis of the dance is not one of them.

Example   "I wouldn't vote for Jim Clinard for anything. You see, I grew up with him. We went to grade school together. He was just one big 'goof-off.' You couldn't depend on him for anything. I shudder to think of his being governor of any state in which I lived."

The speaker here is assuming that Clinard is the same kind of person now that he was when he was in grade school. The speaker overlooks the possibility that Clinard may have matured or changed into quite a different person than he was then.

Attacking the Fallacy   Getting an arguer to disregard the origin or original context of an idea or thing is not easy. Strong emotional responses connected to those origins are particularly difficult to dismiss. Consider, for example, how difficult it is to evaluate objectively the attractiveness of a mate's suit or dress that was selected by a *former* lover. Where a thing comes from does tend to have a rather potent effect on the way we evaluate it. Nevertheless, it is important to try to dismiss such factors in our deliberations about their worth. When an opponent uses such considerations, it would be appropriate to ask what there is about the thing itself that he or she finds either objectionable or worthwhile.

To demonstrate the appropriateness of separating the worth of a thing from how it started, consider an emotional issue such as one's love for a mate. Ask the arguer if he or she would feel any differently about his or her mate if it were just discovered that their first meeting or "date" was part of an elaborate practical joke or, even worse, a case of mistaken identity. Such an undesirable beginning surely would be regarded as irrelevant to the assessment of the present worth of the relationship. If the arguer can make that kind of separation in this case, he or she should be able to do it with regard to the matter in question.

Rationalization

Definition This fallacy consists in using plausible-sounding but usually false reasons to justify a particular position that is held on other less respectable grounds.

Rationalization can be properly described as a violation of the first criterion of a good argument, because the premises are not relevant to the conclusion. The stated premises have very little relationship to the conclusion, because they are not the *real* reasons for the conclusion drawn. Those are unstated or concealed.

This fallacy could also be described as violating the second criterion of a good argument. Since the premises are simply "made up" for the purpose of defending an action or propping up a belief arrived at on other grounds, they are not likely to be acceptable ones.

The general character of rationalization is that of *defending* an idea or belief rather than trying to determine whether it is true. Rationalization, then, is a kind of dishonest substitute for good reasoning. In good arguments, the belief or conclusion follows from the evidence. In rationalization, the "evidence" comes after the belief is already accepted. The rationalizer is simply using premises that make his or her questionable position seem more respectable.

Then why not call rationalization simply a case of dishonesty—or, at best, self-deceit? Why should it be treated as a fallacy? It should be treated as a fallacy because we cannot see into the arguer's mind and determine if there is any dishonesty there. The best that we can do is to work with the argument we have before us, testing it against the criteria of a good argument.

Example After losing a boyfriend to another young woman, Sarah says, "Well, I was going to dump him anyway. It was really getting boring having him around. I should have left him long ago; I just felt sorry for him."

Sarah has to deal with the fact that the relationship with her friend is over. To make that break more personally palatable, she finds fake reasons to justify it to herself and to anyone who cares to listen.

Example   Jane, a senior philosophy major, says to Professor Stone, "I didn't do well on the Law School Admissions Test. You see, I just don't do very well on tests. I never have. Tests just don't show my real ability. Besides, the day before I took the LSAT, I had some real bad news from home."

Jane is rationalizing. She is trying to give plausible-sounding reasons for her weak performance on the LSAT, but the reasons sound hollow. They cannot bear the weight that she places on them. She wishes not only to cover her embarrassment but also to offset the effect of her poor LSAT score on Professor Stone's image of her.

Example   "I suppose I really should go to the wedding of my boss's son, but I really don't know him that well. And I only met the bride one time. She probably wouldn't even remember me. Besides, I really didn't know what to buy them for a wedding gift. From what I hear, they have everything a couple would need. Anyway, there are going to be so many people there, they surely won't miss me."

This bit of rationalization is familiar to most of us. The real reasons for not wanting to go to the wedding are probably less admirable. This person perhaps doesn't want to spend the money for the gift, doesn't want to get dressed up, or simply prefers to watch a game on television. The stated reasons, then, are basically irrelevant to the rightness of the decision made.

Attacking the Fallacy   Let your rationalizing opponent know that you have reason to believe that you have not heard the real argument. You may ask for the arguer to give you the real reasons for the action or belief; but since the rationalizer is engaging in a bit of face-saving behavior—the very reason for the rationalization—it is not likely that you will get a straight story. The rationalizer has a vested interest to protect, and revealing the actual reasons would jeopardize that interest. You therefore may have to concentrate your attack on the stated argument.

One strategy is to ask if the arguer would still hold to the belief or defend the action if the stated premises turned out to be false or irrelevant. If the arguer answers "yes," he or she is admitting that the premises are not relevant to the conclusion drawn and the argument is therefore a faulty one. If the arguer answers "no," you might try to find some way of demonstrating the irrelevance of the premises in order to call what you think is the rationalizer's bluff. If the attack is successful, the best result would be for the arguer to either abandon the belief or alter the action. At the very least, the exposed rationalizer should suffer the embarrassment of holding what is probably an indefensible belief or engaging in what is probably a questionable action.

Drawing the Wrong Conclusion

Definition   This fallacy consists in drawing a conclusion other than the one supported by the evidence presented in the argument.

The fallacy of drawing the wrong conclusion is often referred to as the fallacy of missing the point, as in "missing the point of the evidence." The argument in its conclusion misses the main thrust of the evidence provided. Even though this is one of the fallacies of irrelevance, it is not just a typical case of an arguer using an irrelevant premise or two. This is an argument where a well-developed evidential case for a particular conclusion is presented, at the end of which the arguer simply draws the wrong conclusion from his or her own data. The hearer or reader of the argument is poised to receive the conclusion to which the evidence seems to be leading and is startled when the arguer draws a very different one. Even though the conclusion purports to follow from the evidence, the evidence presented actually supports some other, although perhaps related, conclusion. But it has little or no bearing on the truth or falsity of the stated one.

In some cases, reasoning in a way that draws the wrong conclusion or misses the point of the evidence may be deliberate, as in the case of the prosecutor who is allegedly supporting the claim that a defendant is guilty of rape, yet most of the "evidence" presented supports another conclusion, namely, that rape is a heinous crime. The prosecutor may hope, of course, that the jury will infer the stated conclusion ("the defendant is guilty of this rape") rather than the unstated one supported by the actual evidence presented ("rape is a heinous crime").

More often than not, however, drawing the wrong conclusion occurs because of carelessness in the formation of the argument or because of the subtle, perhaps even unconscious, prejudices of the arguer. We are often more concerned about the conclusion issuing from our own agenda than we are about the conclusion that follows from the evidence.

This fallacy is one of the clearest expressions of the violation of the relevance criterion. Since the criteria of a good argument require that premises have a bearing on the truth or falsity of the conclusion, and since the premises in this kind of argument have little or no relevance to the truth of the conclusion, such an argument cannot be a good one. Given the evidence presented, the arguer should have drawn a different conclusion.

Example "The present method of evaluating public school teachers, which, at best, is an occasional perfunctory check by an administrator, is quite inadequate. If a teacher turns out to be a poor one, there is presently no effective way of getting rid of him or her. Therefore, teachers should be hired for a 'term of service,' after which they will reenter the job market, seeking jobs through the usual screening processes."

There may be good reasons for hiring teachers for terms of service, but that conclusion does not follow from the evidence presented. A more relevant conclusion might be that some method of systematic evaluation should be found that would provide a defensible basis for discharging incompetent teachers.

Example "Americans have a great heritage built on fine ideals, and we should all help to carry on this great heritage by passing it on to our children. That is why families should regularly attend church together."

In this argument, no evidence is given to show the connection between passing on our national heritage and families going regularly to church. We were expecting to hear a conclusion to which the evidence seemed to be pointing. Instead, we got an unexpected or wrong conclusion, with no evidence given in support of it.

Example "Reporters keep the public informed, and we all know that a well-informed public is necessary to bring about any semblance of justice. Besides, reporters keep public officials and others 'honest' by digging out the facts behind their claims and exposing them when they don't tell the truth or when they engage in questionable practices. Therefore, I think that the courts are grossly unfair to newspaper reporters when they force them to go to prison just because they won't reveal the sources of their information."

The weight of evidence in this argument supports the view that newspaper reporters perform a very useful and important service for their readers; it does not support the claim that the courts have been unfair to reporters. That particular conclusion is the wrong conclusion to draw from the evidence presented.

Attacking the Fallacy An argument that draws the wrong conclusion can often be very persuasive, because it can still drive us to a conclusion, even though it is not the arguer's stated one. It might even be helpful to point out what conclusion the evidence *does* support, in order to encourage the arguer to change his or her conclusion to the right one. If the arguer is not interested in the "right" conclusion, that is, the one to which you are led by the evidence, and insists on focusing on the original conclusion, you should point out that that conclusion requires some very different evidence.

Since the arguer is not likely to agree that his or her conclusion was the wrong one to draw from the evidence, be prepared to be patient in helping him or her to line up the right evidence with the right conclusion. If the issue is one about which the arguer feels very strongly, it is likely that he or she will regard almost everything related to that issue as relevant to the claim. For example, if the arguer is concerned about how women are unfairly treated in this society, all the evidence of sexist behavior in society might be brought forth in support of a plea for a particular piece of legislation or even a constitutional amendment on equal rights. But while that evidence may support a claim that ours is a sexist culture, it would not necessarily support the claim that a particular piece of legislation should be passed or that a particular amendment to the Constitution should be ratified. In this case, the arguer should not be allowed to think that the evidence supports the argument.

Using the Wrong Reasons

Definition This fallacy consists in attempting to support a claim with reasons other than the reasons appropriate to the claim.

This fallacy may best be described as the reverse of the fallacy of drawing the wrong conclusion. Just as in the case of that fallacy, this fallacy should not be treated as if it were simply a case of an arguer using an irrelevant premise. In this case, the arguer obviously wants to provide support for the conclusion, but he or she has simply introduced the wrong reasons in support of that conclusion.

The difference between the fallacy of drawing the wrong conclusion and the fallacy of using the wrong reasons is found by looking at where the emphasis lies in the context of the argument. If the arguer, in a rush to get to the favored conclusion, simply misses the point of his or her own evidence, the fallacy of drawing the wrong conclusion has been committed. But if the arguer is attempting to defend a particular conclusion, for which good evidence may be available, but uses some other evidence instead, he or she has committed the fallacy of using the wrong reasons. Typically, in the case of using the wrong reasons, the conclusion is uttered *before* the premises, while in the case of drawing the wrong conclusion, the conclusion is drawn *after* the presentation of the premises.

The place where many of us encounter the kind of faulty reasoning that uses the wrong reasons is the situation where we might tend to agree with the conclusion of an arguer, or at least find it an interesting position to consider, but not for the reasons given in his or her argument. The reasons given are simply not the right ones or the importantly relevant ones for that conclusion.

Why would arguers give the wrong reasons for their conclusions? In some instances, it could simply be a case of rationalization. However, it is probably more often the case that the arguer, for whatever reason, started with the conclusion and then was unable to support it with any relevant or good reasons.

This fallacy is committed perhaps most commonly in the area of political debate. For example, one often hears arguments against a policy or program on the grounds that it does not or would not achieve certain goals. But when these goals are goals that the program or policy was never designed or expected to achieve, the reasons given for the negative evaluation of the policy are the wrong reasons. The arguer has assigned unintended goals and functions to a policy or program and then criticized it for not achieving those goals.

Almost any program, policy, or piece of legislation has certain limited functions or goals that its designers quite readily recognize. Moreover, few programs, when implemented, are such that their most ideal consequences can be or are expected to be fulfilled. Therefore, when these consequences are not achieved, it is not a sufficient justification for abandoning the program. This is especially true if the program has the effect of accomplishing some other important goal or performing some other important function that otherwise probably would not be brought about. There may be some good or relevant reasons for abandoning the programs, but the reasons used are the wrong reasons for that conclusion.

Example   The following is a summary of a typical conversation between many a college philosophy major and his or her critics.

Lynn: Do you really think that philosophy will ever solve all of our problems?
Owen: No, probably not.
Lynn: Then why are you wasting your time studying it?

What the critic fails to recognize is that no philosopher would ever claim that philosophy can solve all human problems. The philosopher simply claims that philosophical inquiry can be very effective in helping us to solve many of our problems. There would be no justification for abandoning it simply because it is not effective in helping us to solve *all* our problems. Lynn has used the wrong reasons for her conclusion that a philosophy major is a waste of time.

Example   Many critics of gun-control legislation have argued that, because gun-control laws probably will not prevent criminals from using guns in the course of committing crimes, there is no good reason to pass such legislation. But those critics are using the wrong reasons to come to their conclusion about gun-control legislation.

As far as the control of crimes is concerned, the proponents of gun-control legislation recognize that it can probably have only limited effect. Indeed, the serious criminal will probably not be much affected by the restricted sale and registration of guns, but the legislation could serve other very important functions, such as making guns less readily available as a means for settling domestic quarrels. Moreover, gun control might have the effect of reducing the number of accidental killings. Hence, in spite of its limitations, proponents think that there are still very good reasons for passing legislation that would control gun use.

Example   "A woman should keep her own name when she gets married. That way she would no longer have to find a mate whose name she would feel comfortable with. It would also keep people from knowing that she is married. Besides, many important people, such as movie stars, keep their own names." There are many good reasons for a woman keeping her own name after she marries, but the arguer, in this case, has used the wrong reasons, or at least not importantly relevant reasons, to defend a position that might be quite defensible on other grounds.

Example   "Certain groups should not be targeted by tobacco advertising. Tobacco has been shown to cause cancer, it is an expensive habit, and it is offensive to family members, associates, and others who have to put up with the smoker's smoke."

The reasons given may all be true and good reasons not to smoke; however, they have very little to do with the main issue here. Since this argument uses the wrong reasons for its conclusion, it is not likely to convince anyone that certain groups should not be targeted by tobacco advertisers.

Attacking the Fallacy   One way to be helpful to the arguer who uses the wrong reasons to support a claim is to say something like this: "I find that you have an interesting thesis, and it might even be a defensible one, but not for the reasons you give." You might even suggest some reasons that seem more relevant and more supportive of the claim at issue.

One way to prevent a critic from inappropriately assigning irrelevant goals and functions to proposed programs and policies as a basis for a negative evaluation is to make every effort to specify the limited goals of the program or policy. It might even be helpful to remind your listener of your awareness of such limitations as often as possible. The critic may thereby be prevented from taking a "cheap shot" at the program. If the critic persists, make it clear that he or she is attacking a claim that no one is making or that a misrepresentation of the claim is being attacked.

Exercises

In each of the following exercises (1) identify the type of fallacy of irrelevance illustrated; (2) explain what specific feature in the example causes it to be properly identified in that way; and (3) explain how the reasoning violates the criterion of relevance:

1. **Henry**: I've gone off my diet. It just isn't working.
   Richard: But I thought it was working real well. Haven't you already lost about 20 pounds?
   Henry: Sure, I've lost weight, but my social life hasn't improved one bit!
2. Many people without Ph.D.s are much better teachers than people with Ph.D.s. Getting a Ph.D. doesn't make one a better teacher. Therefore, I don't think we should hire a person with a Ph.D. to fill this position in our department.
3. Warren Christopher, secretary of state under President Clinton, said in a recent interview in *U.S. News & World Report* that historians will probably describe President Clinton as having developed a very strong, forward-looking, and well defined foreign policy for the post cold-war years.
4. The voters of Massachusetts overwhelmingly defeated a proposed gun-control law in the state, which proves that gun control is really a rotten idea.
5. I could quit if I wanted to. You see, if I didn't smoke I would start gaining weight, and being overweight is just as unhealthy for you as smoking is.
6. Incest must be wrong, because virtually every society, both past and present, has forbidden it in one form or another.
7. I wasn't invited, but I wouldn't have gone anyway. I just don't care to spend my time with such snobs. Besides, I've already been skiing twice this winter.
8. Grades don't really give us much information about a student. If a prospective employer or graduate school were to find from a transcript that a student got a B– in a particular course, very little could be inferred about the particular character or quality of his or her work in that course. Hence, I think that we ought to go to a simple pass-fail system.
9. As far as I'm concerned, the food-stamp program is a total bust. There are still people in this country who go to bed hungry.
10. No, I don't want my boys to join the Boy Scouts. Did you know that the Boy Scouts were organized as a paramilitary organization? They even trained the young boys in accordance with a military scouting manual. The word *scouts* in *Boy Scouts* literally refers to *military* scouts. None of my children is going to join such an organization with my blessing.

11. I think we should hire Karen Johnson as the new third grade teacher. She lives here in the community; she has children in school here; she loves to work with children; and she has been active in the PTA.

12. A pregnant bride should not wear white. A white wedding dress symbolizes purity. And *you, Karen,* hardly qualify!

13. The total number of students enrolled is steadily decreasing. The students are restless and unhappy, and many are threatening to transfer to some other college. It is my opinion that we had better revise our curriculum before it's too late.

14. Janice: Why are you so opposed to the singing of hymns in worship services?

Penny: Don't you know that many hymn tunes used to be drinking songs sung in taverns?

15. I think that we should adopt this new curricular proposal. After all, it has been unanimously endorsed by the college's Board of Trustees. The people who are entrusted with running the college should know what they're talking about when it comes to deciding the best curriculum for the school.

16. Merrill Lynch said in its latest newsletter that now is a good time to invest in the stock market. It went on to say that more money is to be made in buying individual stocks than in investing in various mutual funds. So I bought several Dow stocks. I needed to buy something that can make up for all the money I lost on those CDs I've held for years.

17. Yes, I subscribe to *Playboy*, but I do it for the great articles in there. There was a great piece last month taking a new look at Jimmy Carter's presidency.

18. I am not going to become a public school teacher, because that was the only role that women were traditionally allowed to have. I do not want to help perpetuate that immoral tradition.

19. I don't see why you don't want to take your husband's name when you get married. The vast majority of Americans obviously think it should be done that way. It's hard to believe that that many people could be wrong!

20. Your honor, Dr. Chamberlain is a respected physician and has been a friend of the defendant's family for many years. She will be able to testify as to the state of the defendant's mental health at the time of the crime.

IRRELEVANT EMOTIONAL APPEALS

Appeal to Pity

Definition   This fallacy consists in attempting to persuade others of one's point of view by appealing to their sympathy instead of relevant evidence, especially when some more important principle or issue is at stake.

The prospect that someone may be disappointed or suffer some kind of mental anguish by your failure to give a desired response to a claim or proposal is usually an irrelevant consideration in the determination of the merit of the claim or of the proposed action. One who appeals to pity is actually exploiting emotional sensitivities rather than presenting convincing evidence that a claim is true or that an action has merit.

An argument that uses pity in place of evidence is using an irrelevant premise, which is a violation of the first criterion of a good argument. The introduction of pity can never settle a question of fact, for the pitiable consequences of a claim's being true have absolutely no bearing on the truth or falsity of the claim.

Although feelings of pity will no doubt influence our *action* from time to time, we should be careful not to let them cloud our *judgment* about that action. Even though we may respond positively to a particular appeal to pity, we should be clear in our own mind what we are doing. The effectiveness of the tug of pity should not be mistaken for relevant evidence.

A number of critics have tried to make a distinction between coming to a *belief* on the basis of pity and making a decision about a *course of action* on the basis of pity. They then insist that the fallacy of appeal to pity occurs only in the case of an argument that attempts to get one to come to a belief on the basis of pity. It seems to us if that distinction and the inference drawn from it were maintained, actual cases of appeal to pity would be quite rare, because very few people, if any, ever come to believe something to be true simply on the basis of pity. The introduction of pity can never settle a question of fact, for the pitiable consequences of a claim being true have absolutely no bearing on the truth or falsity of the claim. An argument that uses pity in place of evidence is therefore using an irrelevant premise, which is a violation of the first criterion of a good argument.

Critics also suggest that the appeal to pity is *not* fallacious when it involves a decision about a course of action; for they assume that in those cases the appeal to pity involves inherent moral considerations. While it is true that appeals on the basis of pitiable circumstances sometimes involve implicit moral premises, that is certainly not always the case. Moreover, even when the Principle of Charity requires us to recognize such premises, they still may not be relevant ones. An arguer should not assume that one's own moral principles are always going to be shared by those to whom one addresses an argument. We must also keep in mind that even in cases where such principles may be shared, they may not be relevant to a more important issue or principle that may be at stake.

Admittedly, when the issue is one of action, the line between relevance and irrelevance is often blurred. There may indeed be some situations where the potential hurt to others is a relevant consideration in adopting or rejecting a course of action. Many calls to compassion are in fact moral arguments that appeal implicitly to moral principles. In such cases, the description of the pitiful situation may simply be a device used to call attention to a relevant moral principle. For example, suppose that an older employee were being terminated as part of a cost-reduction plan. If he made a case for staying on until he became eligible for his full retirement benefits in six months, he would probably be implicitly appealing to a principle of fairness to which he would assume his employer subscribed. Indeed, if he were to make such an appeal, it is not likely that anyone would think it to be a fallacious one. The appeal would simply be regarded as a rather good moral argument.

In summary, let us say that an appeal to pity, in a context in which no *defensible* moral premise is lurking about, exploits our vague feelings of generosity or concern for others, while usually neglecting (or at least obscuring) a more relevant principle or issue at stake; therefore, the appeal is fallacious.

Example "Larry, I really think that you ought to take Nicole to the May dance next Friday. She hasn't had a date all year. In fact, she has never been invited to go to any dance. Have you ever thought what it might be like to sit alone in your room every time there is a campus dance, while all your friends are doing what you'd like to be doing?"

Larry may truly feel sorry for Nicole, but the relevant question is whether he should let those feelings play a significant role in deciding whether to invite her to the dance. Since dating is generally regarded as a practice, the purpose of which is to spend time, presumably enjoyable time, with someone to whom one is in some way attracted, the suggestion regarding Nicole would probably be at cross-purposes with that understanding. A nonfallacious argument for inviting Nicole to the dance should provide evidence that spending the evening with her would be a pleasant or enjoyable experience. If he took her because he felt sorry for her, he would be doing it for the wrong or irrelevant reasons.

Example The sympathies that may be aroused by the fact that someone has a physical handicap should not play a primary role in a decision to hire that person. Even though our sympathies may be further aroused by the fact that he or she has had great difficulty getting a job, partly because of the handicap, that, too, does not constitute a good reason for hiring.

The most relevant consideration in hiring someone usually relates to whether the person can do a good job in the position. If the person's handicap is such that he or she could not be effective, our feelings of pity should not play a role in the hiring decision.

Example The owner of an apartment house, who had a tenant who was three months behind in the rent, would probably ask her to move out. If she argued that she had lost her job, had no prospect of a job, and didn't have any place to go, that plea would probably arouse some pity in any decent human being; but it should not constitute a significant factor in the decision to evict or not to evict the tenant.

The primary purpose for owning an apartment house is usually earning some profit on an investment. A nonpaying tenant violates that primary function.

Attacking the Fallacy If you allow yourself to be overcome by the force of an emotional appeal, it is important to remember that you are no less guilty of fallacious reasoning than the one who formulates the appeal. You have allowed the description or projection of a pitiable situation to count as evidence, even though, in most cases, it does not constitute any evidence at all. However, to avoid appearing to be an insensitive brute, it might be wise to acknowledge your aroused feelings openly, yet to state specifically that you are not going to allow them to interfere with the process of coming to a defensible judgment. Point out that accepting a proposal primarily because of those feelings would be doing so, in most cases, for the wrong reasons.

Since arguments with irrelevant premises can sometimes be reconstructed with relevant premises, ask the arguer to try to so modify the argument. If he or she cannot do this, without appealing to pity, then not only was your original assessment of the argument probably correct, but it is not likely that the proposal itself merits your acceptance.

Appeal to Force or Threat

Definition   This fallacy consists in attempting to persuade others of one's point of view by threatening them with some undesirable state of affairs instead of presenting evidence for one's view.

Unfortunately, such intimidation can often gain acceptance of a conclusion in the absence of a convincing argument. There is nothing wrong, of course, with pointing out the consequences of a particular course of action. In fact, if certain consequences are a natural outcome of an action, calling attention to them might be very much appreciated. In some such cases, being aware of the consequences of an action might even cause one to alter one's course. However, if an arguer tries to force another to accept the truth of a claim or the rightness of an action by threatening some undesirable action, then the arguer is guilty of using an irrelevant appeal, which is a clear violation of the first criterion of a good argument.

One particular form of this fallacy is often referred to as *authoritarianism*. Authoritarianism consists in appealing to someone as an authority not because of that person's skill, knowledge, or expertise in a field but because of his or her power or influence over the one to whom the argument is directed. In such a case, a demand for blind submission to that authority takes the place of relevant evidence or good reasons.

In most cases, the appeal to force is used, not to lead another to a particular belief but to a course of action. Lobbyist Trollinger, for example, asks a member of Congress not to believe something but to do something when he reminds the legislator that, as a lobbyist, he represents 10,000 voters in the representative's district.

Similarly, local businesswoman Johnson is asking that something be done, rather than believed, when she reminds the editor of the local newspaper that she spends a lot of her advertising dollars in that paper and would prefer that the story concerning her arrest for drunken driving not appear in it. In both cases, the reasons given are not relevant to the rightness of the action sought. Such implicit threats might lead to the action desired, but not because good arguments were presented. There is no way that such arguments could qualify as good ones, because their premises have no bearing on the merit of their conclusions.

Example   Most of us are familiar with cases of sexual harassment, in which a supervisor may demand sexual favors from someone over whom he or she has control in return for continued employment or continuation in a graduate program. In such cases, the supervisor has not persuaded the victim of the rightness of the action—only that cooperation may be necessary to maintain one's present status. The threat may be effective, even though the argument is a bad one.

Example The following exchange illustrates a familiar example of authoritarian thinking.

>   **Son**: Dad, why do I have to go to church every Sunday?
>   **Father**: Because I'm your father, and I say so, that's why.

The son is asking what good reasons there are for attending church, but his father responds by demanding blind obedience to his will. The father, in this case, is appealing to his power over the boy to force his compliance. His alleged argument is fallacious, for it implicitly gives a threat of force in place of relevant reasons for attending church.

Example One of the most effective appeals of many evangelists and others in reaching possible Christian converts is the threat of eternal damnation. But "burning in hell" is not a relevant reason for accepting the truth or the rightness of the Christian faith. It may be that many people do accept it as true because of their fears, but the prospect of dire personal consequences following on the rejection of a particular religious perspective is not relevant to its truth.

Attacking the Fallacy It is sometimes difficult to withstand the pressure of a threat, particularly when it comes, as it usually does, from someone with the power to place you in a very undesirable situation. Indeed, your ability or inclination to reject such irrelevant appeals may depend on your own sense of personal, economic, and professional security. Nevertheless, one who is guilty of appealing to force or threat should at least be exposed. One way of doing this might be to say to such a person, "I know what you're going to do to me if I don't accept your position, but are there any good reasons for believing your position to be *true* or *right*?"

Appeal to Tradition

Definition This fallacy consists in attempting to persuade others of one's point of view by appealing to their feelings of reverence or respect for some tradition instead of evidence, especially when there is some more important principle or issue at risk.

The comfortable or warm feelings that we may have for a particular traditional way of doing things may be one reason we revere it, but such feelings are not a reason for regarding the tradition as the best way of doing things, especially when a more important principle may be at stake. Good feelings cannot be an appropriate substitute for evidence.

Emotional attachments to the past are common and pleasant experiences for almost all of us. Moreover, it is true that many traditions perform social functions of great importance. They often embody the distilled wisdom of earlier generations and relieve us of the burden of having to invent our own solutions to the problems created by social interaction.

But there is also a dark and negative side to many traditions. Even though most traditions might originally have had good reasons behind them, those reasons may no longer be relevant considerations. Powerful traditions can perpetuate earlier injustices and stifle creative approaches to life or to better ways of doing things. Indeed, the English philosopher John Stuart Mill claimed that "the despotism of custom is everywhere the standing hindrance to human advancement."

To point out that a particular practice has the status of a tradition sheds no light on whether it is a wise or foolish one. When there is no more important principle at stake, the appeal to tradition is neither a fallacy nor a matter that should concern us. But if holding to a tradition threatens to prevent a solution that enlightened reflection supports, then any positive aspects it may embody must be weighed against the damage that it may inflict. If a tradition has serious negative or harmful features connected with it, then the fact that it is a tradition should be a minor consideration in its support—good feelings aside.

An argument that attempts to persuade by an appeal to tradition when other important considerations are at issue is using an irrelevant premise, which is a violation of the first criterion of a good argument. The rightness of an action or the truth of a claim in such a context is not supported by the fact that it is part of a tradition.

Example "Sheila, if a woman loves her husband, she is proud to be called by his name. In our culture, taking a husband's name makes a woman feel married, because she is doing what other women have always done when they get married. If you keep your own name when you marry, you'll be abandoning something that has had a very long and rich history of meaning for all of us."

In this argument, no reason other than tradition is given for a woman to adopt her husband's name. If there are good reasons to continue that practice, rather than each partner maintaining his or her own name at marriage, the arguer makes no use of them. The only alleged evidence is irrelevant to the issue at stake.

Example "But, John, our family has always been Southern Baptist. Your grandfather was a Southern Baptist minister, and you have two uncles who are Southern Baptist ministers. Your mother's family has also always been Southern Baptist. I just don't understand how you could even think of joining the Methodist church."

John's father has pointed out several facts to John in order to impress on him the family tradition. However, the more important ecclesiastical or theological considerations are given no attention at all; only feelings of reverence for a family tradition are considered.

Example "When I was in public school, we had prayer every day at the beginning of the school session. It was a very meaningful thing for me. I just don't see why my children can't have the same kind of experience."

No counterargument is offered here to the Supreme Court position that required prayer in public schools constitutes an "establishment of religion"; the only appeal is to the comfortableness of a tradition.

Example "Virginia Military Institute should not allow women to enter. Ever since Stonewall Jackson, VMI has been an all-male school. My father graduated from there and went on to fight and die in Korea. He would turn over in his grave if he knew that women had been allowed to go to VMI."

A greater issue than tradition is at stake here. Since VMI is a state-supported public school, it should not be allowed to discriminate against women in its admissions policy.

Attacking the Fallacy Assure your verbal opponent that there is nothing intrinsically wrong with doing things in a traditional way. In fact, you might even admit that you, too, often feel more comfortable with traditional ways of doing things. However, you should also point out that if there is a more important principle at stake, then there is a good reason for changing a way of acting or thinking or for not continuing a particular practice. In such cases, a reverence for the past is not a relevant consideration in the process of determining what to do.

Appeal to Personal Circumstances or Motives

Definition This fallacy consists in urging an opponent to accept or reject a particular position by appealing solely to his or her personal circumstances or self-interest, usually when there is some more important issue at stake.

An argument that appeals to the personal circumstances or self-interest of another in an effort to get him or her to accept or reject a particular claim or proposal is using a premise that is usually not relevant to the merit of the question at issue. This is especially the case when there is some larger issue at stake. Even though arguments like these are often quite effective, it is not because they are good ones.

It is ironic that some of the same people who present us with arguments based on personal circumstance or motives think it unscrupulous of us when we accept or reject some *other* proposal on the basis of self-interest. It would seem, therefore, that people who use such appeals are probably aware, in their more reflective moments, that personal circumstances or interests are usually not relevant to the merit of an idea or action.

Example "I really don't see how you can oppose the administration's bill to cut income and capital gains taxes. After all, you're in a tax bracket that will benefit considerably from the cut, and if you sell any of that real estate and those stocks you own you're going to realize a lot more from the sale if the capital gains tax is lowered."

While it may indeed be to the advantage of the target of this argument to have lower taxes, there may be a more important issue at stake here. Lowering income and capital gains taxes could have the effect of curtailing other important governmental programs, of increasing the national debt, or of creating other more serious economic problems for the country. Personal benefit is only one of the considerations.

Example "Nancy, I would have thought that you would be actively supporting an affirmative action program here at the university. Because you're a woman, you of all people should see the merit of using every means available to hire more women to work in areas that have traditionally been dominated by men."

The special circumstance that Nancy is a woman is not a relevant or sufficient reason for her to support such a program. Whatever her reason for not actively supporting affirmative action, being a woman is not a relevant consideration in the determination of her judgment.

Example   One faculty member appeals to the personal interests of another to gain his vote in an important curriculum fight: "Don't you realize, Professor Morris, that if the faculty votes to drop the foreign language requirement, very few of our students will be likely to take a foreign language? Don't you agree that without the requirement it will be difficult to get a decent enrollment in our Latin classes? The requirement helps us to pick up our majors and minors. No one comes to college *planning* to major or minor in Latin."

The question of whether a foreign language should be required of all students should be determined on the basis of factors relevant to the requirement. The fact that it provides majors, minors, and larger classes for Professor Morris should not be the principal concern.

Attacking the Fallacy   If someone appeals to you on a personal level or on the level of self-interest, you can head the debate in a more positive direction if you ask for an alternative argument that makes no reference to what may be of personal benefit to you. Let it be known that you are concerned about the truth or the rightness of the position in question, not whether it will benefit you personally. If a good argument for the idea can be formulated, accept its conclusion without embarrassment, even if it *does* benefit you personally.

Exploitation of Strong Feelings and Attitudes

Definition   This fallacy consists in attempting to persuade others of one's point of view by exploiting their strong emotions or by manipulating their positive and negative attitudes toward certain groups or ideas, instead of presenting evidence for one's view.

Other names for this fallacy are "appeal to the crowd" or "appeal to the gallery." The "gallery" to which an appeal is made refers to the undiscriminating public, which is often easily swayed through a manipulation of their strong feelings and attitudes. Such exploitation has no place in a good argument, because according to the criteria of a good argument, the premises must be relevant to or count in favor of the truth of the conclusion, and premises constituted by manipulative emotional devices have no bearing on the truth of the conclusion.

To exploit or manipulate feelings and attitudes is to employ clever but unfair methods to take advantage of, use, control, or play on another person's feelings and attitudes for one's own end. Some of the strong emotions that are so exploited are fear, envy, jealousy, anger, hate, love, greed, guilt, and shame. Positive sentiments that are frequently exploited are familial concerns, patriotism, national security, group loyalty, and military superiority. Negative attitudes against such things as labor unions, capitalism, liberals or conservatives, taxes, religious groups, political parties, political incumbency, gays and lesbians, racial groups, lawyers, and feminists are often manipulated as a means of persuading others to accept a particular conclusion. The arguer's choice of which sentiment to exploit is, of course, determined by the constituency of the audience or gallery.

There are two distinctive types of exploitation that deserve special attention. One might be called the "appeal to shame." It seeks to elicit a feeling of guilt from a person or group for holding an unpopular opinion or for acting in a particular way, without demonstrating why feelings of guilt would be warranted.

The second distinctive type of exploitation uses an appeal to group loyalty. It attempts to persuade a person to accept a position because of his or her identification with a particular social group that accepts the point of view in question. Neither of these factors, however, is relevant to the task of determining the truth of a claim or choosing an appropriate course of action.

Example   "I'm an old lady, Eddie, and you should be ashamed to charge me for mowing my yard." Eddie, of course, may decide to mow her yard "for free," but there is no reason why he should feel ashamed for charging someone for mowing a yard, especially if the only reason offered for not charging her is simply that she is an "old lady."

Example   "The fact that you witnessed the gang-rape doesn't matter, Felicia. When it is your own brother-in-law who is one of those accused, you just don't get up on the witness stand and spill your guts. It is quite possible that you could help send a member of your own family to prison for 20 years."

This is a clear case of an appeal to loyalty, which is an irrelevant appeal in this context. If Felicia responds positively to this faulty argument of family members, she could very well contribute to a miscarriage of justice, which is probably a more important concern than family loyalty. If no important principle were at risk, family loyalty might serve some very beneficial functions.

Example   The following comment was heard in a conversation between a man and a woman. The woman was apparently angry that the man had not opened a door for her. She said, "Any respectable and decent man would open the door for a lady!" No evidence is given for why the man should feel ashamed or disrespectful, other than the fact that she is a woman.

Example   "I know that you, the hard-working men and women of this town, many of you veterans, are getting tired of paying taxes for the suburban yuppies who worm their way around the tax laws. Send me to Congress, and I'll put some of your burden back where it belongs."

This congressional candidate is obviously playing to the strong feelings and attitudes of small-town America. It is unclear what platform he stands on, but if the exploitation works, maybe it won't really matter.

Attacking the Fallacy   Exploitation of strong feelings is most effective when it is directed toward the uninformed or the uncritical, but even some of the most reflective people can be aroused by appeals to their own feelings and attitudes. Nevertheless, one should make every effort not to allow such appeals to intrude on the process of making a careful judgment about an issue.

Not only should we take care not to allow ourselves to be moved by appeals based on strong sentiments, we should also not allow speakers who attempt to exploit our feelings and attitudes to think that they have offered any relevant reason in support of a claim.

There are several ways in which this might be done. First, you could simply inform your opponent that you are unable to properly evaluate or respond to the claim unless more relevant evidence is offered in support of it.

Second, if your own sentiments correspond with those expressed by your opponent, you might freely admit that fact. Such an admission would probably have a somewhat disarming effect on the arguer. But you should hasten to inform the arguer that you do not intend to allow your feelings to obstruct your careful scrutiny of the issue. In other words, you should make it clear that you are still waiting to be convinced on the basis of relevant evidence.

Third, you could use an example or two to give an additional thrust to your attack. You might point out that even though one's loyalties may be with the home football team, those feelings should not prevent one from recognizing the possible superior abilities of the rival team. Likewise, one's negative feelings toward foreign spies should not play an important role in evaluating the wisdom or propriety of another country maintaining an effective espionage system in behalf of its vital interests, especially in view of the elaborate espionage system maintained by our own country in behalf of *its* interests.

Use of Flattery

Definition   This fallacy consists in attempting to persuade others of one's view by engaging in excessive praise of them, instead of presenting evidence for one's view.

A very effective way of persuading others is to flatter them in some manner. For example, you have probably heard a speaker say something like this: "Because you are a mature audience of highly educated professionals, I'm sure that you can see clearly the merit of my proposal." High praise, of course, is not fallacious by itself. It only becomes fallacious when it is used as a substitute for evidence.

Everyone likes positive affirmation, but whether the device of flattery can successfully manipulate us will probably depend on how confident we are of ourselves and about our way of coming to conclusions or making decisions. If we are clear about what makes a good argument, it is more likely that we will not be taken in by the cheap trickery of those who use flattery to control our thinking.

Example   "Because you have been such good neighbors and have always been so kind to us when we were in trouble, I really hate to ask you this. But we were wondering if you would be willing to feed our dog while we're at the beach next week. I was just telling my cousin on the phone this morning that if all people were as nice as you, there wouldn't be any trouble in this world." Such flattery might be effective in getting the dog fed, but it is hardly relevant to the issue.

Example "I really hate to ask you this, because you have been so understanding when I've had trouble with this class before. But I was wondering if I could take my test over again for a better grade. You know, if all professors were as caring as you, I don't think there would be such a negative stereotype of them among students."

This student has used flattery rather than reasons for her request. In fact, she mentions no reasons at all for why she should be allowed to retake the test.

Example "Dad, you and Mom have always been such great parents. Not many parents have shown as much trust in their children as you have in me. You have always given me the freedom to show that I can be responsible and deserve your trust. I can't imagine how it would be to have parents who are always looking over my shoulder, watching my every move. I know I am only 16, but if Bill and I used the condo at the beach this weekend, would that be any problem for you guys?"

Normal parents would have difficulty not being intimidated by this kind of flattery—so much so that they might not even notice that no evidence is given for the specific request. It makes no difference whether the flattering comments are true or not, for they constitute an irrelevant personal appeal that is used in place of evidence.

Attacking the Fallacy There is no need to insult someone who gives you a compliment, but it should not be allowed to affect in any way your evaluation of the merit of a view or the rightness of an action. Even if you are convinced that the praise was designed to manipulate a particular response, you could still thank the arguer for his or her remarks and then proceed to ask the questions appropriate to the careful evaluation of the merit of the view. An alternative plan might be to ignore the praise altogether, thus disarming the arguer, and then proceed with the evaluation.

Assigning Guilt by Association

Definition This fallacy consists in attempting to manipulate others into accepting one's view by pointing out that the opposing view is held by those with negative esteem, instead of presenting evidence for one's position.

This fallacy involves the manipulation of negative feelings, by pointing out that the opposing view is held by people or groups we don't like or don't usually agree with. This appeal encourages one to accept the arguer's position in order to avoid any guilt by association with those held in such negative esteem.

There is no good reason to assume that a person we might disagree with on one issue would be one we would disagree with on every issue. Indeed, it would be just as absurd to assume that we will agree with those whom we like on every issue. Whether we like or dislike a person who holds a view that we are contemplating could not possibly affect the truth or falsity of that view or the rightness or wrongness of an action.

If the only basis for holding a position is that it can be defended by a good argument, it is not unlikely that even some people we don't like will be persuaded by the same argument and thus come to the same conclusion as we have. After all, it is not just likable people or our close friends and associates who are able to evaluate accurately the merit of arguments.

Example

Notice how Professor Smith attempts to manipulate Professor Jackson's negative feelings in the following exchange.

> **Professor Smith**: You are going to vote with us on this personnel policy at next week's faculty meeting, aren't you?
> **Professor Jackson**: No, I really don't think it is a very good idea.
> **Professor Smith**: Really? Well, neither does Professor Hart or Professor Carter. They're voting against us, too.

If Professors Hart and Carter are people with whom Professor Jackson has always disagreed or predictably opposes, it is possible that he might be tempted to alter his opinion. At least that is what Professor Smith hopes will happen. However, because no relevant evidence was presented for Professor Jackson's consideration, there is no relevant reason for him to move over to Professor Smith's position.

Example

> **Dawn**: Hey, Sean, you *are* going to vote for Dawson for class president, aren't you?
> **Sean**: No, I think I'm going to vote for Kellogg. He impresses me a lot more than Dawson.
> **Dawn**: Well, a whole bunch of people are voting for Kellogg. I understand that virtually every member of every Greek organization on campus is voting for him.

If Sean is opposed to the Greek system of sororities and fraternities, this is a way of trying to manipulate him by associating him with those toward whom he has a negative attitude.

Example   "How could you vote for Senator Willis? He's been endorsed by every gay and lesbian organization in the country. How could you tell anybody who you voted for?" If the person being questioned is homophobic, the strategy of trying to assign some kind of guilt by association just might work—but it shouldn't.

Attacking the Fallacy   Since the attractiveness of character of the holder of a view is irrelevant to the merit of the view, you should forthrightly insist that it makes no difference to you who holds the view, if they do it for the right reasons.

Even if your close friends and associates think that there must be something wrong with you, if you think like the "enemy" or the unliked, you might point out that a consistent application of that principle would reduce it to absurdity. For example, you might ask the arguer, "If we were to discover that the 'enemy' has joined our political party, what do we do? Resign? What if we discover that people that we don't like are on the same diet plan that we are? Do we change diet plans immediately?" Surely the arguer would not want to say that the views and behavior that are appropriate for us are to be controlled by the whims or actions of our rivals.

Exercises

In each of the following exercises (1) identify the type of irrelevant emotional appeal illustrated; (2) explain what specific feature in the example causes it to be properly identified in that way; and (3) explain how the reasoning violates the criterion of relevance.

1. Ed, I just can't vote for him, even though I agree with what you say about the two candidates. It's just that we have always been Democrats. I'm not sure that I could live with myself if I voted for a Republican.

2. Real estate broker: "You mean that after we flew you down here to Florida at no cost to you, put you up in a Miami Beach hotel for three days with all meals provided, took you on a Caribbean fishing trip, and took you to Disney World, you're not going to buy even *one* of our small lots?"

3. Carpet salesperson: "Surely with your obvious knowledge of carpets and expertise in judgment, you will recognize the quality and value of this piece and know that at this price it is a bargain worth having."

4. Are you sure you want to openly oppose this new curricular proposal? You know that both the president and the dean are pushing it pretty hard—and you don't have tenure yet!

5. If you don't marry me, our poor child will go through life without ever knowing who his father was or without having a normal family life. A boy needs a father, John! Please don't deprive him of that.

6. I just don't understand why you are opposing federal aid to parochial schools. Both of us are Catholics committed to the parochial school concept, and you know how badly our schools are in need of financial resources. If this bill for financial assistance to parochial schools doesn't pass the Congress, it will probably mean that many of our schools will have to close their doors.

7. I know that I haven't done very good work in your courses, Professor Letson, but if you don't write me a good recommendation, there is no way that I can get into graduate school. Graduate school means a lot to me. I know that if I get into graduate school I'll do good work, and you won't be sorry that you helped me when I really needed it.

8. I do hope that you will make a sizable pledge to the United Charities Fund this year, Bill. You were the only member of the managerial staff that pledged less than $100 last year.

9. **Senator Baker**: I think it's time we developed some kind of national health care plan.

Senator Bradford: You must be losing it, Buck. That's socialized medicine—the very thing that Ted Kennedy and the other liberals have been trying to shove down our throats for years.

10. David, you can't be serious about going to Annapolis! Our family has *always* been army—your brother, your father, your uncles, and even your grandfather. All of them, as you well know, went to West Point.

11. I think that we ought to give the "Teacher of the Year" award to Professor Davis. Ever since his wife died last year, he just hasn't been the same. I think that this award would really lift his spirits. He always seems so sad. I think this year has really been hard for him. And he's not really *that* bad a teacher.

12. What's wrong with you taking my name when we get married, Sharon? I know that marriage is an equal partnership, as you say, but it wouldn't mean that we weren't equal just because you had my name. It would really be embarrassing to me if we got married and you refused to take my name. In fact, I don't think I would want to be part of a relationship where you would show me that kind of disrespect.

13. If Buchanan is elected to the county board, you can count on him to keep down the tax rate on property. His opponent, Mr. Groseclose, wants to increase substantially the number of county services, and that is going to take a lot more money. With as much property as you have, there should be no question for whom you should vote.

14. If the faculty and staff of this college are not willing to endorse my re-election to Congress, it may be a long time before you get that new exit that you've been wanting—one that leads directly from the interstate to your campus.

15. But, Cynthia, you must have a church wedding. No one in our family has ever been married outside the church. Your father and I, your grandparents, and your brothers and sisters have all been married in the church.

16. Car advertisement: "Most buyers are misled by gimmicky commercials and glitzy packages, but not *you*. *You* are a discriminating customer, who demands the best for the most economical price. So come by Kingston Motors and drive away in a new Lexus today."

17. I just can't believe that you're going to support the President on this bill, Richard. The way I see it is that if we Republicans vote with the president on any issue, we are simply giving aid and comfort to the enemy.

18. Surely you are not going to urge the county board to vote against raising the county property tax rate. As a teacher, you know that the best way to assure yourself of a raise this year is to have an increase in county revenue.

19. We must continue to fight against any further expansion of gun-control laws. All they do is promote more government control of our private lives, even our hobbies, while making it easier for the crooks.

20. If I were you, I don't think I would stand up there and defend the right of the Klan to march in the parade Saturday. You can't keep people from drawing their own conclusions, you know.

Additional Exercises

In each of the following exercises (1) identify, from among all the fallacies we have studied, the fallacy illustrated; (2) explain what specific feature in the example causes it to be properly identified in that way; and (3) explain how the reasoning violates the criterion of relevance.

1. Bill, I would have thought that, as a coach, you would favor a new NCAA rule lowering the academic eligibility requirement for first-year athletes. That would allow you to have a much larger pool of recruits, and being a nonscholarship school, we need all the help we can get.

2. I was going to *let* Matt win the match anyway. I haven't been feeling well lately, and I was tired of playing in the hot sun. Besides, I hadn't eaten anything since breakfast.

3. Coach, I sure hope my son gets some quality playing time this season. I sure wouldn't want to reconsider my $50,000 pledge for the new stadium project.

4. I am a strong supporter of capital punishment. The present way of trying to rehabilitate criminals isn't working; released convicts and parolees always seem to find their way back into prison.

5. I really think that you ought to give her the job. She may not be the best qualified, but she has three children and can't even afford to feed or clothe them, since her husband walked out on them six months ago and moved out of the state.

6. Barbara-Lyn: I've been going to Weight Watchers religiously twice a week for over a year.

    Tom: Why Weight Watchers?

    Barbara-Lyn: Well, Weight Watchers says that their program is the only way to lose weight safely and effectively.

7. I know that you have good reasons for supporting the administration's proposal, but you know that most of the faculty is opposed to it. And if you stand up and speak for it, many faculty members will just assume that you are one of the administration's "wimps."

8. The Surgeon General has said that AIDS cannot be transmitted by swimming in a pool with an infected person. But *nobody* believes that is true.

9. We should oppose the opening of a new restaurant in our town. It will certainly take away some of the customers from our restaurant and cut into our profits.

10. You have always been so helpful and supportive of me whenever I needed you. I've always known that I could depend on you. I need you now. Would you please talk to my mother about Joe and me moving in together? She won't listen to me.

11. No matter how hard I study, I still don't do well on tests. I always seem to study the wrong stuff. I guess I should just not study at all and take the test blind.

12. This is an idea that most people simply couldn't accept 40 years ago. But now people, like yourselves, are better educated and more informed about their world and clearly see the merit of this proposal.

13. I would never go to Emory & Henry college. It used to be an all-male school. They are still probably sexist and don't give women the same rights and privileges as they do men.

14. I can't believe that you won't donate any money to the American Cancer Society—especially since your father has been diagnosed as having lung cancer.

15. Men should not be expected to do housework, because cleaning, washing, and child care has always been considered a woman's job.

16. You just can't turn your back on the coalition that has made the Democratic party what it is. Even Republicans have trouble understanding how liberal Democrats can vote for a trade agreement opposed by organized labor. This is our constituency! Don't let them down.

17. The sweetener aspartame is really bad for you. I heard the other day that it breaks down DNA particles.

18. I can't believe that you are having both your Mom and your Dad walk you down the aisle at your wedding. No one in our family or anyone I know has ever had her Mom walk her down. People expect certain things to happen at weddings. You should simply do it the way we've *always* done it, Diana.

19. The local factory is not meeting the current standards for either waste disposal or air pollution. There ought to be stiffer laws than the ones currently in place.

20. I don't see how the administration could possibly be serious in telling us to change our pledging program. The pledging activities we engage in have been used for over 50 years to "test" those men who are pledging to us. My father went through those same tests 30 years ago. You can't put restrictions on them. They are part of who we are. There's no way we could change the program.

21. I think that we should build a new residence hall for men on the campus. The dorm for first-year men has rooms that are too small, and the other two dorms are hot and noisy.

22. Dad, we would like to go to the beach at spring break, but we need a car to get there. Could I borrow the van for the last week in March? Bob, Ed, and Ben have already asked their parents, but none of them are willing to let us use their car. I can't believe it! They don't even trust their own sons. I told them that I was confident that you were not like their parents—that you trusted me. You do, don't you?

23. But Mr. President, you must see that if you don't show your allegiance to the religious right, you just might lose this election. You just have to do it!

24. I know there are some people who oppose capital punishment, but there is no way that you can say capital punishment is morally wrong. After all, over 80 percent of the American people approve of it.

25. Professor Morgan, all you have to give me is two points to raise my grade to a "B." If you don't, I'll lose my scholarship. Without that scholarship I won't be able to stay in college. That would break my mother's heart.

26. My mother told me of the practice of hazing by all sororities when she was in school here. I would never join a sorority because I do not want to participate in such degrading practices. I don't think hazing is right.

27. Son, both your mother and I want you to go to Washington & Lee University. If you want us to pay for your education, Washington & Lee had better be your first choice. Okay?

28. Vitamins are an important supplement to our daily diets. They help make up for what we miss in our food. So everyone should take at least 200 milligrams of Vitamin B every day.

29. We need to build a new swimming pool for the community. We should do this because swimming is one of the most effective exercises for cardiovascular improvement; it doesn't require any special equipment; and it can be used as a life-long form of regular exercise.

30. The reason that I failed all my classes last term is that the teachers didn't like me. I compared my tests with those of several other students, and they always got a higher grade for basically the same answers. Besides, my parents were having marital problems.

V

Fallacies That Violate the Acceptability Criterion

The premises of a good argument must meet the criterion of acceptability. An *acceptable premise* is a premise that a reasonable person *ought* to find acceptable. To assist in the task of determining the acceptability of premises, we earlier suggested some *conditions of acceptability*. A premise is acceptable if it expresses any of the following: (1) a claim that is a matter of undisputed common knowledge or of one's own personal knowledge or evidence; (2) a claim that is adequately defended in the same discussion or at least capable of being adequately defended on request or further inquiry; (3) a conclusion of another good argument; (4) an uncontroverted eyewitness personal testimony; or (5) an uncontroverted report from an expert in the field.

An alternative way of employing the acceptability criterion is to apply what might be called the *conditions of unacceptability*. A premise should be regarded as unacceptable if it expresses any of the following: (1) a claim that contradicts the evidence, a well-established claim, a credible source, one's own personal knowledge, or other premises in the same argument; (2) a questionable claim that is not adequately defended in the context of the discussion or in some other accessible source; (3) a claim that is self-contradictory, linguistically confusing, or otherwise unintelligible; (4) a claim that is no different from, or as questionable as, the conclusion that it is used to support; or (5) a claim that is based on a usually unstated but highly questionable assumption.

The premises of an argument, then, should be regarded as acceptable if *each* of them conforms to at least one of the conditions of acceptability and if *none* of them conforms to a condition of unacceptability.

The 22 fallacies treated in this chapter that violate the criterion of accept-ability are divided into three groups: (1) fallacies of linguistic confusion, (2) begging-the-question fallacies, and (3) unwarranted assumption fallacies.

FALLACIES OF LINGUISTIC CONFUSION

Each of the fallacies discussed in this section results from some misuse of or confusion in the meaning of a key word or phrase used in the premise of an argu-ment. For that reason, the premise is an unacceptable one.

As pointed out above, if the meaning of a premise is not clear or under-standable, it cannot be an acceptable premise. Since the criteria of a good argument require that an argument have acceptable premises, an argument whose language is confusing is a flawed one.

Words, regardless of how carefully they are chosen, are always a potential source of misunderstanding. A change in context can cause a subtle change in the meaning of a word or even a whole sentence. If careful attention is not given to this phenomenon of language, our arguments will be ineffective, may be misunderstood, or may cause others to draw unwarranted conclusions. Therefore, anyone who is in-terested in good reasoning must attend to the problems of the imprecision of our language. Some of the most common kinds of linguistic confusion found in claims and arguments follow here.

Equivocation

Definition   This fallacy consists in directing an opponent toward an un-warranted conclusion by making a word or phrase, employed in two different senses in an argument, appear to have the same meaning throughout.

One who equivocates has either intentionally or carelessly allowed a key word to shift in meaning in midargument, while giving the impression that all in-stances of the word have the same meaning. As long as this equivocation is not rec-ognized, the conclusion *seems* to follow from the premises. Indeed, the argument may appear to satisfy all the criteria of a good argument. Once the equivocal terms are recognized, there is a disruption in the logical connection that was assumed to exist between the premises, because the key terms lack a uniformity of meaning that is required to relate the premises. When such confusion severs the connection be-tween the premises, the premises are rendered unacceptable and no conclusion can logically be inferred from them.

In a good argument, the words or phrases employed must retain the same meanings throughout the argument, unless a shift in meaning is understood or spec-ified. Equivocation makes it appear that two words have the same meaning, when in fact they do not; they simply give the *appearance* of having the same meaning. A fail-ure to recognize that a word or phrase is functioning in one part of an argument in quite a different sense than it does in another can make it look like support is being given to the claim at issue, simply because the words have the same appearance or sound. Deception of this kind is particularly difficult to detect in long arguments in which the transition in meaning can be well concealed.

It should be pointed out that a pun, by definition, depends on the possibility of a word's having multiple meanings. What makes a pun clever or humorous is that the listener will momentarily fail to recognize that the term in question has shifted in meaning. In no way am I suggesting that one should avoid the happy practice of punning. I would insist, however, that if you are seriously attempting to justify a substantive claim, you should guard against allowing the words in an argument to shift their meaning.

Finally, remember that the listener bears as much responsibility for avoiding fallacious reasoning as the person who presents the argument. For example, if you fail to recognize a shift in the meaning of a term within the context of another person's argument, you also will be guilty of committing the fallacy of equivocation, because, through your own carelessness, you are allowing a fallacious argument to be a convincing one.

Example   "I don't see any reason why we should listen to the superintendent of schools on this textbook issue. We need to hear from someone who has some authority in the field of education. Our superintendent doesn't even have enough authority to keep the students or the teachers in line. Nobody respects her orders."

The first use of the word *authority* refers to a person who is competent in a particular discipline or field of inquiry. The second use of the word *authority* refers to the ability to maintain order or to command respect for or compliance with one's wishes. The issue, of course, is whether the superintendent has sufficient training and competence in the field of educational theory to be considered an authority in the first sense. If she is such an authority, her judgment deserves to be heard. However, the undetected shift in the meaning of the word *authority* to its second sense could lead one to conclude that she is not an authority in the first sense and that therefore her judgment does *not* deserve to be heard.

Example   "You claim that all of our actions are determined, but I know some people who never seem to know what they are going to do or how they are going to behave. They simply never give thought to their actions ahead of time. Hence, I would say that, at least for those people, it would not be accurate to say that their actions are determined."

The first use of the word *determined* refers to the view that all human behavior is the result of prior events in one's life and could not be otherwise. The second use of the word *determined* refers to behavior that is deliberate or carried out with firm convictions. If we do not detect the respondent's shift in the meaning of the word, we could be misled into thinking that he or she has provided evidence against the claim that the actions of all people can be accounted for in terms of prior causes.

Example   "My college adviser suggested to me that I should take logic because logic, he said, teaches one how to argue. But I think that people argue too much as it is. Therefore, I do not intend to take any course in logic, and I am of the opinion that perhaps logic shouldn't be taught at all. It will only contribute to increasing the tension that already exists in the world."

The first use of the word *argue* refers to the process of carefully supporting claims with evidence and sound reasoning. The second use of the word refers to a bitter controversy or to a kind of disagreeable haranguing between individuals. The shift in the meaning of the word could cause one to come to the unwarranted conclusion that a course in logic teaches one how to be disagreeable.

Attacking the Fallacy   If you have reason to believe that you are being confronted with an argument involving equivocation, there are at least three ways of dealing with its fallacious character. One way would be to identify the problematic word or phrase and point out to your verbal opponent the two different ways the word functions in the argument in question. If there is some dispute about whether the arguer has equivocated, you may ask for precise definitions of the suspected words or phrases. If the definitions are different, then the charge will be proved.

A second way is to translate the word in one of its instances with words that clearly express what you think is the exact meaning of the term and then use the translation in its other instances. If the argument then makes no sense, it thereby loses its appearance of being a good argument.

A third way to demonstrate the fallacious nature of reasoning that involves equivocation is to use the absurd example method. For example:

Since only man is rational,

and no woman is a man,

_____

Therefore, no woman is rational.

The equivocation on the word *man* leads to a conclusion that is obviously absurd.

Ambiguity

Definition   This fallacy consists in presenting a claim or argument that uses a word, phrase, or grammatical construction that can be interpreted in two or more distinctly different ways, without making clear which meaning is intended.

This confusion usually arises in the presentation of the premises of an argument. If one does not know how to interpret a particular premise, then it is an unacceptable one, because it makes a claim whose meaning is unclear or not known. An argument with such a flaw violates the second criterion of a good argument. Hence, no appropriate conclusion can be drawn, because the truth or falsity of a conclusion depends on how the premises are understood.

There are two ways in which this fallacy is committed. The first way is that an arguer may use a word or phrase with two or more meanings in a claim or argument. This kind of ambiguity is sometimes referred to as *semantical ambiguity*. Since a majority of the words in our language have more than one meaning, there is obviously nothing fallacious about using a word with more than one meaning. The fallacy is committed only when the context does not make clear which of the several meanings of the word or phrase is intended. That lack of clarity could render the listener unable to draw any conclusion at all or cause him or her to interpret the word in an unintended way and thus arrive at a false or inappropriate conclusion. Semantical ambiguity can be remedied by a clarification of the meaning of the particular ambiguous word or phrase.

A second way in which this fallacy is committed is in presenting a claim or argument that can be legitimately interpreted in two or more distinctly different ways because of its syntactical construction. This *syntactical ambiguity* is distinguishable from semantical ambiguity by virtue of the fact that it can be remedied by a grammatical reconstruction of the sentence. Some of the most typical grammatical errors that render a sentence ambiguous are unclear pronoun reference ("Claude never argues with his father when he is drunk"); elliptical construction, where words are omitted but supposedly understood ("John likes logic better than his wife"); unclear modifier ("I have to take my make-up test in an hour"); careless use of *only* ("The tennis courts will be available to members only from Monday to Friday"); and careless use of *all* ("All of the fish Doug caught weigh at least 15 pounds"). Such ambiguous constructions are often referred to by grammarians as *amphiboles*.

Example Suppose a friend said to you, "Yesterday we moved into our new house." This is a case of semantical ambiguity. It is not clear from the context whether the "new" house is a different house or a recently constructed one. Hence, it would be inappropriate for you to draw any conclusion about the kind of structure in which your friend now resides.

Example Newspaper headlines are often ambiguous. If you read only the following headline, it would be difficult to draw any justifiable conclusion: ELIZABETH TAYLOR LOSES APPEAL. In this example of semantical ambiguity it would be impossible to know, without reading the article, whether Ms. Taylor had ranked low in a recent poll ranking the world's most beautiful women, whether she is now no longer a box-office attraction, or whether she had just lost a case that she had appealed to a higher court. The newspaper editor has therefore committed the fallacy of ambiguity, and the reader should draw no conclusion without reading the article.

Example Consider the semantical ambiguity involved in this familiar scene with two people driving in city traffic.

Laura: You'll have to tell me how to get there.
Eleanor: Okay. Turn right here. [Laura turns right.] Hey, I didn't
   mean for you to turn right! Couldn't you see that I was pointing left?

In this case, of course, Eleanor meant for Laura to turn *immediately*, but as Laura did not happen to see Eleanor's pointing, her verbal directions were surely ambiguous.

An even more familiar semantical ambiguity encountered in the context of driving is as follows.

Laura: Do I turn left here?
Eleanor: Right!

No matter whether Laura subsequently turns right or left, Eleanor's directions must again be pronounced ambiguous, because it is unclear whether Eleanor is simply confirming Laura's assumption or suggesting another direction.

Example   Suppose you were to read a brochure about a school of carpentry that said, "Come to our school and learn how to build a house in six weeks." It would be unclear whether you were going to be taught how to build a house in a six-week instruction period or whether you were going to be taught a way to complete the construction of a house within a six-week building schedule. A reorganization of this syntactically ambiguous sentence could clarify the intended meaning.

Example   Two faculty colleagues who live near each other are preparing, after a late afternoon meeting, to leave the campus for their homes. Their homes are in walking distance of the campus, but because it is raining, one says to the other, "How about a ride home?"

It is quite possible that the one to whom the question is addressed might think that he is being offered a ride home in the automobile of the asker. On the other hand, it may be the case that the asker is himself seeking some means of transportation home. If the one who was asked the question answers "Okay," it is not clear whether he is agreeing to give the asker a ride home or accepting the asker's offer of a ride. If neither had an automobile parked on campus and if the ambiguity were not cleared up before they walked to the parking lot, it is quite possible that the two colleagues might find themselves standing in the rain looking stupidly at each other in the middle of an empty parking lot. At least that was the way I experienced it a few years ago. The false conclusions and embarrassment to which we were led by the syntactical ambiguity of my question could have been avoided if I had been more careful in formulating it.

Attacking the Fallacy   As in the case of the fallacy of equivocation, you should identify the word, phrase, or problematic syntactical construction and, if possible, ask the speaker for the intended meaning. Make it clear why you are asking for a clarification. Don't be deterred by the accusation that you are being "picky," for it is not being "picky" to ask for help in understanding something that you do not understand. Find some way to communicate to the arguer that you cannot assess the worth of his or her claim or argument until you understand it.

It obviously makes no sense to draw a conclusion from an unintelligible premise. If your opponent still fails to understand this dilemma, counter with a similar but absurd argument of your own. Utter a clearly ambiguous claim, draw a conclusion, and then ask your opponent what he or she thinks of your argument. If the claim is genuinely ambiguous, that is, the opponent really does not know what is meant by the culprit claim, he or she will not be able to answer your question about the merit of the argument.

If you do not understand the meaning of an arguer's claim, and the arguer is not immediately available to provide clarification, use your own knowledge of the arguer's larger perspective as a clue to the possible intended meaning. If you are unable to ask your opponent for clarification and you have no knowledge of any larger perspective, perhaps you should draw no conclusion at all. If you must do so, you might hypothesize about the intended meaning and draw a very tentative conclusion based on that speculation. If the conclusion is consciously tentative, it can be more easily changed with additional information or clarification.

Finally, be careful not to falsely accuse an opponent of ambiguity when none is present. Your opponent has not committed the fallacy of ambiguity if the context makes clear the proper interpretation of the language. If *you* interpret a word, phrase, or sentence in an unjustified way because of your own careless attention to the context, it is you who has committed the error. Such an error might be called "false ambiguity." For example:

> **Buck**: How can they afford to do that?
> **Lila**: Do what?
> **Buck**: Give pizzas away!
> **Lila**: What do you mean?
> **Buck**: Belah's Pizza! It says right here in the ad, "Belah's Pizzas Delivered *Free!*"

Buck has no right to make such an interpretation of the advertisement. The grammar of the ad is perfectly clear; *free* refers only to the *delivery* of the pizzas.

If someone draws an improper conclusion from your statement when its context makes the meaning clear and then attempts to place the blame on you, don't be intimidated. Shift the responsibility back to your opponent as quickly as possible by showing how the context of your statement did not allow for such an interpretation.

Improper Accent

Definition   This fallacy consists in directing an opponent toward an unwarranted conclusion by placing improper or unusual emphasis on a word, phrase, or particular aspect of an issue or claim. It is sometimes committed by taking portions of a quotation out of context in a way that conveys a meaning not intended by the person quoted.

Improper accent may be given in at least two ways. The first has to do with placing emphasis on a word or phrase by either voice inflection or word placement in a way that misleads a hearer or reader. This error is sometimes quite difficult to detect, because it can result from the slightest change in the speaker's voice inflection. Such stress is sometimes given by means of a sarcastic or mocking intonation. Many sentences can take on quite different meanings depending on which word is being stressed or given an unusual emphasis. If such accenting causes a listener to come to an unwarranted conclusion, even though the words themselves might not express an untrue statement, the speaker is guilty of misleading the listener.

The second way of giving improper accent is to lift something out of its context. Entire statements or even paragraphs can be wrongly accented by being taken out of a larger context. The speaker or writer commits the fallacy of accent in this case by omitting important contextual meanings or qualifications of a claim.

The second criterion of a good argument requires that the premises be acceptable. One who emphasizes (or fails to emphasize) certain words or phrases, thereby causing another person to arrive at a probably false or misleading conclusion, is using an unacceptable premise, because it creates a confusion that is not resolved in the context of the argument. Hence, an argument that employs such a confusing premise cannot be a good one.

Example If a father were speaking of the problems of raising his three children and said of his oldest daughter, "*She* won't listen to me" (stressing *she*), you might conclude that the other two children *do* listen to him. If it is not the case that the other two children do respond positively to him, the father might be justifiably accused of directing his hearers to a false conclusion, even though the words that he uses express a true proposition.

Example A student says, "I often see Professor O'Neil, but never with his *wife*." The particular stress on the word *wife* in this sentence would probably suggest that Professor O'Neil spends a great amount of time with someone other than his wife or that he never takes his wife anyplace. The sentence itself, without stress on any particular word, may express a true proposition—namely, that the student has not seen Professor O'Neil with his wife. However, because of the accent on the word *wife,* a listener may be falsely led to infer one of the other two interpretations of the statement.

Example Newspaper headlines and titles of magazine articles often commit the fallacy of improper accent. Again, the actual words of the headline or title may be the vehicle for a true statement, yet the statement may be misleading in that it suggests some additional claim because of an unusual stress. Such headlines or titles often lead to understandings that are put into proper perspective only by the articles to which they are attached. This is commonly the case with supermarket tabloids. Suppose the following headline were printed in your local newspaper: BILLY GRAHAM FAVORS HOMOSEXUALS. The headline might lead one to infer something about Reverend Graham's sexual interests or his support for gay rights, whereas the article might be simply an item from an interview in which Graham said that he saw no reason why repentant homosexuals should not be ordained into the ministry.

Example One of the most frequently committed forms of the fallacy of accent is lifting a phrase or sentence out of its context.

Karen: If Ben doesn't stop harassing me, I'm going to report him to my supervisor.

Mark (speaking to Ben later): Karen was talking to me today about your harassing her, and she said that she was going to report you to her supervisor.

In this example, Mark's conveying of the message from Karen leaves out the important antecedent in Karen's hypothetical statement. If the entire message had been delivered, Ben would probably conclude that ceasing the harassment would probably keep his job intact. But without the important "if" statement, Ben would probably draw a very different conclusion—that his days at his job are numbered.

Attacking the Fallacy In most cases, one can confront the fallacy of improper accent much like one does the fallacy of ambiguity. Point out the part of your opponent's argument or claim that you suspect of being inappropriately accented, and ask for a clarification. It is, of course, difficult to get someone to "take back" a voice inflection after it has had its misleading effect.

You can also guard against being led astray by improper accent by taking some precautionary measures. Always read or ask for the larger context of any statement you suspect of being accented. You might preclude the possibility of being misled by questionable headlines or titles by determining, if possible, to read the articles to which they are attached. At least you can be very cautious about drawing an inference based on a headline or title alone.

In general, it is always wise to follow the rule "When uncertain, ask." Don't be embarrassed to ask about something you don't understand. It is better to run the risk of appearing naive or uninformed than to come to a false conclusion.

Illicit Contrast

Definition This fallacy consists in a listener directly inferring from a speaker's claim some related but unstated *contrasting* claim by placing improper or unusual emphasis on the words or phrases in the statement.

This fallacy is very closely related to the fallacy of improper accent, but in this case it is clearly the listener, rather than the speaker, who does the accenting. It is also very similar to false ambiguity, where one interprets a claim in a way that is not justified by the context. In the case of illicit contrast, one is claiming that the speaker accented some particular part of a claim, which led to the inference drawn, even though there is no evidence that any such emphasis was introduced by the speaker. Indeed, it is the listener who has introduced the misleading emphasis. He or she has inappropriately extended the meaning of the speaker's claim. The listener has taken the speaker's claim that "X is true of Y" and extended it to also mean that "X is *not* true of the *contrast* of Y." For example, if the speaker claims that logic teachers are very smart, the listener would be inappropriately extending the meaning of that claim if he or she infers that the speaker is also saying that professors in other fields are *not* smart. In this case it is the listener who has employed an unacceptable premise, and an argument with such a premise is a flawed one.

Example If a young woman, after an unhappy love affair, claimed that men are insensitive brutes, it would be fallacious to infer from her statement that she was implicitly contrasting males to females, saying that females are *not* insensitive people. The young woman was probably not trying to characterize the differences between men and women; she was probably just responding emotionally to her own hurt feelings. Moreover, even if she were making the claim that all men are insensitive, nothing should be inferred about her thinking regarding the sensitivity of women.

Example   If a Catholic cardinal were dealing with a problem in which a young priest had been discovered to be relating sexually to a married woman, he might caution all the priests in his diocese that "it is improper for priests to relate sexually to married women." It would be fallacious, since it would be unjustified by the context, to assume that the cardinal is suggesting that it is not improper for priests to relate sexually to unmarried women.

Example   The following conversation between my two daughters and me took place several years ago in my home.

> **Father**: Isn't that Diana's dress you have on, Cynthia?
> **Cynthia**: It's mine now. Diana gave it to me. It's too little for her.
> **Father**: Well, it looks very nice on you.
> **Diana**: Then you don't think it looked nice on me?

In this short domestic exchange, Diana committed the fallacy of illicit contrast, because she falsely accused me of accenting the word *you* when I said, "It looks nice on you." The case was, however, that I did not stress the word *you*; I was simply describing how the dress looked on Cynthia. I was making no implicit comment on how it looked or might have looked on someone else.

Attacking the Fallacy   Because your opponent is falsely claiming that you have accented some particular part of a claim that led him or her to the questionable contrasting claim, you should insist that the burden of proof is on the opponent to demonstrate that the context or your voice inflection encouraged such an interpretation. You, of course, have a peculiar advantage, because you can almost always point out that the contrasting claim was not specifically uttered. But your opponent has already acknowledged that you did not actually utter the claim in question; the issue is whether you *implicitly* made the claim and whether you are prepared to defend it.

No person should be required to accept responsibility for any claim not made. If you think you have been mistakenly heard making a claim that you have not made, you could express your willingness to examine the unstated contrasting claim in question, while making it quite clear that your original statement had in no way implied that claim. Unless you wish to reserve judgment about the merit of the issue, you could even deny the questionable claim outright—in addition to denying that you implicitly made the claim. Denying that you made the claim and denying the claim itself are two different issues, and that point should be made clear to your opponent.

Argument by Innuendo

Definition   This fallacy consists in directing one's listeners to a particular, usually derogatory, conclusion, by a skillful choice of words or the careful arrangement of sentences that implicitly *suggest* but do not *assert* that conclusion. The force of the fallacy lies in the impression created that some veiled claim is true, although no relevant evidence is presented to support such a view.

This method of arguing is commonly used to attack a person, group, or idea when there is little or no evidence to justify a straightforward claim or accusation. The power of suggestion is used in this way to compensate for the lack of relevant evidence. Because no actual claim is made, it could be said that a person using the argument by innuendo is not guilty of outright lying or of making an unjustified claim. Indeed, such a speaker would probably deny that any outright claim had been made and would refuse to accept responsibility for any inference that might be drawn from his or her utterance.

The conclusion of an argument by innuendo does not merit our acceptance, because the speaker has chosen and arranged the words of a claim (the asserted one) in such a way that a very different claim (the suggested one) is being made. Not only is the suggested claim confused with the asserted claim, but the suggested claim is one for which no evidence is or is likely to be given.

Nevertheless, the speaker wishes you to draw a particular conclusion on the basis of the claim; but since the claim is a confusing one, it is an unacceptable one. It therefore cannot be part of a good argument.

Example Sometimes the addition of a single word or phrase in an utterance can lead to a false or unjustified conclusion, even though the words together do not express anything that is not true. Suppose that a dean of students at a college is asked by an employer if a prospective employee had ever been in any kind of disciplinary difficulty while attending college. The dean might look at the records and say, "No"; or she might say, "No, we were never able to convict him of any violations of college rules." The latter response, unfortunately, would probably have a negative effect on the prospective employee's chances for employment, even though it might express a true proposition.

Suppose that the prospective employee were still a student at the college in question and the dean said in response to the same question, "No, not yet!" The addition of the last two words transforms a straightforward negative answer into one filled with innuendo. Moreover, the conclusion that the employer might draw from such a response is one for which the dean would probably not wish to accept responsibility.

Example Suppose that you heard the following statement uttered by one of the candidates in a hard-fought gubernatorial race: "If you knew that one of the candidates in this race was receiving money from illegal sources, would that affect your voting decision? Look into the matter and see where the campaign funds of my opponent are coming from. The facts might surprise you." The speaker has allegedly made no serious claim against his opponent that requires any kind of defense, but the power of suggestion has done its work.

Example The power of innuendo usually depends on the tone of the speaker.

Ginger: Are Allison and Eddie still going steady?
Luci: Well, according to Eddie, they are.

The straightforward claim is that Eddie believes that he and Allison are going steady. The tone of the response could suggest that Eddie is unaware that Allison thinks differently about their relationship or even that Allison is dating other men—a fact unknown to Eddie.

Attacking the Fallacy   In spite of the fact that the speaker usually will not wish to take responsibility for the unspoken claim, you should perhaps spell out the conclusion to which you have been led and ask the speaker to justify it. In no case should you accept an implicit claim without being satisfied on evidential grounds, because an implicit assertion requires the same justification as does an explicit one. If the speaker is not inclined to defend the claim in question, suggest that he or she specifically both deny the implicit claim and take definite steps to counterbalance the effect that it has had. Finally, be especially careful that you do not read innuendoes into utterances when they are not there.

Misuse of a Vague Expression

Definition   This fallacy consists in attempting to establish a position by means of a vague expression or in drawing an unjustified conclusion as a result of assigning a very *precise* meaning to another's word, phrase, or statement that is quite *imprecise* in its meaning or range of application.

A person is not guilty of committing this fallacy simply because he or she employs vague expressions. There is nothing wrong with using vague language. Almost all of us use vague expressions as a part of our linguistic style. Indeed, they usually function quite well for us when nothing of importance is at stake. The fallacy occurs when vague expressions are *misused*.

Vague terms may be misused in two ways. First, vague expressions are misused when they are key words in premises used to establish a position. Used in this way, the support is at best dubious. Since the term is quite imprecise in its meaning, it is not possible to evaluate the acceptability of the claim in which it is employed. Such a claim is also impossible to refute. Since we do not know the range of application of most vague terms, we cannot know at what point counterevidence may do some damage to the claim in which the terms appear. For example, if we wished to argue against an employee's claim that she is overworked, we must know precisely what it means to be overworked before we can know whether the counterevidence we might have weakens or refutes the claim.

The second way in which a vague expression may be misused is for a listener or reader to infer a very particular conclusion from an obviously vague expression. A listener is usually not sufficiently informed to specify the intended meaning of another's vague expression. Hence, the specification would be an arbitrary one, and any inference from it would be equally arbitrary. Vagueness, then, becomes a problem when its presence might encourage a false or unjustified conclusion.

Whether it is the listener drawing a very specific conclusion from a vague term used by the speaker or the speaker using a vague expression to support a specific conclusion, an unacceptable premise is being used. A claim with a key term whose meaning is unclear cannot be used as support for any other claim, nor is it one from which any specific claim can be inferred.

Example At a faculty meeting several years ago, the president of our small college told us that our student enrollment figure was moving us toward a financially dangerous low point and that perhaps we should show a little more concern for some of our weaker students, some of whom were dropping out of school because of failing grades. In response to the president's remarks, one faculty member indignantly exclaimed that he would quit before he would let the president force him to give a passing grade to a student who did not deserve it.

The faculty member, in this case, gave a particular interpretation to the president's vague request to "show a little more concern for some of our weaker students." Of course, if previous experience gave the faculty member reason to believe that "show a little more concern" was a euphemism for "don't fail any students," then his interpretation would have been justified. In this instance, however, such was not the case.

Example A Supreme Court ruling regarding pornography included the view that what is "pornographic" should be determined in accordance with "community standards." However, a prosecutor who tried to establish a case against a distributor of pornographic materials on the grounds that he or she had acted in violation of "community standards" would have to assign a very precise meaning to that very vague criterion—a precision to which it does not lend itself.

Legal concepts are often expressed in very vague language, and those who apply them to particular situations sometimes cannot avoid assigning more specificity of meaning to those words. In doing so, however, one must not assign a meaning in a particular context that is more precise than the original language could possibly support. For example, if one were to assume that the specific meaning of the Supreme Court's notion of "community standards" could be reduced to a formula like "whatever presently offends more than 50 percent of the people in the community" and then to use that highly questionable assigned meaning of a term to draw a conclusion about the illegality of an act, then one might reasonably be charged with misusing a vague expression.

It would be just as fallacious, of course, to argue a case by means of an *untranslated* notion of "community standards." For example, it would be a misuse of vague language to argue that "since this act involving pornographic materials was not in accordance with 'community standards,' then this act should be regarded as against the law."

Example During a textbook controversy in southwest Virginia, some people claimed that the use of a particular series of textbooks constituted a violation of a state law that requires public schools to engage in "moral education." The critics claimed that to use literature with profane or obscene language taught students to be immoral—the very opposite of what the state had mandated the schools to do. In this case, a very particular interpretation has been given to the vague term *moral education*.

Attacking the Fallacy   In most cases, vague expressions can be attacked in the same way ambiguous expressions can; that is, you can insist on further clarification or stipulation of meaning. If a word's range of application is indeterminate, ask for a more precise meaning of the expression. Such a procedure is particularly important if the issue is a significant one and it is desirable to continue the debate. If nothing of significance is at stake, you can, of course, simply ignore the imprecision.

If you do not wish to be misunderstood yourself, avoid using imprecise language as much as possible when dealing with important or controversial issues. Find new words to replace those that have become hopelessly vague, or at least specify the meaning of any words that may have become too vague in ordinary usage to convey your intended meaning clearly.

If you do not give specificity to your words, there are other people who will be quite happy to do so. Vague language, by its very nature, invites others to impose precise meanings on your words. For example, if someone were to say to you, "If you were really concerned about the pollution problem, as you say, you would help us pick up highway trash this Saturday," he or she would be giving an unduly precise meaning to your use of the word *concerned*. But there is no legitimate basis for drawing such a specific conclusion; therefore, you should not be intimidated by this manipulative tactic. Your words do not have to mean what somebody else says they mean.

When an opponent attempts to support a particular claim with statements that contain vague words, challenge the acceptability of the premises on the grounds that you cannot assess their evidential value as long as the meaning of the vague term remains unspecified. A statement that is not understood surely cannot provide convincing support for some other claim.

Distinction Without a Difference

Definition   This fallacy consists in attempting to defend an action or point of view as different from some other one, with which it is allegedly confused, by means of a very careful distinction of language. In reality, however, the action or position defended is no different in substance from the one from which it is linguistically distinguished.

Probably the most common occasion of this fallacy is when an arguer wishes to diminish the possible embarrassment he or she feels in holding what is probably an untenable position or when one's behavior is questionable. One is free, of course, to stipulate the meaning of any term he or she uses, but if the new meaning functions in the same way that the original meaning functions, no difference is made by the attempted distinction. Moreover, since the fallacy is usually committed in response to some form of accusation, the alleged distinction, because it really constitutes no difference in meaning, does not blunt the force of the accusation.

An argument that rests on a fundamental confusion about the meaning of a key claim cannot be a good one, for such a confusing premise could not qualify as an acceptable one. In the case of the fallacy of distinction without a difference, not only is it difficult to distinguish between two claims that may be confused with one another, but there is reason to believe that the claims are substantively the same. Hence, a premise asserting that they are distinguishable notions would be a questionable and therefore unacceptable premise.

Example   Suppose the question is whether a particular person is a good driver. It is generally agreed that the ordinary "good driver" obeys the rules of the roads, keeps his or her mind on the task of driving, and is courteous to other drivers. Suppose that the individual in question is easily distracted by events taking place along the road and frequently turns and talks to other people in the car, thus failing to see and respond appropriately to important road signs. The response to the accusation that he is not a very good driver might be, "I'm not really a bad driver; I just don't pay much attention to the road." The accused person has made a distinction that exhibits no real difference. Hence, the force of the accusation against the driver has not been blunted.

Example   "We must judge this issue by what the Bible *says*, not by what we *think* it says or by what some scholar or theologian thinks it says."
The radio preacher who made this claim apparently thought he was making an important distinction, but it is no distinction at all. If the Bible requires interpretation, and it does, then all persons are interpreters. The Bible or any other text doesn't say anything until it is interpreted by someone—either by a scholar, by a theologian, by an ordinary reader, or by the radio preacher. Therefore, there is no intelligible distinction to be drawn between what the Bible says and what someone says it says. In this particular case, the preacher apparently thought he was telling us what the Bible said, but as a matter of fact, he was merely telling us what *he* thought it said.

Example   "I'm not saying anything against feminism; I just happen to sincerely believe that the male should be the head of the household."
This is an example of an attempt to hide one's opposition to the antisexist movement. At best it represents a confusion concerning the feminist perspective. In any case, the distinction drawn is an empty one.

Attacking the Fallacy   Because many people are unaware that their attempted distinctions are not true differences, the first step that you might take is to try to point out to them the futility of their efforts. If your verbal opponent takes issue with your assessment, which is likely, you might ask for an explanation of just how the alleged distinction differs in meaning. If you are unconvinced by this explanation, you may be inclined to offer a lesson in semantics. But as that would probably not be fully appreciated, why not settle for the absurd example method? Consider the following example: "I wasn't copying; I was just looking at her paper to jog my memory." Such an example should clearly illustrate how very different words can function in very similar ways.

Exercises

In each of the following exercises (1) identify the type of linguistic confusion illustrated; (2) explain what specific feature in the example causes it to be properly identified in that way; and (3) explain how the reasoning violates the criterion of acceptability.

1. **Vic**: In the college handbook concerning cafeteria regulations, it says, "Appropriate dress is expected at all times."
   Chad: That's terrible. Why should I have to wear a coat and tie just to eat in the cafeteria?

2. **Frank**: Here, let me run the projector; I'm good at things like that.
   Jason: What's the matter? Don't you think I am capable of running the projector?

3. **Lori to Francine**: "Your husband seems to have to work late at the office a lot. Does his new female assistant usually have to work also?"

4. Last term I took logic and introduction to philosophy. I hope I have more exciting courses this term.

5. I don't know anything about Elliott, except that he's a liberal, so I didn't vote for him. I didn't want to add another voice to the ranks of the critics of the military in the Congress.

6. Sally is starting her cooking class next week.

7. Gambling should be legalized because it is something we can't avoid. It is an integral part of human experience; people gamble every time they get in their cars or decide to get married.

8. **Dave**: I sure feel good today.
   Dan: I didn't realize that you had not been feeling well.

9. A new play in town was reviewed by the local newspaper's drama critic as being "a great success, considering the lack of facilities and the poor quality of actors with whom the director had to work." The play was then publicized as "a great success."

10. What is right should be required by law. To vote is a right in the United States. Therefore, there should be a law requiring people to go to the polls and vote.

11. A headline in a country newspaper reads, TWO DOCTORS FOR 50,000 PATIENTS. The article to which it is attached explains that there are only two veterinarians for the estimated 50,000 animals in the county.

12. I didn't lie to you; I merely stretched the truth a bit.

13. Senator Phillips reported that the changes in the bill introduced by the Democrats have improved it considerably.

14. **Susan**: Is Valerie helping with the charity show this year?
    Ami: Well, she comes to our meetings!

15. According to our judicial system, a person is innocent until proven

guilty. Hence, the investigation of William Grant, the president's security adviser, was simply an effort by the media and the Senate to damage the reputation of an innocent man.

16. My wife wouldn't come into the office with her sister, because she still had her hair up in curlers.

17. An impartial arbitration committee should not take sides when settling a dispute. But the so-called impartial committee that was supposed to arbitrate the issue between the students and the administration decided in favor of the administration and suspended the students. So how can they claim to have been impartial?

18. We didn't steal this stuff; we just liberated it from the bourgeois capitalist elite.

19. Denise: No, I don't think I should go out tonight. I take my studies very
seriously, and I just *have* to get some work done tonight.

Jim: What makes you think that I don't take my studies seriously?

20. Senator Fisher has been a faithful spokesman for the state's manufacturing interests. It is not particularly surprising that, since his election 12 years ago, he has become one of the richest members of the state legislature.

BEGGING-THE-QUESTION FALLACIES

It is not uncommon to encounter an argument that smuggles the arguer's position on the claim at issue into the wording of one of the premises. Such an argument may be said to beg the question. Even though the conclusion is clearly not warranted by the evidence, the listener is, in effect, "begged" to accept it anyway. There is, of course, the appearance of evidential support, but at least a part of the "evidence" is actually a form of the conclusion in disguise. Such arguments violate the second criterion of a good argument—that the premises or assumptions must be acceptable. A premise cannot be acceptable, according to the conditions of unacceptability, if it is no different from, or if it is as questionable as, the conclusion that it is used to support.

There are many different ways of arguing that could be characterized as question-begging. Some of the most common of these types of argument will be discussed in this section.

Arguing in a Circle

Definition   This fallacy consists in either explicitly or implicitly asserting, in one of the premises of an argument, what is asserted in the conclusion of that argument. Moreover, it uses a premise that probably would not be regarded as true, unless the conclusion were already regarded as true.

The circular argument uses its own conclusion as one of its stated or unstated premises. Instead of offering proof, it simply asserts the conclusion in another form, thereby inviting the listener to accept it as settled when, in fact, it has not been settled. Since the premise is no different from and therefore as questionable as its conclusion, a circular argument violates the criterion of acceptability.

Since premises are those statements that are used to make it more reasonable to believe a conclusion, they should be at least more acceptable than the conclusions they support. If the premises in a particular argument would be accepted only by someone who had already embraced the conclusion, it is obviously not those premises that make it reasonable to accept the conclusion.

Consider, for example, the person who argues that God exists because he or she does not want to be sent to hell. Such a person would be concerned about the prospect of being sent to hell only if he or she already believed that a God exists who could send someone there. Therefore, such an argument is a circular one.

When the conclusion appears as a premise, it is usually stated in different words or in a different form. The circularity of the argument is therefore not always easy to detect. Moreover, those who reason in a circle rarely put their premises and conclusion close enough together to make detection obvious. Indeed, an instance of circular reasoning is sometimes spread over the whole of an essay, a chapter, or even a book.

It should probably be pointed out that a circular argument may be formally valid, in the sense that the conclusion cannot be false if the premises are true. The validity of an argument, however, does not at all establish the truth of its conclusion, especially in the case of the circular argument where at least one of the premises is no different from the conclusion. For the conclusion of a valid deductive argument to be true, the premises must be true or acceptable, and that is the very question at issue. If the premise is simply the not-yet-accepted conclusion in disguise, the premise is obviously not acceptable and cannot support the conclusion.

The circular argument, it could be said, only *pretends* to establish a claim. Once you have recognized the structure of a circular argument, you will see that it says nothing more significant than "A is true, because A is true."

Example   "Mr. Baker cannot be regarded as a competent music critic, because he is biased against all forms of modern, especially atonal, music. I think that the reason he doesn't like modern music is that he is too uninformed to appreciate it; he simply doesn't have the qualities needed to make sound artistic judgments."

The circularity of this argument can be shown by pointing out its basic structure:

Since Baker is biased against modern music,

and the reason Baker doesn't like modern music is that he is uninformed and does not have the qualities needed to make sound artistic judgments,

---

Therefore, Baker is an incompetent music critic.

The claim that Baker is "uninformed," and without "the qualities needed to make sound artistic judgments" means the same thing as the claim that Baker is "incompetent." Hence, Baker's incompetence is given as a reason for his bias, and his bias is given as a reason for his incompetence.

Example   One of the simplest and most easily detected forms of circular reasoning uses a single premise that is actually only a restatement of the conclusion in different words. Consider the following argument: "To use textbooks with profane and obscene words in them is immoral, because it is not right for our children to hear vulgar, disrespectful, and ugly words." The form of the argument is clear: "A, because A."

Example

Amy: This college is very paternalistic in its student policies.
Lori: What reasons do you have for saying that?
Amy: Because they treat the students like children.

In this circular argument, Amy may think that she is giving a reason for why the college is paternalistic, but at best she is only explaining what the word *paternalistic* means. But Lori did not ask for a definition of paternalism. She apparently already knew what the term meant. She asked her for "reasons" for making the claim. Amy, however, gave her no such reasons; she merely repeated her claim.

Attacking the Fallacy   If you are to avoid being misled by those who argue in a circle, it is necessary to keep a very keen eye on the logical structure of the argument in question. Make sure that no premise is simply an equivalent form of the conclusion or that no implicit or explicit premise assumes the truth of the conclusion. If the argument is a long one or one with a number of "chain links," carelessness in attention or a faulty memory may allow the sameness of premise and conclusion to go undetected.

You may directly attack circular reasoning by calling attention to the fact that the conclusion has already been assumed to be true as a part of the evidence. You will need to carefully identify for your opponent the questionable claim that is repeated. This can probably best be done by putting the argument into standard form. After demonstrating how the premise and the conclusion actually make the same claim, indicate why you think that the premise would not have been accepted but for the arguer having already accepted the conclusion.

The fallacious character of arguing in a circle might also be demonstrated by an obvious or absurd instance of it. For instance, if you said, "Reading is fun, because it brings me lots of enjoyment," it should be clear to your opponent that no claim has been established by such an argument. Yet it clearly has the same form as the more subtle examples given above, namely, "A, because A."

In many cases, those who argue in a circle will readily agree that they assume the conclusion to be true—because they are genuinely convinced of its truth. Such arguers need to be reminded that in an argument, one's personal beliefs or convictions concerning the truth of a claim cannot be evidence for the truth of the same claim.

Question-Begging Language

Definition   This fallacy consists in discussing an issue by means of language that assumes a position on the very question at issue, in such a way as to direct the listener to a particular conclusion about the issue.

Question-begging language prematurely assumes that a matter, which is or may be at issue, has already been settled. In such cases, the listener is subtly being "begged" to infer a particular conclusion, although no good reasons are presented for doing so. A plaintiff, for example, who testifies in a contract dispute that he or she was "cheated," when the very purpose of the court proceeding is to decide that issue, is using question-begging language. A nonquestion-begging way of testifying would be to *describe* what happened and then let the court decide if he or she were "cheated."

Slanted or loaded language is logically objectionable when it assumes a position or an attitude on an issue yet to be decided—without providing evidence for that position. Because prejudicial language often influences the outcome of an inquiry by generating a response other than what the facts might support, a special effort should be made to use only descriptive or neutral language when there is an important issue to be decided.

No premise is acceptable if it is as questionable as the claim to which it allegedly lends support. Hence, a premise that employs a question-begging expression cannot be an acceptable one, for it includes within itself a position on the very question at issue.

Example   The chair of the city council announces, "Today we have several issues to consider, one of which is to decide whether to accept or reject these ridiculous recommendations of the Zoning Commission." Although the context is allegedly one of open inquiry, the chair, by prejudging the recommendations as "ridiculous," has begged the very question at issue, that is, whether the recommendations are worthy of acceptance.

Example   Often an allegedly objective analysis of an idea will end with an emotion-laden question-begging expression that has the effect of leading the listener, without evidence, to the speaker's conclusion. Consider a proposal before Congress that concludes with the comment "The whole idea smacks of socialism." Or suppose that a theologian describes another theologian's view as "dangerously close to pantheism." In each case, the speaker is attempting to lead the listener to reject the proposal in question because it leads to something presumably undesirable, although no reasons are given for its undesirability.

Example   Suppose that you are engaged in a discussion of the moral permissibility of abortion. One of the more important issues related to abortion is whether the fetus is to be considered a human being. If one of the discussants constantly refers to the fetus as *the baby*, he or she has begged the question on one of the very points at issue.

Attacking the Fallacy   Question-begging language is not likely to show up in the reconstruction of your opponent's argument, and for that reason it is sometimes difficult to attack directly. Perhaps the best way to confront a person who has committed this fallacy is to point out how his or her very language might prevent the discussion of the issue from being a genuinely open one.

If your opponent will not acknowledge that his or her language may prevent an objective mutual assessment of the merit of the claim, it may be an issue about which he or she cannot be objective. If, for example, your opponent insists on representing your action with words like *double cross* or *blackmail*, and genuinely believes that he or she is simply being "descriptive," it may not be possible to get that person to help assess the action impartially on the basis of the evidence available.

Above all, do not be intimidated by the language of the question-begger, particularly when he or she introduces a claim by such phrases as *obviously, any ten-year-old knows*, or *any fool knows*. This language suggests that the speaker thinks that the issue is not really an issue that deserves any further discussion or investigation. Such expressions function as defenses against attack, and if you wish not to be the victim of such tricks, you must risk the appearance of being naive, uninformed, or even mentally deficient by announcing, "Well, it's *not obvious to me*."

Loaded or Complex Question

Definition   This fallacy consists in formulating a question in a way that presupposes that a definite answer has already been given to some other *unasked* question, or in treating a series of questions as if it involved only one question.

A respondent cannot answer a complex question without granting a questionable assumption or without giving the same answer to each of the two or more questions involved. Nearly all questions are complex in the sense that they make assumptions, but a question does not rise to the level of being a fallacious complex question if the questioner has good reason to believe that the respondent would be quite willing to grant those assumptions. An argument begs the question only when it forces the respondent to grant an assumption that is dubious or when it improperly assumes that the same answer will be given to each question in a series of questions.

In most cases, the complex-question device can be construed as an unacceptable premise, because it implicitly assumes a position on a questionable issue and then uses that position to oblige one to accept an even more questionable position. But as we have seen in all question-begging fallacies, a dubious conclusion cannot be properly supported by an equally dubious premise.

Example   The most common form of this fallacy asks two questions, one of which is implicit and the other of which is explicit. Consider the young man who asks a fellow sophomore, "What fraternity are you going to pledge?" Or the pushy salesclerk who asks, "Cash or charge?" long before you have decided to buy the merchandise. Or even the worried mother who asks her bachelor son, "When are you going to settle down and get married?" In each case, the questioner has assumed a positive answer to an implicit question, namely, that the sophomore has decided to pledge some fraternity, that the customer has decided to buy the merchandise, and that the bachelor has concluded that he will some day get married. The questioners were using unsupported assumptions or premises in concluding what they did. Apart from appropriate evidence, their conclusions were probably unwarranted, and a respondent's direct answer to any of the questions would also be unwarranted, because an answer would have to make the same questionable assumptions.

Example   In a different version of the complex question, a series of questions is treated as if it involved only one question. Suppose that I am asked, "Are you and Nancy going to the wedding and the reception afterward?"

This question involves at least three different questions. It asks if I am going to the wedding, if I am going to the reception, and if my wife, Nancy, will be my companion at these events. It might be the case that I would wish to answer positively in response to two of the three questions but negatively in response to the third. Yet the question is asked in such a way that only one answer can be given. Interestingly, this question could conceivably be an even more complex question, for it could be further divided by asking if Nancy were going to accompany me to the wedding and if she were also going to accompany me to the reception. Indeed, a careful analysis of the original question might reveal 16 different questions if all possible combinations involving the four variables were considered. If the question is not divided, the questionable assumption that is granted to the questioner is that the same answer will be given to each of the questions.

Example   "Why is it that the children of divorce are emotionally more unstable than those children raised in unbroken homes?"

This is a complex question, for the questioner has assumed a position on a questionable claim, namely, that children of divorce are emotionally more unstable than children raised in unbroken homes. That claim must be established before the question calling for an explanation of such a phenomenon can be appropriately asked. Indeed, if the substantive claim can be shown to be false, the call for explanation would be out of order. However, as it was originally asked, the question does not consider the possibility that the substantive claim may be false. Hence, the respondent is "begged" to grant the truth of that assumption.

Attacking the Fallacy   There are a number of ways you might respond to a complex question. First, refuse to give a straightforward *yes* or *no* to such a question. Second, point out the questionable assumption and deal with it directly. Third, insist, if necessary, that the question be appropriately divided, so that each question can be answered separately. Remember that even standard rules of parliamentary procedure provide for "dividing the question"; indeed, a motion to divide the question has a priority status.

If you yourself are accused of asking a loaded question, make sure that your accuser is using the term *loaded* correctly. Sometimes when people do not want to answer a question because their answer might be personally embarrassing, they will accuse the questioner of asking a loaded question. In logic, however, a question is not loaded unless it contains an unwarranted assumption. There is nothing fallacious about asking a question that might be personally embarrassing for the respondent to answer.

Leading Question

Definition   This fallacy consists in "planting" a proposed answer to a question at issue by the manner in which the question is asked.

A leading question usually involves asking only one question. This question contains an unsupported claim, in that it unjustifiably assumes a position on what is probably a debatable, or at least an open, issue. Furthermore, the questioner is, in effect, asking another to assume the same position on the issue yet fails to provide any adequate justification for the respondent to do so. The questioner is therefore simply "begging" or coaxing the respondent to come to the same conclusion.

As in the case of the complex question, the leading question can be construed as a case of unacceptable premise. The arguer is inviting us to accept a conclusion on the premise that he or she believes it to be true. The circular or question begging character of the exchange is clear. Consider the following example of a leading question: "You will support me in my effort to get this judgeship, won't you?" This could be construed as an argument with the following form:

Since you will support me in my campaign,

Therefore, you will support me in my campaign.

Such a premise is surely unacceptable, since it is not defended and is obviously no different from the conclusion itself, and an argument that has such a premise as its only premise cannot be a good one.

Example   Suppose that a long-time friendship between two people is seriously threatened with dissolution because one of the friends has committed an act that the other considers very "unfriendlike" in character. The perpetrator of the act asks, "Our friendship will never die over something as trivial as this, will it?" The questioner has assumed that the matter in question is a trivial one, and is begging the friend to accept it as trivial, when the triviality or nontriviality of the act is the very question at issue.

Example   Consider the courtroom lawyer who leads her client in the following manner: "You did plan to return the money that you borrowed from the cash drawer, did you not?"

In this case, the defense lawyer is "leading" the witness, by assuming a position on the very question at issue—namely, whether the defendant embezzled the money or whether he inappropriately "borrowed" it. Even though the lawyer may be convinced that it was simply borrowed, that is, that her client is innocent, a proper procedure for getting at the truth of the matter would be to encourage the witness to explain the circumstances related to the taking of the money. This would be evidence for the conclusion being argued, that is, that the money was simply borrowed. In this way, the claim of the defense would be a supported one. Planting a proposed answer is not only likely to be disallowed by the judge, it is also a procedure that is likely to weaken the case for the defense.

Example Suppose a faculty member approaches one of his friends just before a faculty meeting at which a vote on an important curricular matter is to be taken and asks, "I don't suppose you would turn your back on your friends by voting against us on this issue, would you?"

The questioner here is making an unsupported or questionable claim, which he is "begging" the friend to accept, namely, that voting on the other side of the issue is equivalent to being a traitor or unfriendlike. The questioner begs the question by telling the respondent how to answer without explaining how voting in accordance with one's own convictions is a traitorous act. A proper approach to such a situation would be to give the friend some good reasons for supporting the proposal. Such a procedure would probably also be more successful; it might gain the support of the friend on the issue in question.

Attacking the Fallacy To confront the leading question tactic, you must find some way to reveal to the questioner that he or she is asking you to grant an assumption that is at least part of the very question at issue. When that issue is clear, you might point out that you think the position you are asked to adopt requires more evidential support than it now has, or at least that you are not now willing to give the questioner's "begged-for" answer on the basis of the available evidence. Of course, if the position held by the questioner seems self-evidently true or is one you find well supported, then from your perspective, no fallacy has really been committed.

Question-Begging Definition

Definition This fallacy consists in attempting to establish an irrefutable position in an argument by means of a questionable definition. What appears to be a factual or empirical claim is often rendered impervious to counterevidence by being subtly, and sometimes unconsciously, interpreted by the claimant as a definitional statement. The claim at issue thereby becomes "true" by definition.

The question-begging definition begs the question at issue because it tries to settle an empirical or factual question, which supposedly can be resolved only by observation or experiment, with a highly questionable definition of the key term in the debate. A clue that such a deceptive technique is being used could be the presence of such modifying words as *truly, really, essentially,* or *genuinely* before the key term in the discussion of an issue. Even though the speaker may strongly believe that such a term should be defined in the way that he or she has done it, if the very definition of a key term has the effect of making a controversial empirical claim true by definition, then the fallacy of question-begging definition has been committed.

A definitional claim that poses as an empirical one cannot be an acceptable premise. It is unacceptable for two reasons. First, it tries to settle an empirical claim by sustaining a confusion about the nature of the claim. Indeed, its persuasiveness as a premise depends on the listener not recognizing the confusion. Second, it tries to settle an empirical issue without a proper consideration of relevant evidence. To be acceptable, a premise of an empirical argument would not only have to be free of confusion, but also provide credible empirical evidence for the conclusion.

Example   Suppose that Paul maintains the empirical claim that "true love never ends in separation or divorce." When he is presented with examples of true love followed by divorce, he insists that such cases were not *genuine* cases of true love. His "evidence" that they were not cases of true love is that they ended in divorce. Paul is hereby settling the issue by definition, for his judgment is that any marriage that ends in divorce could not have been a case of true love. No evidence is allowed to count against his claim. Indeed, it is the presentation of counterevidence that is typically the occasion for the claimant's reinterpreting the empirical claim into a definitional one.

If Paul wishes to define *true love* as love that would not end in separation, that is his prerogative, although such a definition is a highly questionable one from the perspective of ordinary language. However, Paul's claim has the appearance of being a factual assertion, which is an assertion for which empirical evidence is appropriate. If Paul had intended his claim to be a definitional one, he should have made that clear from the beginning.

Example   When a popular politician switched from the Republican party to the Democratic party several years ago, a number of his critics, especially Republicans, claimed that he had obviously not been a "true-blue" Republican or he wouldn't have switched political parties. The primary "evidence" the critics could cite for his "non-true-blue" Republicanism was that he switched parties. It was obvious that little evidence would have been allowed to count against the claim. This is, therefore, a case of the fallacy of question-begging definition; the *definition* of a "true-blue" Republican is apparently one who would never leave the Republican party. Hence, the only matter that is actually in dispute is whether the definition is an appropriate one; there is no empirical claim at issue.

Example   Several years ago, in an effort to defend the relevance of philosophy to the students in my introductory philosophy course, I announced that "all philosophical questions are solvable." To emphasize my point, I added that it was unlikely that I, a professor of philosophy, would have taken up on myself the lifetime task of studying philosophical questions if I thought they were inherently unsolvable. I claimed that if a "philosophical question" were such that there were no realistic possibility of solving it, then it wasn't really a philosophical question.

When an alert student pointed out the question-begging character of my claim, I then had to admit that I *defined* a philosophical question as one that has the possibility of being answered. It then became clear to me and to my students that I was not at all making an empirical claim about all the philosophical questions that I had encountered; I was simply explaining how I was using the term *philosophical question*. Since that is a controversial definition, I was clearly guilty of committing the fallacy of question-begging definition.

Attacking the Fallacy   If you suspect a question-begging definition, ask the speaker directly what kind of statement he or she is making. If the speaker is puzzled by your question, it might be necessary to explain, as simply as possible, the difference between a definitional and an empirical claim. If the claim is found to be definitional, it is obviously not subject to falsification, although the speaker should be prepared to defend the definition against alternative definitions based on ordinary language or the thinking of relevant authorities. If the claim is found to be empirical, the arguer has the burden of providing empirical proof for the claim and must, of course, be willing to consider any counterevidence to the claim.

Exercises

In each of the following exercises (1) identify the type of begging-the-question illustrated; (2) explain what specific feature in the example causes it to be properly identified in that way; and (3) explain how the reasoning violates the criterion of acceptability:

1. Mr. St. Clair says to his nephew David, who is a high school senior, "Where will you be going to college next year, David?"

2. **Marie**: The criminal mind simply cannot be rehabilitated.
   Homer: That's not true. I know several criminals who have been completely rehabilitated.
   Marie: Well, then, those people must not have been real criminals.

3. It's supposed to be in the low twenties tonight, so surely we're not going to the football game, are we?

4. **Roy**: But how do you know that the Bible is actually divinely inspired?
   Dorothy: Because it says right in the third chapter of II Timothy that "all Scripture is given by inspiration of God."

5. One of Senator Fisher's constituents asks, "Are you going to vote for the proposed cut in the defense budget—a cut that will surely weaken our military posture around the world?"

6. Professor: "Unless someone wishes to add anything further to the discussion of this absurd issue, I suggest that we move on to the next topic."

7. **Richard**: Only the fittest of organisms survive.
   Shirley: How do you know?
   Richard: Well, if they survive, they must be fit.
   Shirley: Yes, but how do you know that it is only the most fit of the organisms that survive?
   Richard: Those creatures who have survived obviously have survived because they are somehow adapted for survival.

8. Academic Dean: "The faculty is supposed to vote next week on the committee's newest 'hodgepodge' curricular proposal."

9. **Carl**: Human beings are creatures of despair. To be genuinely authentic, human beings must experience some despair.

Ida: But I don't ever have such experiences. I really don't. I think you are wrong.

Carl: Well, obviously you are simply deceiving yourself if you never allow such feelings of despair to come to full consciousness. Being a creature of despair is what distinguishes humans from nonhumans.

10. Cynthia, do you really want me to have to sit through another one of those horrible PTA meetings tonight?

11. **Phyllis**: A Christian would never drink alcoholic beverages.

Leslie: That's just not true. I know several Christians who occasionally take a drink. In fact, I know some Christian ministers who do.

Phyllis: Then as far as I'm concerned, they couldn't be real Christians.

12. You're not going to vote for a man who would give an interview to a magazine like *Playboy*, are you?

13. Diana, did you empty the dishwasher and clean the kitchen while I was gone, as I asked you?

14. Legal measures that would put some controls on corporate monopolies are clearly in the public interest, because the good of the community would be decidedly improved if we could find some legal way of preventing the total control of the production and distribution of a particular service or product by a single corporation.

15. **June**: I say that "once saved, always saved." A person who is once saved or redeemed cannot fall from grace, that is, fall away from the faith. I suppose that's why we Baptists differ from you Methodists.

Harold: But I know some people who now have nothing to do with the church, speak ill of it, and hardly lead lives that would be considered saved or Christian, yet they did have experiences of salvation when they were in their early teens. Are you saying they have not fallen away from the faith?

June: Well, if those people act as you say they do, they must not really have been saved in the first place.

16. I think that capital punishment for murderers and rapists is quite justified; there are a number of good reasons for putting to death people who commit such crimes.

17. **Jason**: What do you think about this issue, Gloria?

Gloria: About what?

Jason: About the college spending our tuition money on something as silly as campus beautification projects.

18. You aren't *serious* about nominating Professor Reiff as "Teacher of the Year," are you?

19. Professor Letson, I would like to talk with you sometime about the unfair grades you've been giving me.

20. Waitress to customer: "What may I bring you for dessert?"

UNWARRANTED ASSUMPTION FALLACIES

The patterns of argument discussed in this section are fallacious because they employ highly questionable, although sometimes popular, assumptions. Typically, these assumptions are implicit or unstated but nevertheless crucial to the force of the argument. Because these implicit yet unacceptable assumptions are used to support premises in arguments, the premises built on them are likewise unacceptable, for one of the conditions of unacceptability states that a premise is unacceptable if it "is based on a usually unstated but highly questionable assumption." Hence, such premises cannot serve as premises of good arguments.

Many of these assumptions are a part of our conventional wisdom because they seem to have a "ring of truth" about them. They may even *be* true in some contexts. However, no argument would be a good one if its conclusion were based on the imagined truth of any one of these common assumptions.

An argument that rests on an unwarranted or unacceptable assumption may have its faulty character blatantly exposed by spelling out the beguiling assumption as part of a reconstructed argument. Articulating the assumption in this way is by itself sometimes sufficient to convince even the arguer of its unacceptability. Once the unacceptable premise is recognized as being crucial to the force of the argument of which it is a part, then the argument too will be assessed as a faulty one.

Fallacy of the Continuum

Definition   This fallacy consists in assuming that small differences in a sequence of things are insignificant or that contraries, connected by intermediate small differences, are really very much the same. Hence, there is the failure to recognize the importance or necessity of sometimes making what might appear to be arbitrary distinctions or cut-off points.

The assumption involved in this fallacy is a very common one, and it is not always easy to persuade others of its dubious character. It is often expressed in the common claim that "it's only a matter of degree." This "only a matter of degree" kind of thinking implicitly claims that small differences have a negligible effect or that to make definite distinctions between things on a continuum is impossible or at least arbitrary.

A more graphic name for this fallacy might be the "camel's back fallacy" as in "One more straw won't break the camel's back." Anyone who has played the child's game "The Last Straw" knows that one more straw *can* break the camel's back. The game rules specify that each player be given a handful of very lightweight wooden "straws." Then each player in turn places a single straw in a basket on the camel's back. The player who places the straw that breaks the camel's back, that is, causes it to collapse, loses the game. There *is* a straw that makes the difference between the camel's back breaking and not breaking. Similarly, there is a distinction that can be made on a continuum between one category and its contrary. Nevertheless, clear distinctions between these categories are sometimes very difficult to draw. Vague words particularly lend themselves to this difficulty. At what point, for example, does a warm evening become a cool one or a girl become a woman?

The fallacy of the continuum is not committed by those who neglect to make precise distinctions in ordinary conversation, but by those who make the unwarranted assumption as a part of an argument that such distinctions cannot be made. There *is* a difference between a warm evening and a cool evening just as there is a difference between a girl and a woman. To make distinctions may in some cases seem somewhat arbitrary, but it is appropriate in some contexts that distinctions be made. At any rate, it would be fallacious to assume in one's thinking that such distinctions could *not* be made.

The ancient name of this fallacy is the "fallacy of the beard." Such a name probably originated in the context of the ancient practice of debating such a question as "How many hairs would one have to have in order to have a beard?" We would be reluctant—because it would appear arbitrary—to specify a certain number of hairs, but obviously there is a difference between having a beard and not having a beard. Must there not, then, be a cut-off point between the two?

This fallacy may be committed not only when dealing with conceptual issues, such as the questions of when death occurs or when the fetus becomes a human being, but also when dealing with questions of behavior. For example, it is often argued that if one is justified in taking a small step in a particular direction, such as drinking one more beer, additional steps seem to be justified as well; there seems to be no good reason to stop at any particular point—as long as the steps are small ones. Nevertheless, to avoid the fallacy of the continuum, we *must* develop criteria for imposing appropriate stopping points.

The implicit premise used in the fallacy of the continuum, namely, that small differences are unimportant or that contraries connected by intermediate small changes are not significantly different, is simply false. For that reason, the premise is an unacceptable one and cannot be used as part of a good argument.

Example   Arguments using the assumption involved in the fallacy of the continuum are very persuasive. Indeed, even students who have carefully studied the fallacy have been heard to argue in the following manner: "Professor Morris added five points to every student's final numerical average. It seems to me that if he added five points, he could have gone on and added six points. Then I would have passed the course. After all, there is very little difference between five points and six points. Yet that one point made the difference between passing and failing the course. Clint had a 60 average after the five-point addition, and I had a 59. He passed and I didn't; but does he really know that much more philosophy than I?" It is probably the case that the student with the 59 average did not know much less philosophy than the student with the 60 average, but some cut-off point has to be established somewhere in order to avoid making extremes—for example, knowing and not knowing philosophy—indistinguishable.

Example A number of people have sometimes been convinced by a clever salesclerk that a little larger monthly payment isn't going to make very much difference.

> **Customer**: I just can't afford that much for an air conditioner right now.
> **Salesclerk**: Why don't you just put it on your MasterCard?
> **Customer**: But the monthly payment on my account is already $215 a month.
> **Salesclerk**: But if you buy the air conditioner now, you can have it all summer, when you really need it, and it will add only a few dollars a month to your minimum payment.

Such reasoning, if it leads one to a purchase, need occur only a few times before the customer might be in serious financial difficulty.

Example What person on a diet or trying to cut down on smoking has not been deceived by the argument that one little doughnut or one more cigarette surely can't make any real difference?

Attacking the Fallacy If there are any doubts about whether the fallacy of the continuum is really a fallacy, ask your verbal opponent who uses this fallacy for the definition of some vague term such as *rich person*. Try to get him or her to be very specific about the amount of assets in dollars that a person would have to have in order to qualify as *rich*. Let us call that amount X. Then subtract a small amount, for example, ten dollars, from that number and ask if a person having X minus ten dollars would still be rich. Your opponent will no doubt say "yes." Repeat the question again and again, subtracting a few more dollars each time. Your opponent will probably continue to say "yes" every time, until it becomes clear that it is his or her own assumption that small differences are unimportant that renders him or her vulnerable to such manipulation. If your opponent does not recognize such fallacious reasoning, he or she will soon be assenting to the claim that a person having X minus X dollars is rich, which is an absurd claim.

It would be naive to deny that making distinctions is sometimes very difficult; at the same time, it should be insisted on that distinctions can and sometimes must be made. For example, there must be a difference between failing and passing a course and between staying on a diet and not staying on a diet. Moreover, hot and cold are discernible distinctions, even though hot and cold are extreme points separated on a continuum by a large number of small intermediate differences. Surely your opponent would not wish to say that a hot day is really not much different from a cold day because "it's only a matter of degree."

Fallacy of Composition

Definition This fallacy consists in assuming that what is true of the parts of some whole is therefore true of the whole.

The fallacy of composition is committed principally in those cases where a "whole," because of the particular relationship of its parts, represents something different from simply the sum or the combination of those parts. In such cases, the whole either takes on a new characteristic because of its composition or at least does not take on or maintain particular characteristics attributed to each of its parts. The fallacy, then, is to attribute to the whole those characteristics that are attributed to each of the parts making up that whole, simply because it is a whole made up of those parts.

A person who commits such a fallacy has ignored or failed to understand that the way the parts relate, interact, or affect each other often changes the character of the whole. For example, the fact that each of the players on a football team is an excellent player would not be a sufficient reason to infer that the football team is an excellent one.

This fallacy should not be confused with the fallacy of inferring something about a whole class of things on the basis of one or a few instances of that thing. The fallacy of composition is committed when we infer something about the characteristic of some whole because of some characteristic of *each one* of its parts.

The implicit premise used in the fallacy of composition, namely, that what is true of the parts of a whole is therefore true of the whole, is an indefensible or unwarranted assumption. While that assumption may be true in some cases, it does not merit our acceptance as a general claim. Moreover, any argument with a premise supported by such an unwarranted assumption cannot be a good one.

Example   If we were to infer that the United States is a strong and efficient country because each of the 50 states is strong and efficient, it would be a clear case of the fallacy of composition. In fact, the strength or efficiency of each of the states might suggest that each state has a kind of independence that would detract from the possibility of a strong and efficient nation. In such a case, the whole might not take on the characteristics of its parts.

Example   Who has not heard this fallacy committed in the most casual comments? "Dan is a fine young man, and Becky is a fine young woman. They'll make a lovely couple."

The whole called marriage *is* more than a sum of the parts that make it up. Hence, the parts, by virtue of their relationship in the marital whole, might create something very much lacking in loveliness or fineness.

Example   It is often quite hard to recognize the subtlety of the fallacy of composition. I have often heard comments like the following: "Professor Elliott and Professor Carruth are going to team-teach a course next spring in the philosophy of science. They are two of our best teachers, so it really ought to be a good course."

If Professors Elliott and Carruth are good teachers in the sense that term is ordinarily used in an academic context, it could very likely be the case that the team-taught course would be a poor one. Many "good" teachers are good by virtue of their total and singular control of the classroom. A team-taught course usually does not allow for such control. There could also be other reasons, of course, why the professors might not work well together. Assuming that they will is falling into the fallacy of composition.

Attacking the Fallacy A careful attempt should be made to show the person who commits this fallacy just *how* a whole may very well represent something different from simply the sum of its parts. Try an obvious example: If it is the case that Diana has a very pretty blouse, a pretty skirt, and pretty shoes, they will not necessarily make a beautiful outfit together. The clash of patterns or colors could render the outfit quite ugly.

It is important to keep in mind, however, that wholes are not *always* different in character from their parts. For example, if every cup of punch in the punch bowl is sour, it would be entirely warranted to draw the conclusion that all the punch in the punch bowl is sour. In this case, there is nothing about a cup of this punch that, when it was mixed with all the other cups of punch, would change the taste or character of the whole bowl of punch.

Furthermore, in a number of cases *some* evidence for a claim about a whole *is* provided by facts about the parts. For an "attack" strategy, then, you might say to your opponent that you understand why he or she might have drawn a conclusion about a characteristic of the whole based on a characteristic of the parts, for in some cases the parts do provide evidence for a claim about the whole. At the same time, you might use a few examples to illustrate how such an understandable assumption can lead to absurd conclusions in other cases. The problem, you might point out, lies in assuming that a characteristic *automatically* passes over to a whole from the parts.

Fallacy of Division

Definition This fallacy consists in assuming that what is true of some whole is therefore true of each of the parts of that whole.

The fallacy of division is the opposite of the fallacy of composition. Rather than assuming that a characteristic of the parts is therefore a characteristic of the whole, it assumes that a characteristic of the whole is therefore a characteristic of each of the parts. However, as we have seen, a whole often represents something quite different from its parts. We could not assume, for example, that an excellent choir has equally excellent individual voices.

One of the most common ways of committing the fallacy of division is to infer something about a particular member of a class on the basis of a *generalization* about the whole class. In this case, the characteristic of the whole should not be applied to the parts, because the characteristic of the whole is only a statistical generalization based on the characteristics of *most* of the parts. Such a characteristic of the class is attributable to many of its parts, but because it is impossible to know to which members of the class the generalization may apply, it would be fallacious to assume, without additional evidence, that the characteristic accurately describes any particular member of the class.

The implicit premise employed in the fallacy of division is an unacceptable one. It is simply false that what is true of some whole is always true of each of the parts of that whole or that what has been generalized to be true about a class of things is true of every member of that class.

Example   It may be true that John has a handsome face; yet it may not be true that any part of his face, for example, the nose or the mouth, is handsome apart from the rest of his face. In this case, a characteristic of the whole is not necessarily a characteristic of the parts.

Example   Although normal human beings are conscious entities, we should not infer from such a characteristic of the whole that individual cells or molecules of that whole are conscious entities.

Example   Suppose that a high school senior rejected the idea of attending a large university on the grounds that he or she preferred small, intimate classes. To think in this way would be to commit the fallacy of division, because the student could not infer that a large university would have only large classes. Even if it were statistically true that large universities have large classes, the student could not logically infer that any of the classes of any particular large university would be large or that any particular class in a large university would be a large one.

Attacking the Fallacy   The attack on the fallacy of division is similar to the attack on the fallacy of composition. Say to your opponent that you understand why he or she might have drawn a conclusion about a characteristic of the parts based on a characteristic of the whole, because in *some* cases evidence for a claim about the parts is provided by facts about the whole. Then you might use a few examples to demonstrate how such an understandable assumption could lead to absurd conclusions in some cases. For example, you might point out how absurd it would be to assume that a particular state is diversified in terms of its climate or industry simply because it is a part of the United States, which is so diversified.

The following absurd example might seal the case against drawing conclusions about members of a class based on a generalization about the whole. If it is statistically the case that Maytag washing machines do not break down during their first three years of use, it would be absurd to exclude the possibility that your *particular* Maytag machine might break down during its first three years.

False Alternatives

Definition   This fallacy consists in assuming too few alternatives and, at the same time, assuming that one of the suggested alternatives must be true.

Because a reduction in the number of alternatives often results in only two extreme alternatives being presented, this fallacy is sometimes referred to as the black-and-white fallacy. The fallacy of false alternatives, however, is not just thinking in extremes; it is an oversimplification of a problem situation by a failure to entertain or at least recognize all its plausible alternative solutions.

A common form of the fallacy of false alternatives derives from the failure to differentiate properly between contradictories (negatives) and contraries (opposites). Contradictories exclude any gradations between their extremes; there is no middle ground between a term and its *negative*, for example, between *hot* and *not hot*. Contraries, on the other hand, allow a number of gradations between their extremes; there is plenty of middle ground between a term and its *opposite*, for example, between *hot* and *cold*.

A common mistake in our thinking occurs when contraries are often treated as if they were contradictories. In the case of contradictories (a term and its negative), one of the two extremes must be true and the other false. It is either hot or it is not hot. In the case of contraries (a term and its opposite), it is possible for both extremes to be false. It could be neither hot nor cold. To assume that it must be either hot or cold would be to treat contraries as if they were contradictories and thereby commit the fallacy of false alternatives, that is, to assume too few alternatives and to assume that one of the alternatives must be true.

Thinking in extremes requires much less mental effort than looking diligently for all possible solutions to a problem. The implicit premise that all plausible solutions to a problem can be reduced to a small number, usually two, can be shown to be false by a minimum of imaginative effort. The phony "either-or" premise is therefore an unacceptable one and cannot be part of a good argument.

Example   A case of treating contraries as if they were contradictories is seen in one of the well-known sayings of Jesus: "If you are not for me, you must be against me." A similar instance may be found in the claim that if one is not a theist, then one must be an atheist. Neither claim seems to allow for the alternative of neutrality (or agnosticism).

Example   One would clearly commit the fallacy of false alternatives by assuming that a particular political candidate was running on the Democratic ticket simply because she was not running on the Republican ticket. There are a number of alternative tickets on which one might run, or one could be running on no ticket at all.

Example   Suppose that Professor Morton insists that a certain activity is either morally right or morally wrong. If *morally right* means morally obligatory and *morally wrong* means morally prohibited, then the fallacy of false alternatives has been committed, because there may be other alternatives. One such alternative might be to treat the activity as morally permissible. The terms *right* and *wrong*, then, must be regarded as contraries or opposites rather than as contradictories.

Example   Absolutistic thinking or thinking in extremes is quite frequently found in political rhetoric. The issue of national health care is often presented in terms of false alternatives: "Either we allow the government to take total control of the field of medicine or we must allow our physicians to be free of governmental restrictions." Surely there are a number of middle ground alternatives to the problem of health care.

Attacking the Fallacy   Genuine "either-or" situations are very rare. If you are presented with one, it probably would be a good idea to treat it with a bit of skepticism—unless, of course, the either-or is a set of contradictories. In almost all other cases, more than two alternatives are usually available, although those additional alternatives might have been ignored by the arguer. As a means of attacking an argument based on limited alternatives, ask the arguer two questions: First, do these alternatives that you set forth exhaust all the plausible alternatives? Second, don't you think that if we really tried, we could be imaginative enough to think of some others? If the arguer is unable or unwilling to come up with any additional alternatives, point out a number of them yourself, and challenge the arguer to show why they do not qualify as plausible solutions. Once all the plausible alternatives have been considered, then the question becomes that of determining which of the plausible alternatives is best supported by the evidence or by good reasons.

Is-Ought Fallacy

Definition   This fallacy consists in assuming that because something is now the practice, it *ought* to be the practice. Conversely, it consists in assuming that because something *is not* the practice, it *ought not* to be the practice.

The is-ought fallacy is permeated by moral or value overtones. The "way things are" is regarded as ideal or morally proper simply because "things" are as they are. No good reasons are given for the appropriateness of a thing's being the way it is; it is simply assumed that if it *is*, it must be right, and if it *isn't* that must be right, and the possibility of changing it is not seriously entertained.

This fallacy can easily be confused with the appeal to tradition. However, in the case of the is-ought fallacy, it is argued that the status quo should be maintained not out of reverence for the past, as is the case with the fallacious appeal to tradition, but simply because it is the status quo. It is assumed that if it *is* the status quo, then that fact is sufficient reason for the appropriateness of it being so.

The is-ought fallacy can also be confused with the fallacious appeal to common opinion. The appeal to common opinion is usually used in an attempt to establish the truth of a claim; that is, an opinion or judgment is erroneously assumed to be true because it is held by a large number of people. The is-ought fallacy, however, is used to establish the rightness or appropriateness of a particular kind of behavior or practice simply because it is presently engaged in by a large number of people. Although the distinction is sometimes very subtle, the appeal to common opinion should be primarily understood as a faulty method of establishing the *truth* of a *claim*, while the is-ought fallacy should be understood as a faulty method of establishing the *rightness* of a *practice*.

A premise that embodies an is-ought assumption is not an acceptable one, because the fact that a particular practice is current says nothing about the defensibility of it. To support a judgment about its rightness, other and independent evidence would be required.

Example "Smoking marijuana is illegal, son! If there were nothing wrong with it, it wouldn't be illegal. Don't you understand?"

The fact that marijuana is illegal constitutes no reason whatsoever for the propriety of that status. In other words, there is no logical justification for claiming that because it *is* illegal, it *ought* to be illegal.

Example "Public school teachers and professors should not seek to engage in collective bargaining. After all, very few teachers are presently involved in such practices. There is simply very little interest in that sort of thing in our profession." The fact that very few teachers are currently members of labor unions is not a sufficient reason for concluding that such involvement is not a good idea.

Example

Professor Taylor: Students should be allowed to be more involved in the decision-making processes at this school.
Professor Smith: The fact is that a college is just not very democratic in character. So let's not tamper with the institutional structure. Let's concentrate on some other important things that need our attention.

Professor Smith does not even entertain the possibility of introducing more democracy into the institutional structure, simply because of the "way things are."

Attacking the Fallacy An argument always requires evidence or good reasons to support its conclusion. If no evidence or reason is given other than the status quo, you should point out that fact and insist that some specific evidence or reasons be provided. If the arguer is able to provide such support, you can then evaluate that evidence to determine whether the conclusion merits acceptance. For example, the fact that people *are* being discriminated against because of their gender is not a good reason for sex discrimination. However, if an opponent has other reasons for the view that people should be treated differently on account of their gender, that support should be presented for proper evaluation.

If necessary, resort to the absurd example method. You should have no trouble finding good examples, but consider this one: "Since the majority of people *do not* wear their seat belts, people *should not* wear seat belts." The faulty character of this argument should be transparent to even the most committed users of the is-ought.

Wishful Thinking

Definition This fallacy consists in assuming that because one *wants* something to be true, it *is* or *will be* true. Conversely, it consists in assuming that because we do not want something to be true, then it *is not* or *will not be* true.

All of us spend a lot of our time wishing that things were a particular way. This way of thinking is erected into the fallacy of wishful thinking when one uses a wish as if it were a premise in an argument, that is, when one implicitly assumes that wanting something to be so will somehow make it so. Such thinking has both a positive and negative form. We sometimes *accept* a claim because of our wish that it *be* true, or we *reject* a claim because of our wish that it *not* be true.

This fallacy is sometimes difficult to distinguish from rationalization. The rationalizer attempts to establish a claim by means of a phony argument, while the wishful thinker tries to establish a claim directly from his or her strong desires—indeed from the implicit premise that whatever one wants to be true is or will be true.

This implicit premise is an unwarranted assumption, because our feelings or emotions about a particular claim have no bearing on the truth or falsity of that claim. Nevertheless, many of our strong religious and other ideological beliefs seem to be built on no more of a foundation than our intense wish that those beliefs be true. Some writers have even suggested that wishful thinking could be called the "fallacy of belief" or even the "fallacy of faith." "If you have faith," we are sometimes told, then it will be true. We are even told that something can be true "for you" if you believe it to be so. Such thinking is a clear case of wishful thinking. While it may be true that wanting something to be true may give you the motivation to try to help bring it into being, believing does not make anything so.

Since there is no reason to believe that our wishes affect the truth of claims, the implicit premise used in wishful thinking is an indefensible one. Moreover, an argument that uses such an unacceptable premise cannot be a good one.

Example "My husband has been missing for over ten years, but I know he's still alive. He just couldn't be dead." He may still be alive, but her wishing him to be alive has no bearing on whether that is true.

Example "There is a perfect marriage partner out there for everyone in this world. That is what everyone wants—a perfect marriage. If you look hard enough for it and then work hard enough at it, you'll have a perfect marriage."

Sometimes our wish that something would happen can have some effect on whether it does, but only in those cases where we are directly and dynamically related to the situation. Even then, we would rarely have total control over it, especially something as complex as marriage.

Example One of the more serious arguments for life after death put forth by a British theologian goes like this: "There must be a life after death, because almost all people desire it. It is a part of the very nature of human beings to desire it. If there were no life after death, then why would all humans desire it? Like the desires for food, water, and sex, all of which are satiable, the desire for life after death is universal."

Even if the claim about the universality of the desire for the afterlife is true, it is quite conceivable that a universal desire could go totally unsatisfied. Consider, if you will, the desire of most of us to have more money than we presently have. Wanting something to be the case, even if it is universally wanted, does not make it so.

Attacking the Fallacy One method of attacking the fallacy of wishful thinking would be to offer strong evidence for a claim that is contrary to the claim at issue and to ask your opponent to evaluate that evidence. The serious believer will presumably want to find some way to counteract the force of that evidence, and in order to do so will have to abandon his or her exclusive reliance on a wish premise.

Another strategy would be to state a belief of your own contrary to the arguer's belief and to cite as your only "evidence" your wish or belief that it is true—the same "evidence" that your opponent cites for his or her alternative view. Since your conclusions are contrary to one another, at least one of you must be wrong. Determining who is wrong may require, if all goes right, a cooperative evaluation of other or independent evidence.

Finally, you might try an absurd example. Ask your opponent if his or her wish-based thinking is any different in form from a friend believing that she is not pregnant, simply because she does not *want* to be pregnant.

Misuse of a General Principle

Definition This fallacy consists in assuming that a generalization or rule has no exceptions, thus misapplying it in a particular instance. Conversely, it consists in attempting to refute a generalization or rule by means of an exceptional case.

One who commits this particular fallacy overlooks the fact that there are usually implicit qualifications of almost any rule, principle, or generalization that render it inapplicable in some unusual cases. The fallacy occurs when one makes the unwarranted assumption that the principle can be applied in *every* case, no matter what the circumstances are, or when one assumes that unusual or exceptional cases would falsify or refute such a principle. In other words, the arguer applies a general rule or principle to a situation for which it was not intended and then draws an unwarranted conclusion. These unusual circumstances do not affect the general truth or rightness of the principle. The arguer has simply failed to take into account the principle's restricted range of application.

Because this fallacy involves the problem of dealing with unusual or accidental circumstances, it is often referred to as the "fallacy of accident." Regardless of what it is called, it is an argument that uses an unacceptable premise. The implicit premise that a general rule has no exceptions or that an unusual case can refute a general principle represents an inaccurate understanding of the nature of rules, principles, or generalizations.

Example A general principle to which most of us subscribe is that people are entitled to use their own property in whatever way they wish. But it would be a misapplication of this principle to say that no restrictions should be imposed, for example, on the driving of one's own automobile while intoxicated. Intoxication is a special circumstance in which the general principle is inapplicable because of the serious potential harm to others.

Example If the rule with regard to X-rated movies shown at a drive-in theater is that "no one under 18 will be allowed into the theater," it would be a misapplication of this rule for an attendant to refuse to allow a couple to bring their infant child with them. Surely the rule was not intended to be applied in such cases.

Example The opposite form of this fallacy might be shown by an argument that attempts to refute the principle that "lying is wrong" by pointing out that a psychological counselor surely would be justified in lying to keep from betraying a confidence. This exception to the principle against lying would not allow the arguer to draw the conclusion that lying is *not* wrong. It should simply be the occasion to recognize the fact that moral principles often come into conflict and that a choice must be made between them, usually in terms of which principle has the greater worth or priority in the context.

Attacking the Fallacy One way of pointing out the fallacious character of a particular misapplication of a principle is to analyze very carefully what the purpose of that particular rule or principle is and then to discuss how exceptions would be in order when that purpose is not being fulfilled or is superseded by some more important, conflicting principle. Then try to show in the particular case that either the exception is not inconsistent with the purpose of the principle or that there is a more important principle at stake. In other words, an attempt should be made to show that the unusual case in question really is an exception to the principle by virtue of its special or unusual circumstances.

Another line of attack might be to find some general principle with which your opponent would agree, and then find an exception to that principle with which he or she would also agree. If the arguer recognizes legitimate exceptions in your illustration, he or she should be willing to acknowledge possible exceptions to the principle being misused. For example, your opponent would probably agree that parents have the responsibility to raise their children in whatever way they think best, but he or she would probably also agree that parents do not have the right to use physical torture as part of their method.

Fallacy of the Golden Mean

Definition This fallacy consists in assuming that the moderate or middle view between two extremes must be the best or right one simply because it is the middle view.

Another name for this bit of faulty thinking is the "fallacy of moderation." It is assumed—indeed it is a part of our conventional wisdom—that a position on an issue that is somewhere in the middle is always the best simply because it is in the middle. In many situations, a moderate view may in fact be the best or most justifiable position to take, but it is not the best simply because it is a moderate position. In some cases, the so-called extreme or radical solution to a problem is the most defensible one. The fact that a particular position is a moderate one has nothing to do with its worth.

Although a compromise is sometimes necessary to settle a dispute or resolve a conflict, it cannot be assumed that a compromise solution is always the best one. It might well be the case that the position of one of the parties involved in the dispute or conflict has no legitimacy whatsoever. Therefore, though it could be said that it is *not* a fallacy to compromise in order to settle a dispute, it *is* a fallacy to assume, apart from evidence, that a compromise solution is the best one.

The implicit premise that the moderate or middle position is best is a highly questionable assumption, which is not warranted by any evidence. It therefore is an unacceptable premise whose use would violate the second criterion of a good argument.

Example "I have difficulty accepting the notion that all human events are the inevitable results of prior causes, but I also have difficulty with the view that human beings can act apart from prior causes in their experience. In other words, I find both determinism and indeterminism untenable. Surely the most defensible view is somewhere between those extremes."

This is the somewhat common dilemma that the introductory philosophy student encounters. The solution does not lie in finding a middle view between these extremes. Determinism and indeterminism are contradictories. Either all events are determined or it is not the case that all events are determined. There is no middle ground.

Example Consider the following argument that is sometimes put forth regarding the Israeli-Arab conflict: "Both the Arab and Israeli points of view represent extremes. Therefore, some kind of compromise must be the best solution." Compromise may be the only way that this dispute can be finally settled, but it is a different thing to say that a compromise per se is the best solution in that conflict.

Example Suppose you are looking for a used refrigerator for your apartment and you find one that seems to be the right size at a used furniture store. The seller wants $300 for it, and you offer $200. Because the two of you are far apart on the price, you suggest "splitting the difference" at $250. Although such a compromise may seem fair to you, it may not be the best solution to the problem. On the one hand, it is possible that the seller already has almost $250 invested in it and needs to make some profit. On the other hand, it is possible that it may not even be worth $250 in the used furniture market. Indeed, your original offer may have been a very fair one.

Attacking the Fallacy If an arguer proposes a middle position with regard to an issue, insist that he or she justify the merit of that position itself, without reference to its middle status. In the example above, presumably both the offer of $200 and the asking price of $300 for the refrigerator could be construed as the conclusions of previous arguments that could be objectively evaluated. If either one of the arguments turns out to be a genuinely good one, the "splitting the difference" option could not be regarded as a defensible one.

It might also be helpful for all parties to keep in mind that there are two ways of understanding the notion of "best position to take" in any particular situation. A compromise may be the "best" way to resolve a difficult situation. For example, it may prevent continued economic deprivation, bloodshed, or mental anguish. However, it may not be the "best" in the sense of being the most accurate, justifiable, or morally responsible solution to the problem. Although you may sometimes have to accept the compromise "best position to take" in order to settle the issue, you may want to make it clear that you do not think it the fair or most justifiable "best position to take."

If your direct attack on the faulty assumption of the golden mean is unsuccessful, you can always try an absurd example. Ask your opponent if the best way to behave in the voting booth would be to "compromise" and vote for exactly one-half of the Republicans and one-half of the Democrats.

Faulty Analogy

Definition   This fallacy consists in assuming that because two things are alike in one or more respects, they necessarily are alike in some other respect.

Those who commit this fallacy overlook the possibility of significant differences in compared cases and therefore draw a questionable conclusion from a comparison. Commonly, two compared things are alike only in unimportant ways and are quite different in important ways, that is, in ways that are relevant to the issue at stake in the argument. The analogy often appeals to similarities that are very superficial and thus fails to support the particular conclusion sought.

The implicit premise that two things alike in one or more respects are alike in some other respect is a very dubious assumption and thus cannot qualify as an acceptable premise. Therefore, any argument concerning compared cases where an inference is drawn from such an assumption cannot qualify as a good argument.

Even if the premises of the analogical argument made observations about the more relevant and important similarities in the compared cases, there could still be a problem with the argument. Because analogies are by nature usually only suggestive, those who use them should be prepared to offer evidence in addition to pointing out any observed similarities. If a conclusion is drawn about one case from another case, then there should be evidence presented to show precisely *how* the compared cases are alike in the significant way that is relevant to the claim at issue. An observed similarity, by itself, does not constitute evidence.

Example   Suppose someone defended open textbook examinations with the following argument: "No one objects to the practice of a physician looking up a difficult case in medical books. Why, then, shouldn't students taking a difficult examination be permitted to use their textbooks?"

With very little reflection, it will be clear that there is little similarity between the compared cases. The only thing that seems at all similar is the act of looking inside a book for some assistance in solving a problem. But there the alleged similarity stops. Very different purposes are served by such an act in the two situations. One is specifically designed to test a person's knowledge; the other functions as a means of helping the physician to diagnose a patient's problem. The physician's basic knowledge has already been tested by virtue of his or her status as a licensed physician. For this analogical argument to be nonfallacious, the arguer would have to present evidence to demonstrate that the two functions do not significantly differ.

Example "Smoking cigarettes is just like ingesting arsenic into your system. Both have been shown to be causally related to death. So if you wouldn't want to take a spoonful of arsenic, I would think that you wouldn't want to continue smoking."

Although it is true that both the ingestion of arsenic and the smoking of cigarettes have been shown to be causally related to death, there are some significant differences in the character of those causal relations. A single heavy dose of arsenic poisoning will bring about immediate death, whereas the heavy smoking of cigarettes would be likely to bring about premature death only as a result of a long process of deterioration or disease. In one case, then, death is immediate and certain; in the other, death is statistically neither immediate nor certain. Thus, the analogy is a faulty one.

Example "If one were to listen to only one kind of music or eat only one kind of food, it would soon become tasteless or boring. Variety makes eating and listening exciting and enriching experiences. Therefore, it could be concluded that an exclusive sexual relationship with only one member of the opposite sex for the rest of one's life—that is, marriage—does not hold out much hope for very much excitement or enrichment."

Although such an argument might have some initial force, in order for it to be a strong argument, the arguer would have to demonstrate that an exclusive sexual relationship is not essentially different from an unchanging food diet or an unchanging musical diet. Because human relationships are so complex and so full of a variety of possibilities, it seems likely that a successful counter to such a claim could be produced. However, the burden of proof is on the person who wishes to extend the disadvantages of narrow diets of food and music to exclusive sexual relationships.

Attacking the Fallacy One of the most effective ways of blunting the force of an argument from analogy is to formulate a counteranalogy, which allows you to draw a conclusion that directly contradicts that of the arguer. Such a device would at least demonstrate the inconclusiveness of an argument from analogy.

If you are using a counteranalogy to make a serious counterclaim, rather than to provide an absurd example, make sure that you can provide convincing evidence that the compared cases are similar in important or significant ways. If you are not able to come up with a counteranalogy or if you are not interested in making a counterclaim, all you may be able to do, when confronted with a weak or faulty analogy, is to point out that the two compared cases resemble each other only in unimportant or irrelevant ways. Therefore, no inference should be drawn concerning the claim at issue. In no case, of course, should you allow a clever user of analogies to think that simply pointing out interesting similarities qualifies as evidence for any claim.

Fallacy of Novelty

Definition   This fallacy consists in assuming that a new idea, law, policy, or action is good simply because it is new.

There is nothing inherently worthwhile about something novel simply because it is novel. Every idea, law, policy, or action requires a defense independent of its novel character. A pattern of reasoning that assumes that whatever is novel is better would result in the absurd consequence that every proposed alternative to the present way of doing things would demand one's acceptance.

Nevertheless, such reasoning is not uncommon, although the assumption is usually not stated so blatantly. It usually takes a more subtle form. For example, many of us at one time or another have thought that the problems in our church would be solved if we got a new minister, or that our country's problems would be solved when a different administration with fresh ideas took over in Washington.

The implicit premise that whatever is new is better can be clearly shown to be an unacceptable premise. It is a claim that is clearly contradicted by the evidence. Moreover, since it fails to meet the standards of premise acceptability, it cannot function as part of a good argument.

Example   A sign in front of a restaurant or service station with the words "Under New Management" is usually intended to convey to the passerby that the food or service will be better than in the past. However, no reason is usually given for believing such a claim. If we patronize such a place in the expectation of better food or service, we have committed the fallacy of novelty no less than the person who erected the sign.

Example   Consider this argument presented by Dean Henderson to an unconvinced faculty: "We *have* to institute this new curriculum if we are going to meet the challenge of the future. I just don't understand why you are dragging your feet against our attempts to improve our programs here."

The dean has presented no argument for the superiority of his curriculum except that it is new. The dean simply assumes that the novelty of the curriculum is sufficient reason for its adoption. Interestingly, it would seem incongruous if a member of the academic community, whose very function is to instruct in the art of careful inquiry, were to vote to accept a curriculum simply on the basis of its newness.

Example   "Our baseball record last year was a miserable two wins and 18 losses. But things will be better this year, because we're getting a new coach."

"Things" may indeed get better, but they could stay the same or even get worse. Without information about the coach other than his "newness," we can infer virtually nothing about how "things" will be.

Attacking the Fallacy Attacking the fallacy of novelty is not an easy task, because the advertising industry has acculturated all of us to the idea that "new" is tantamount to "improved" or "better." Indeed, it is common sense to believe that energy is expended in developing new products, legislation, or ideas primarily because of the desire to make them better. It is not unreasonable to believe that most new things *are* better in some way.

However, the fact that most new things may be better should not lead to the conclusion that every new thing is better. The problem, then, becomes that of convincing those who commit this fallacy that they should not assume that any particular product or idea is better simply because of its newness. One way of doing this might be to confront your opponent with some new idea or product he or she would obviously find worse than an earlier one or at least not better. This demonstration should raise serious questions about the soundness of the opponent's "new is better" assumption and encourage him or her to eliminate novelty as a consideration in an evaluation of worth.

Exercises

In each of the following exercises (1) identify the type of unwarranted assumption illustrated; (2) explain what specific feature in the example causes it to be properly identified in that way; and (3) explain how the reasoning violates the criterion of acceptability.

1. People who have to have a cup of coffee every morning before they can function have no less a problem than alcoholics who have to have their alcohol each day to sustain them.

2. If a physician is justified in deceiving a sick person, and if there is nothing wrong with telling children about Santa Claus, then we must reject the view that "lying is wrong."

3. **George**: No, thank you. I don't care for any decaffeinated coffee. It just doesn't taste right.
    Mildred: But this is better. It's a completely new way of preparing it.

4. I don't see why you have criticized this novel as implausible. There isn't a single incident in it that couldn't have happened.

5. Anyone who eats meat tacitly condones the killing of animals. We might just as well condone the killing of human beings, for how do we draw the line between one form of animal life and another?

6. Harvard University is one of the best universities in this country, so it must have an outstanding philosophy department. Why don't you apply to do graduate work there?

7. The way I see it is that we must either spend enough money on our football program to make us competitive with some of the better teams in this region or simply drop the program altogether.

8. **Maxine**: Give me some time to think about it. I want to consider very carefully whether to have sex with you. I want to try to make a rational decision about this.

Eugene: Look, Maxine! Having sex with someone is not something people make rational decisions about.

9. God must exist; otherwise, life would be unbearable.

10. Judge: "I have heard contradictory testimony from the two principal witnesses in this case. I can only conclude that the truth must lie somewhere in between."

11. Each of the members of the Board of Trustees has demonstrated superior judgment and skill in handling his or her personal affairs. Therefore, I think we can be assured that the Board will exercise superior judgment and skill in handling the affairs of this institution.

12. Some students want our college dorms to be completely "open" to members of the opposite sex, 24 hours a day. Others want a "closed" dorm policy—that is, one that makes the dorms off limits to any member of the opposite sex, anytime. Wouldn't the best solution be to have the dorms open about 12 hours in a day, perhaps from noon to midnight?

13. Because the Democratic party supports a program of national health insurance, I assume that Congressman Foster, who is a member of the Democratic party, will support such a program.

14. Because human bodies become less active as they grow older, and because they eventually die, it is reasonable to expect that political bodies will become less and less active the longer they are in existence, and that they too will eventually die.

15. Farmer to son: "Son, if you pick up that newborn calf over there *once* every day, your muscles should develop to the point that you would be able to lift it when it is a full-grown cow. The calf will gain just a tiny bit of weight each day, and that little bit of weight can't make any significant difference in your ability to lift it. If you can do it one day, you should be able to do it the next day."

16. My husband is being cared for in one of the best hospitals in the country. They use all the latest techniques there.

17. Did you vote for him for president because he is a Democrat or because he promised to reorganize and simplify the federal bureaucracy?

18. But, officer, you shouldn't give me a parking ticket for parking here! People park here all the time and never get tickets. I myself have been parking here for several months and never once received a ticket. No one pays any attention to the "No Parking" sign in this alley.

19. **Resort Manager**: I'm sorry but you cannot bring that pet in here. We have a rule against any pets.

Vacationer: That's my wife's seeing-eye dog; she is blind.

Resort Manager: I'm sorry, but we have to enforce the rule or we would have a whole menagerie here.

20. Young gymnast to another: "I think our gymnastic show tomorrow will be a very good one, since this is the only time that our parents will be able to see us perform, and obviously we want to do a really good job for them."

Additional Exercises

In each of the following exercises (1) identify, from among all the fallacies we have studied, the fallacy illustrated; (2) explain what specific feature in the example causes it to be properly identified in that way; (3) indicate which criterion of a good argument is violated; and (4) explain how it violates that criterion.

1. I heard that Kenneth got an "A" on his test last week. I also heard that Susan, who sits directly in front of him, also received an "A."

2. Snake handler: "If one has enough faith in God, one can be bitten by a snake or drink poison and not die."

3. **Ruth**: I have Mutual Homeowner's Insurance on my house. It's the cheapest and has the best service.
   Roland: I never heard of it. How did you find it?
   Ruth: Don't you listen to Paul Harvey? He endorses only those products and services that he really believes in. He says this is the best homeowner's insurance available.

4. It is hard for me to see how my neighbors and I can be blamed for discrimination when it comes to deciding who is to live in our neighborhood. We make discriminations all through life. If people are not allowed to discriminate, how can they make decisions in life between right and wrong? Indeed, how can they even act responsibly if they must be indiscriminate in their choices?

5. *Man* has always been used as a generic pronoun. There's no need to change a way of speaking and writing that everyone understands.

6. **She**: I love you, but I don't want to get married yet.
   He: If you don't want to get married, then you must not love me.

7. **Perry**: Do you mind if I smoke?
   Mack: Do you mind if I blow asbestos dust in your face?

8. **Cynthia**: I just don't understand what could have happened to the $50 that I had in my desk drawer.
   Virginia: Why don't you ask Denise? She's been out shopping all day today. She just came back with a whole bunch of new stuff. She's in her room now, I think.

9. The president fell flat during a recent campaign trip.

10. I know that you are very busy with your classes, but I was wondering if you could fill out a recommendation for me for graduate school. The reason that I am asking you is that your classes were the most enlightening and intellectually stimulating of my college career. I know you would do a good job for me. A favorable letter written by you would be almost any student's dream.

11. Perry is good-looking and so is Lottie. They should have really beautiful children.

12. We're finally going to get some competent medical care in this town. I'm switching to the new physician opening up a practice next month. I already have an appointment.

13. **John**: I just drove the new Mazda. You know, these Japanese cars are great cars.

Dawn: I don't know why you are putting down American cars. There are some excellent cars built in America.

14. Why would you support a ban on smoking cigarettes? Have you forgotten that you own stock in several tobacco companies?

15. Some people think that there should be no restrictions on gays in the military. Others think that no gays at all should be allowed to serve in the armed forces. The best solution, I suppose, would be to institute a policy of "don't ask, don't tell."

16. The Constitution grants me the right of free speech, so there is no way you can stop me from talking anywhere I please. What makes you think that you, a college librarian, can deny me my basic right of free speech?

17. Plaintiff's attorney to witness: "You would *agree*, wouldn't you, Dr. Birkitt, that a good physician always dates the entries he or she makes in a patient's chart?"

18. I know that the sign says that the safe speed for these curves is 25 miles per hour, but if 25 miles per hour is safe, then 30 miles an hour shouldn't give me any problem. After all, there's not a whole lot of difference between 25 and 30 miles per hour.

19. **Jessica**: Why do you say that Mr. Poe is not capable of being a good congressional representative?

Nancy: Because he just can't do the job!

20. Judge to plea-bargaining defendant: "Before I agree to this plea bargain for possession, which will mean that you will do no jail time for this crime, I want you to tell me who sold you the stuff."

21. Surely you don't call this piece of bent metal *good art*, do you?

22. Now that you are settled into your new home, what church are you going to join?

23. **Larry**: No…I don't think that I'll join your group. I'm really not a very religious person.

Paul: Really? I never knew that you didn't believe in God.

24. We do not advocate censorship. We are simply protecting students from reading material that is morally objectionable to us.

25. Lawyer to judge: "Since women are generally more nurturing than men, and since a young child needs a nurturing parent, I think that you should award custody to my client, Ms. Cox."

26. Protestants and Catholics disagree about a number of issues. But I see no reason why they can't get along. Each side is going to have to give a little. The truth surely must lie somewhere in the middle.

27. **Jenny**: That suit you have on makes you look much thinner.

Clint: Look, I'm *on* a diet and exercise program. What more can I do? Besides, I looked like this when you married me.

28. Teresa and Mark are getting married? They are two of the most unhappy people I know. There's no way that can be a happy marriage.

29. Why is it that men have to pay higher auto insurance rates than women, even though men are better drivers?

30. The Philosophy Department at the University of Virginia has been given national recognition as an outstanding department because of the quality of their

undergraduate teaching. One of their staff, Professor Dawsey, has applied for our opening in philosophy here. I think we should hire him immediately. How could we go wrong?

31. I really think that you should turn down that job offer in Los Angeles. I realize that the salary they are offering would be substantial, and that this is the professional opportunity you have been hoping for, but you know how important it is to your mother for you to live close by her here in Virginia. She *lives* for your weekly visits to her house.

32. **Laura**: If a man really loves a woman, he wouldn't let her work outside the home.

Eleanor: But doesn't your daughter teach school? And her husband surely loves her.

Laura: Oh, he acts like he loves her, but I'm not so sure about that. If he really loved her, he would insist on being the sole provider.

33. Captain of cheerleaders: "We have to decide whether we want to cheer to the empty bleachers at the women's basketball game or the packed fieldhouse for the men's games."

34. No, I don't believe you. Sara would not do that to me. She loves me; she would not be unfaithful. If she has been cheating on me, as you say, it would destroy a beautiful relationship. She's my whole life, Phil. She just wouldn't do that to me.

35. I'm sure I could pass calculus if they got a new professor to teach it.

36. Senator, I just don't understand how you can give your support to this trade treaty. Its chief supporters are the Fortune 500 and reactionary Republicans. In the past we always counted *you* as one of the "good guys."

37. We told you to be home at a reasonable hour, Dawn, and you come dragging in here at midnight. We thought you could be trusted, but I guess we were wrong.

38. As a defense for his act of spray painting the car of the person who spray painted his car, Wayne says, "Well, you know what Jesus said, 'An eye for an eye!'"

39. Prosecutor to witness: "Would you tell us, Ms. Powers, about the nature of your relationship with the rapist, Mr. Graham?"

40. I know that you are not a wealthy man, but I hope that does not embarrass you. There's nothing wrong with being poor.

VI
Fallacies That Violate the Sufficient Grounds Criterion

The fallacies discussed in this chapter are particular ways that insufficient evidence can cause an argument to go wrong. Some arguments use too little evidence or no evidence at all; others use biased evidence or only the appearance of evidence. Still others omit key or crucial evidence from the mix. Arguments that commit the so-called "causal" fallacies draw conclusions about causal relationships that are not sufficiently supported by appropriate evidence.

In a variety of ways, all of these patterns of reasoning fail to provide sufficient grounds for an argument's conclusion, which is a violation of the third criterion of a good argument. If the premises are not sufficient in number, kind, and weight, they may not be strong enough to establish the truth of the conclusion. Additional or different premises may be needed to make the case.

The 16 fallacies that violate the criterion of sufficient grounds are divided into two groups: (1) the fallacies of missing evidence and (2) the causal fallacies.

FALLACIES OF MISSING EVIDENCE

Insufficient Sample

Definition   This fallacy consists in drawing a conclusion or generalization from too small a sample of cases.

The evidence used in a case of insufficient sample is usually acceptable and relevant, but there is not enough of it to establish the conclusion of the argument. This fallacy is sometimes called a "hasty generalization," because an arguer has been too quick to draw a conclusion, given the skimpiness of the evidence.

The flaw, then, has to do with the *sufficiency* of the evidence. The quantity is too limited or the sample of data is too small to constitute evidence sufficient to lead one directly to a particular conclusion. It is not uncommon for some people to draw a conclusion or generalization based on only a few instances of a phenomenon. In fact, a generalization is often drawn from a single case, an act that might be described as committing the "fallacy of the lonely fact." In the face of such limited evidence, it would be fallacious to draw any conclusion at all, for to do so on insufficient grounds would violate one of the criteria of a good argument.

It is usually difficult to determine just what constitutes a sufficient number of instances for drawing any particular conclusion. The sufficiency of the sample is partially determined by each context of inquiry, but it should not be assumed that an increase in the number of instances means that the claim for which they are evidence will be more reliable. There is a point beyond which the increase in the number of instances has a negligible effect on the truth or falsity of the claim.

Some areas of inquiry have become quite sophisticated in developing guidelines for determining the sufficiency of a sample, such as in voter preference samples or television viewing samples. There are many more areas, however, where there are no such guidelines to assist us in determining what would be sufficient grounds for the truth of a particular conclusion.

Example   "I'm convinced that Vitamin C really works. Every member of my family used to have at least one winter cold every year. Last fall each of us started taking 1,000 milligrams of Vitamin C a day, and there hasn't been even a sniffle at our house in over nine months."

Such data may be interesting enough to encourage some people to consider a regular program of Vitamin C consumption, but the argument hardly makes the case for the program's effectiveness. A number of other good reasons could possibly account for the no-cold phenomenon in a particular nine-month period. The speaker, of course, may have other evidence for the effectiveness of Vitamin C, but that evidence is not presented as a part of the argument. On the basis of the limited evidence given, to draw any conclusion about the cold-preventing effects of Vitamin C would not be justified.

Example   A common experience is that of occasionally stopping by a grocery store other than where we normally shop to pick up a few items. If we discover that the prices on several items are lower than the prices on those items at our regular store, we may infer that we should switch grocery stores in order to save on our monthly grocery bill. However, such an inference would be unwarranted, because the sample used is too small. Only the positive results of a more comprehensive comparative survey of the prices on the items we typically buy during the month could possibly justify such a conclusion.

Example   "My experience with my ex-wife was such a bad one that I have no intention of ever marrying again. In fact, I would not recommend marriage to anyone." This reasoning is based on too small a sample. His one experience with marriage apparently convinced him that marriage was not a worthwhile institution for himself, his friends, and probably anyone else. It is quite possible, however, that his one negative experience with marriage could be attributed to his own flaws or to those of his wife, rather than to flaws in the institution itself. It can at least be said that the conclusion concerning the value of marriage deserves more evidence.

Attacking the Fallacy   Those who present you with an argument based on a single case or an insufficient sample are usually quite convinced of the truth of their claim. Perhaps the reason that it seems so convincing to them is that it often involves or comes out of a significant personal experience. You should, however, find some way to make it clear that an existential insight falls far short of being a good argument.

It is possible, in some cases, that what appears to be a one-instance generalization may not be intended as an argument at all; it may simply be the expression of an opinion. To clarify the matter, you might even ask, "Are you just expressing an opinion or do you have good evidence for what you say?"

If your opponent denies that he or she is just expressing an opinion, rather than giving evidence for a claim, a reconstruction of his or her argument may be helpful. A reconstruction of the argument, which spells out the implicit premise that is being used, namely, that *one* or a *few* cases constitute sufficient grounds for drawing a conclusion about all cases, should clearly demonstrate to the arguer the flawed character of his or her argument. If it doesn't, an absurd example might: "Faculty kids are real brats. I babysat with one the other night, and he was spoiled, rude, and uncontrollable." If necessary, put the argument into standard form:

Since the faculty child I babysat for recently was a brat,

(and one faculty child is a sufficient sample of faculty children to determine what is true of all faculty children),

Therefore, all faculty children are brats.

It is highly unlikely that your opponent could embrace, without embarrassment, the second premise, once it is spelled out, and therefore could not continue to hold to a similar premise in his or her own argument.

Unrepresentative Data

Definition   This fallacy consists in drawing a conclusion from exceptional cases or from unrepresentative or biased data.

Unrepresentative data are data that are not proportionately drawn from all relevant subclasses. For example, if one wished to generalize about the opinion of the American people on a particular issue, it would be appropriate to consider data proportionately drawn from subclasses based on race, age, educational and professional status, sex, geographical area, and perhaps even religion. In most cases, data from other subclasses, such as body weight and hair color, would not be relevant.

It is also important to avoid using data that may be biased. This can occur in at least two ways. First, the data collected may be tainted by virtue of the bias of the gatherer. Opinion data gathered by a political party or by an advocacy group should be immediately suspect. Second, data purporting to support claims about any matter are biased data if collected from one or only a few subgroups of the target population—especially if data are collected from groups that might have strong positive or negative opinions about the matter at issue. For example, if one were interested in assessing campus opinions about college athletics, one would not survey just the members of the campus athletic teams. Neither would one survey just the nonathletes.

Likewise, if one were interested in the quality of a recent film release, it would not be a case of good reasoning to form one's judgment exclusively on the basis of evaluations collected from readers of a single magazine. Subscribers to a particular magazine are a subgroup with special interests and tastes. Of course, if you already share those same tastes, and you are looking for a film consistent with them, the data may be important evidence to consider in your decision to go to or rent the movie.

Another kind of atypical data might be data of differing quality. If one compared statistics gathered with modern techniques of statistical reporting and analysis with statistics gathered under very different methodological and technical conditions, any conclusion would be highly questionable. For example, if one were to compare statistics on the number of violent crimes committed in the United States in 1993 with statistics on similar phenomena in 1940, the comparative conclusion would be suspect.

Example "We had a mock election on campus today, and the Democratic candidate won. So I am pretty confident that she will win the election in November, especially because over 2,000 students voted. That seems to be a big enough sample. Don't you agree?"

A college population hardly qualifies as a representative sample of voters, even if the size of the sample is actually larger than the number usually polled by sophisticated polling organizations. A sample not only must be large enough, it must also be genuinely random. If it is not drawn from relevant representative subclasses, the size of the sample is of no consequence.

Example "It has been concluded from a recent study involving over 100,000 people in the state of Florida that 43 percent of the American people now spend at least two hours a day in some form of recreational activity."

To draw such a conclusion about the leisure-time activities of the American people would not be warranted. The state of Florida is populated by a disproportionate number of retired and recreation-oriented people, so data based on a Florida population alone would be unrepresentative.

Example "A recent study of how Americans spend their vacations revealed that 52 percent of the people spend at least five or more days a year at ocean beaches. The study of 50,000 Virginians also revealed that 85 percent of American women buy a new bathing suit every year.

A sample of 50,000 Americans from the state of Virginia surely seems to be large enough, but it is hardly representative. Most areas of Virginia are close enough to many popular beaches within the state itself as well as in North and South Carolina that a disproportionate number of the residents of Virginia, when compared with those from many other states, spend a part of their vacations at the beach. Moreover, a study based on data collected exclusively from Virginia residents does not provide sufficient evidence to draw any reliable conclusion about the frequency that American women buy new beachwear.

Attacking the Fallacy   Suggestions for a proper response to those who use unrepresentative data are similar to those given for dealing with too small a sample. If you encounter a case where someone has used suspect data, you might devise a similar argument with an absurd conclusion. For example:

> Since most of the people in attendance at the county dog show own dogs,
>
> and what is true of the people at the dog show is true of the entire population,

---

Therefore, most people own dogs.

If your opponent sees nothing wrong with the second premise, no attack against unrepresentative data may turn out to be successful, but you might try one other strategy. Threaten your opponent with the possibility of gathering another set of data of the same size as support for a claim that most people *do not* own dogs. For example, threaten to survey all the people living in a local nursing home about their ownership of dogs—a survey that should yield very different results. If samples of equal size can support two contradictory conclusions, it should be clear that there is something wrong with the quality of the data.

Arguing from Ignorance

Definition   This fallacy consists in arguing that a claim is true because there is no evidence or proof that it is false or because of the inability or refusal of an opponent to present convincing evidence against it. Conversely, it consists in arguing that a claim is false because there is no evidence or proof that it is true or because of the refusal or inability of an opponent to present convincing evidence for it.

Arguing from ignorance is a tactic many people use to defend some of their favorite unsupported beliefs. They simply point out that since the view in question has not been disproved, it must be true. But this is hardly a fair way of arguing, for if an idea were so absurd or trivial that no one even bothered to address it, an arguer could win by default.

To argue from ignorance is to use the lack of evidence against a claim as positive evidence for its opposite. For example, if I were to argue that the lack of evidence for the claim that my students *do not* like me is positive evidence that they *do* like me, I would be arguing from ignorance. In such an argument, the alleged "evidence" for the claim that my students like me is actually no evidence at all. My conclusion would be supported by my *ignorance* or by my lack of evidence, rather than by my *knowledge* or by positive evidence. The absence of evidence for a claim does not constitute sufficient evidence for the opposite claim.

Another possible name for this fallacy is the "fallacy of shifting the burden of proof," because it violates a standard methodological principle that the burden of proof for any claim generally rests on the person who sets forth the claim. When one commits this fallacy, one is attempting to shift the obligation of proof to another person, usually to someone who is unconvinced by or skeptical about the claim. This is typically done by insisting that the *critic* has the responsibility to disprove the claim or provide support for the contradictory claim.

There are some situations of inquiry in which this kind of reasoning seems to be acceptable. In our judicial procedure, for example, a defendant is assumed to be innocent unless proven guilty. It should be noted, however, that *innocent* in this context is a highly technical term, which actually means *not proven guilty*. Moreover, when a jury pronounces a verdict of *not guilty*, it is not claiming that the defendant did not commit the act as charged; it is only claiming that the evidence is not weighty enough to prove such a charge. In a judicial proceeding, for practical reasons, some decision must be made. Hence, it has been determined that, for legal purposes, a person should be regarded "as if" he or she were innocent unless convincing evidence exists to the contrary. It should be pointed out, however, that even in this case, the methodological standard is intact. The burden of proof is still on the one who makes the positive claim—the prosecutor who says that the defendant is guilty.

This fallacy probably gains its *appearance* as a good argument from a *legitimate* way of arguing that appears to be similar to it in form. If standard methods of proof are available, and if they have been used in a sincere effort to prove or disprove the claim in question and have failed, then the negative or contradictory claim can usually be legitimately inferred. For example, if a thorough examination produces no evidence to support the claim that there are termites in a house, then the effort to prove the claim has failed. It is then justifiable to conclude logically, and by common sense, that there are probably no termites in the house. This sounds like the argument from ignorance, but there is a crucial difference. The negative inference is based on the actual assessment of the evidence relevant to the claim that there are termites in the house. It is not an inference based solely on the fact that no proof is offered or attempted for such a claim.

An argument that employs an appeal to the "evidence" of no evidence does not satisfy the third condition of a good argument. It obviously fails to provide sufficient grounds for the claim at issue, because evidence is missing altogether.

Example "Since my opponent has not clearly indicated his *opposition* to the new federal gun-control bill, he obviously is in *favor* of it." The only "evidence" offered in support of such a claim is the fact that the opponent has not addressed the issue. Interestingly, the arguer could have defended the opposite claim with the same evidence: "Since my opponent has not clearly indicated his *support* for the new federal gun-control bill, he obviously is *opposed* to it." Any evidence that could lead to either a positive or negative conclusion with equal strength cannot be sufficient grounds for an argument.

Example "I didn't see any 'No Trespassing' sign, so I assumed that it was all right to walk through his field." The fact that there is no sign indicating that an act *is not* permissible does not entitle one to assume that the act *is* permissible.

Example

Connie: Did you get that teaching job at the University of Virginia?
Neil: No. I sent in my application over two months ago, and I never heard a word from them.

Neil is assuming that he has been rejected by the university, even though the only "evidence" for a rejection is that there is no evidence for any other claim regarding the status of his application. However, it would be inappropriate to conclude that he had been rejected for the teaching job on the basis of no communication from the university, especially because the institutional procedure required for filling a teaching position is usually a very long and involved one.

Example "What's all this business about equal pay for women? The women who work in my office must be satisfied with their salaries, because not one of them has ever complained or asked for a raise."

The speaker is assuming that the situation of a group of people must be satisfactory, simply because no complaints about that situation have been expressed. In other words, the absence of evidence *against* the satisfactory character of a situation is regarded as evidence *for* the satisfactory character of that situation. Making such an inference is so distinctive a form of the fallacy of arguing from ignorance that it is often given a separate name—the fallacy of quietism. But from the fact that a person or group is "quiet," that is, makes no complaint, one could in no way infer that there is nothing to complain about. There may indeed be many good reasons why the complaints are not openly voiced.

Attacking the Fallacy If the absence of proof against a claim could be regarded as proof for it, then even the most bizarre of claims could allegedly be proved. If your opponent makes what you consider a highly questionable claim and supports it by pointing out the lack of evidence against it, you could show the faulty character of that kind of reasoning by making what you think he or she would consider an equally questionable claim and support it by the same method.

You could also show how one could be led to logically contradictory conclusions if the pattern of thinking in question were not fallacious. Suppose someone suggests that because psychokinesis has not been proved false, it must be true. Some other person could argue that because psychokinesis has not been proved true, it must be false. Such reasoning would lead us to the contradictory conclusion that psychokinesis is both true and false.

It also might be helpful to point out a special problem with the burden of proof. If you claim that since you have no reason to believe that a claim is true, it is therefore false, you have actually made a claim for which you now have the burden of proof—a task for which you might not be presently inclined or prepared. A careful distinction should made between asserting that "I have no reason to believe that X is true" and asserting that "X is false." The first does not entail the second. Each is a distinct claim. The first explains why one is not now prepared to affirm or deny the claim; the second is a negative claim for which one must assume the burden of proof. In the absence of a thorough investigation of the issue, the best response might be simply to say that you have no reason *to believe* the claim in question rather than to assert its denial.

Another way of dealing with this matter on a practical level would be to simply act "as if" the negative claim is true, without making the denial—especially if you do not have the time, energy, or inclination to defend it. For example, you may not be prepared to *prove* that ghosts do not exist; but if, on the basis of the available evidence, you do not *believe* that they exist, you could simply act "as if" they do not, without denying their existence. Otherwise, you might be asked to prove your claim. This is a way of contending daily with one's world without having to defend every belief or assumption on which one acts.

Contrary-to-Fact Hypothesis

Definition This fallacy consists in making a poorly supported claim about what might have happened in the past if other conditions had been present, or about an event that might occur in the future. This is done in such a way as to treat hypothetical claims as if they were statements of fact.

Because *empirical* evidence for claims about nonexistent events is obviously not available, any alleged "evidence" must be regarded as part of an imaginative construct. Even though there is usually no way of knowing what might have been or what may be the consequences of an event that did not occur or has not yet occurred, there may be good reasons or other evidence for a well-supported hypothetical construct about it. Such constructs might be helpful in understanding the past and in planning for, or avoiding undesirable consequences in, the future. However, it must be remembered that such constructs are only speculative and thus quite uncertain. They are at best "likely stories."

The question arises, then, as to whether there is any fallaciousness in constructing an imaginative hypothesis. Making a claim about an unfulfilled hypothetical event is fallacious only insofar as it is not well supported or its speculative character is not acknowledged. The contrary-to-fact hypothesis is fallacious, then, if it is a weak hypothesis or if it is treated as a statement of actual fact.

This fallacy, insofar as it refers to past "events," is sometimes called "Monday morning quarterbacking." Nearly every avid football fan is known to make claims about what would have happened in last weekend's game if the quarterback had just called a different play or had executed differently the one called. But there is no way of knowing with any degree of certainty what would have happened in the past if something that *did* happen had not happened and if something that *did not happen* had happened. The evidence for a claim that is contrary to the facts is simply not available. For this reason, the contrary-to-fact hypothesis that is treated as if it were fact or that is only weakly supported violates one of the criteria of a good argument, because it draws a conclusion without sufficient grounds for doing so.

Example Consider the following contrary-to-fact hypotheses, none of which is provided with any support: "If you had only tasted the stewed snails, you would have loved them." "If I hadn't goofed around my first year in college, I would have been accepted at medical school." "If I had only been there for him last night, he wouldn't have killed himself." "If only I had practiced a little more on my backhand, I could have won that tennis tournament."

Such claims are usually lacking in adequate support and therefore rarely merit acceptance. There may indeed be good reasons to accept such constructs, but we have not been provided with any of those reasons.

Example Consider the number of students who have convinced themselves or their parents, with something like the following argument, of the wisdom of moving out of campus housing: "If I could just live off campus, I could get a lot more studying done, my grades would improve, and I'm sure I would get a lot more sleep." No doubt the student thinks that there are good reasons to support these claims; yet listeners are expected to accept such claims without hearing those reasons.

Example Even history professors have been known to commit this fallacy: "If Hitler had not invaded Russia and opened up two 'fronts,' the Nazis would have won World War II." "If the Democrats had won the election of 1860, then the War between the States would never have erupted." These are such highly speculative claims that it is difficult to imagine how sufficient evidence for such claims could ever be found.

Attacking the Fallacy Because the formulation of imaginative constructs is a vital part of planning for the future and understanding the past, in no way would I encourage anyone to pounce on every hypothetical construct or to refrain from exercising one's own imagination. However, if you are confronted with a substantive contrary-to-fact claim that is highly questionable, I would suggest that you find some way of getting your opponent to recognize and to admit to the speculative character of the claim. Sometimes the very act of admitting that a claim is speculative will lead one to be more open to counterarguments and to take more seriously the task of supporting the claim. The fact that one may clearly admit the speculative nature of a claim does not, of course, relieve one of the obligation to provide good reasons in support of it.

One effective way of confronting an unsupported hypothetical claim might be to inform your opponent that you are in no position to respond to the claim in the absence of evidence. You might say, "Well, you may be right, but I would have no way of determining that, as I am not aware of your evidence for such a claim." Your opponent will probably feel obligated to make some attempt to provide you with evidence, and that should at least get the discussion on a constructive track.

Improper Use of a Cliché

Definition　This fallacy consists in using an aphorism or cliché in place of relevant evidence for a claim.

The fallacy commonly takes the form of using a cliché or aphorism to express an argument or opinion and failing to show that the proposition expressed by the cliché is reliable. Indeed, the fact that many clichés or aphorisms seem to contradict each other suggests that depending on a cliché for one's insight or direction is highly questionable. Do not the following sets of aphorisms seem to give contradictory advice? (1) "Two heads are better than one" and "Too many cooks spoil the broth." (2) "Where there's smoke there's fire" and "You can't tell a book by its cover." (3) "He who hesitates is lost" and "Fools rush in where angels fear to tread." (4) "Better safe than sorry" and "Nothing ventured, nothing gained." (5) "A new broom sweeps clean" and "Many a good tune is played on an old fiddle." (6) "Where there's a will, there's a way" and "If wishes were horses, beggars would ride." (7) "Birds of a feather flock together" and "Opposites attract."

Aphorisms or clichés are not really arguments at all; they are simply expressions of popular wisdom, and the "wisdom" expressed in many aphorisms can easily be contradicted by the "wisdom" expressed in others. Hence, apart from other evidence, there is no reason to regard an aphorism as reliable support for any claim or course of action. The attempt to argue by means of a cliché is a clear violation of the third criterion of a good argument—that there be sufficient grounds for a claim. A cliché or aphorism does not constitute such grounds.

Example　Suppose that a counselor tells a young woman that she can't have a serious relationship with two different men at the same time. In an attempt to convince her, he says, "You just can't have your cake and eat it too." Such an aphorism is inapplicable in this particular instance. Having or keeping a piece of cake and consuming that same cake are logically incompatible, but there is nothing logically incompatible about being in a serious relationship with two people at the same time. To make the case, the counselor would have to demonstrate why the two are unworkable or practically incompatible.

Example　A typical campus cliché expressed by one student to another the night before an important test is "Well, if you don't know it now, you never will." No evidence is usually given for such a questionable claim; indeed, there is considerable evidence to suggest that it is a false claim. As far as performance on tests is concerned, it is probably safe to say that a conscientious student might learn a significant amount of material during the hours immediately before a test.

Example   Sometimes a cliché is simply used as a substitute for good reasons or an appropriate response. Suppose that a parent, before leaving for the day, gives very clear instructions to a child to mow the yard. On returning, the parent finds that only about half of the grass is cut. When the child is asked why the job is not completed, his or her response is "Rome wasn't built in a day." It is true that 24 hours isn't enough time to build a city the size of Rome, but 6 to 8 hours does provide enough time to cut an average-sized yard. In this case, the familiar proverb is an inappropriate or meaningless response to a legitimate question.

Attacking the Fallacy   Because clichés, like analogies, are at best only suggestive, no argument wholly constituted by a cliché should be treated as a serious one. If the cliché were accompanied by a thoroughly developed argument that demonstrated why the cliché or aphorism expressed an important and defensible insight, the cliché itself would add nothing to the argument; it would be, at best, only a clever way of expressing the argument's conclusion.

In no way should you be intimidated by the allegedly obvious wisdom of a popular cliché. A cliché or aphorism, like any other not so cleverly expressed opinion, requires evidential support or good reasons to make it worthy of acceptance. If an arguer attempts to let an argument rest on a cliché, challenge it directly; or better yet, counter it, if possible, with a cliché that gives contradictory advice. The arguer would then have to show why his or her cliché is better founded than yours.

Inference from a Label

Definition   This fallacy consists in assuming that evaluative or identifying words or phrases attached to people or things constitute a sufficient reason for drawing conclusions about the objects to which such labels are attached.

This is a fallacy many advertisers expect the typical consumer to commit; thus they advertise in a way that lends itself to such faulty inference. The manufacturer of Super-flite golf balls would like weekend golfers to infer, from nothing more than the name, that using such balls will lengthen their drive. The discount houses would like consumers to infer, simply from the fact that they are called "discount" houses, that name-brand goods may be purchased there for lower prices. The manufacturers of an auto wax would like possible users of their product to assume that the wax is simple to apply just because they have what they call an "easy applicator." And who has not been tempted to stop for coffee when the sign reads "The World's Best Cup of Coffee"? While evaluative or descriptive labels may whet our appetite or increase our interest in investigating particular claims, it would be foolish, without further inquiry, to infer from them anything about the objects to which they are attached.

This kind of faulty reasoning is one in which no evidence at all is given to support the claim in question. The arguer has simply inferred a claim from an expression of the same claim on a sign or label. Since a good argument requires that sufficient grounds be provided for a claim, an argument constituted by such an inference cannot be a good one.

Example   Probably we have all had the experience of being tired and hungry after driving a long time on an automobile trip and have found ourselves mildly elated when a sign tells us that there are "delicious food" and "clean restrooms" ahead. However, in some cases the only valuable thing about the stop was that it gave us one more opportunity to learn about the importance of not inferring anything from signs.

Example   "Emory & Henry College must be a good school, because the college catalog says that it is a fine liberal arts college of the highest caliber." Emory & Henry may indeed be a fine school, but that could not be legitimately inferred solely from the description in its catalog.

Example   "What do you mean by saying that the Democratic party doesn't express the will of the people? The very name of the party means that everyone has a voice in what is done." There is no more reason to believe, on the basis of a name, that the Democratic party is democratic than to infer, for the same reason, that "health foods" are healthy.

Attacking the Fallacy   In spite of what has been said about the folly of inferring anything from signs or labels, you need not be skeptical about evaluatively neutral signs such as "You are now entering Yellowstone National Park." There does not seem to be any good reason to question whether you are actually entering Yellowstone Park. However, if a sign in any way includes an evaluation or a description with evaluative overtones, then there is good reason to be skeptical about that part of the claim. For example, if you see a sign at the service station indicating that it has clean restrooms, that would be sufficient reason to believe that the station has restrooms; but there is not sufficient reason to infer, simply from the sign, that they are clean.

While you should avoid becoming a "sign skeptic," you should not fall victim to the schemes of advertisers and others who are trying to manipulate you into making faulty inferences. In other words, refrain from making any inference from evaluative descriptions until you have something more than a label on which to base your conclusion.

Fallacy of Fake Precision

Definition   This fallacy consists in making a claim with a kind of mathematical precision that is impossible to obtain.

It is not uncommon for an arguer to introduce statistical precision into a claim as a means of persuading a listener of the point at issue. A fallacy is committed when this precision is simply guessed at, when approximate data are treated as if they were precise, or when one uses data that cannot be known or obtained with the degree of precision claimed.

It is commonly assumed, and perhaps correctly so, that the more precision one can introduce into one's claim, the more likely it is that a listener will regard it as true. For example, if your favorite television program has just been canceled because, according to the network, not enough people were watching it, you might possibly be skeptical about such a claim. However, if the network claimed that in the last four weeks the highest proportion of the national viewing audience watching that program in any one week was 3.9 percent, you would be more likely to accept the claim as true and the cancellation as appropriate. The fact that statistical precision can have such effects is one of the reasons it is sometimes fabricated to strengthen a weak claim.

Probably no one of us is free from the tendency to introduce a kind of frivolous false precision into even the most casual of our claims. For example, it is not unusual for a parent to say something like the following: "Three-fourths of the time, my children pay no attention to what I say" or "Ninety percent of the time I don't have any idea what I have in my bank account." The purpose of expressing a claim with such alleged precision is probably to make the claim more pointed or dramatic. When nothing of substance is at stake, and no one takes such claims as representing accurate data anyway, the fake precision can probably be safely ignored.

However, when there is something at stake, that is, when someone is making a serious claim and backing it up with data that purport to be accurate data, but that could only be approximate at best or at least virtually impossible to determine with the accuracy claimed, one has clearly committed the fallacy of fake precision. The evidence only has the *appearance* of being sufficient evidence.

The use of fake precision, then, is a way of reasoning that fails to satisfy the sufficient grounds condition of a good argument. When the claim at issue cannot be backed up by data that support the degree of precision claimed, the argument must be regarded as a faulty one.

Example   Consider the claim that "one-third of all forest fires are intentionally set." It seems justifiable to assume that there is no way to obtain reliable data from which such a conclusion could be drawn, because the cause of many forest fires is unknown. Even if it were known that a fire started, for example, because of a cigarette, it would be virtually impossible to determine whether the cigarette was deliberately used to start the fire or whether it was the result of a careless toss into combustible material.

Example   One of the primary reasons cited for engaging in transcendental meditation is that "most of us use only 10 percent of our creative potential." Such a scientific-sounding claim has no doubt impressed many people with the possibilities of tapping the other 90 percent of their creative resources through meditation. However, one would have to know what constitutes 100 percent of one's creative potential in order to know what constitutes 10 percent of that potential, and it seems reasonable to assume that information about such a vaguely described possibility is not available or at least not precisely calculable. Nevertheless, many people would probably give much more credence to a claim stated with mathematical precision than they would to a more defensible, and therefore nonfallacious, form of the same claim, for example, that "there is a lot of creative potential in each of us that we never use."

Example   "There is no way that we can successfully teach that crime doesn't pay, because every time that a thief gets caught, there are 115 times that that same thief does *not* get caught. Those are pretty good odds, don't you agree? Besides that, even when we do punish people for their crimes, we punish the wrong ones. Over 40 percent of the persons behind bars right now did not commit the crimes with which they were charged."

It may be difficult to prove that "crime doesn't pay" or that the criminal justice system doesn't work, but the case does not gain strength by presenting data that would be impossible to obtain with such precision. It is reasonable to assume that many thefts are unsolved and that some innocent people go to jail, or at least go to jail for the wrong reason; but the precise claims presented appear to be the work of a fertile imagination.

Attacking the Fallacy   The first step in confronting this fallacy is not to be intimidated or impressed by such tactics. Remember that if you give additional credence to a claim or assume it to be more accurate than it really could be, simply because it is expressed in precise mathematical language, you also are committing the fallacy of fake precision.

You might be tempted to counter an overly precise claim with a claim of your own that exhibits an even more absurd kind of precision, as an oblique method of exposing the questionable character of your opponent's claim. However, the counterclaim approach may be so oblique that your opponent might miss altogether what you are attempting to do, and your device would turn out to be simply diversionary.

A better approach might be a direct one. Ask some very pointed questions about the overly precise data used in support of your opponent's argument. For example, in response to the claim that "we use only 10 percent of our creative potential," you might ask several direct questions, such as "How did you arrive at such a precise figure as 10 percent?" or "Is it not the case that one must know what amount of creativity constitutes 100 percent in order to determine what 10 percent of such potential might be?" or "Do you really mean 10 percent or is that just another way of saying that we use 'very little'?" This direct approach will at least force your opponent to respond seriously to your attack.

Special Pleading

Definition   This fallacy consists in applying principles, rules, or criteria to another person, while failing or refusing to apply them to oneself or to a situation that is of special personal interest, without providing sufficient reason to support such an exception.

Exceptions to normal rules or principles must be justified. If a double standard is to be applied, some reason must be given for treating differently what appear to be similar cases. Special treatment is sometimes called for, but not unless a special case can be successfully made for it.

Almost every example of special pleading occurs in a context in which it is assumed and understood that a rule, principle, or law applies to all persons alike in the situation. Since the special pleader usually accepts the relevant principle, the occasion of special pleading may come about as a result of a memory lapse or a faulty understanding or deliberate violation of that principle. In most cases, however, one who engages in special pleading wishes to make himself or herself an exception to the principle at issue.

Acceptable evidence for making an exception of oneself is simply missing from a special pleading argument. It violates the criterion of a good argument that says that the grounds must be sufficient in number, kind, and weight to establish the truth of the conclusion. Hence, any argument for a special treatment claim that fails to provide sufficient evidence cannot qualify as a good argument.

Example   Sometimes it is with a subtle use of language that we make a special case of ourselves: "Whereas I (and my friends) am confident, you are arrogant; I am aggressive, you are ruthless; I am thrifty, you are cheap; I am frank, you are rude; I am flexible, you are inconsistent; I am clever, you are conniving; I am thorough, you are picky; I am curious, you are nosy; I am excited, you are hysterical; I am firm, you are pig-headed; I am friendly, you are flirtatious; I am a free spirit, you take license."

But if the behaviors are the same, how can one justify a positive assessment of one's own behavior, while negatively assessing another's, without being inconsistent? When charged with inconsistency, special pleaders often respond with "Well, this is different!" But if they cannot convincingly make that distinction stick, they are clearly guilty of the fallacy.

Example   Jane and Joyce are roommates and come into conflict over the use of their dorm room. Jane wants to play her music and Joyce wants to take a nap. Whose interest should take precedence? The relevant principle that roommates assume is that neither one's interest is more important than the other's. If Joyce claimed that her interest was more important than Jane's, we would say that she was engaged in special pleading. There is no obvious reason why one of the roommates should be granted special treatment. Probably the way to settle the matter would be to negotiate a compromise arrangement.

Example   James claims that he is too tired to share in the chores of cooking, cleaning, or caring for the children after working all day. If he claims that those domestic jobs are his wife's responsibility, even though she too is tired from her full-time job outside the home, he is engaged in special pleading. Being tired from a full day's work outside the home presumably excuses him from domestic chores, while it apparently does not excuse his wife. James is applying a principle to himself that he is not willing to apply to his wife, and he has presented no evidence for such an exception.

Attacking the Fallacy   An attack that is most effective is to accuse your opponent of applying a double standard, playing favorites, or being inconsistent. Each of these charges is commonly understood outside logical circles and has strong negative connotations, with which your opponent will not wish to be associated.

There may, of course, be some situations that call for making oneself a special case, but these are rare, so the careful thinker should always be suspicious of any preferential treatment claim. Ask the arguer to spell out the reasons why he or she should be treated differently from others or why the relevant principle should not apply in this case. The arguer, of course, will almost always have reasons. The question is whether he or she can provide sufficient reason to merit acceptance of the claim. For the hard to convince, try an absurd example:

> Since the law with regard to the payment of income tax should be applied in all cases,
>
> and I am an exception because my case is not like that of others, for I need that money for other things,
>
> _____
>
> Therefore, the income tax law should not be applied to me.

The second premise should sound absurd to even the most inveterate special pleader, and he or she should be prepared to show why the special treatment he or she is requesting is not equally absurd.

Omission of Key Evidence

Definition   This fallacy consists in constructing an argument that fails to include some of the key or principal evidence that is critical to the support of the conclusion.

The sufficient grounds criterion of a good argument is perhaps most clearly violated when crucial or key evidence that is necessary to support a particular conclusion is simply absent from the premises of an argument. It is not unlike the situation of preparing a mixed drink and leaving out the alcohol. The context of each thesis that we might wish to defend requires evidence of specific kinds. For example, if you are trying to make a case for buying a cute little puppy in the pet shop, it isn't enough that it is cute and that your child wants it. Look at this reconstructed argument:

> Since this puppy is cute,
>
> and my daughter wants it,
>
> _____
>
> Therefore, we should buy it

Such an argument looks exceedingly skimpy. Some of the crucial pieces of evidence that are missing from this argument are that you can afford to buy and maintain the dog, that you have a place to keep it, that your child has promised to take care of it, and that you and your spouse like dogs also. If we were to add those missing premises, we would be looking at a pretty good argument for buying the dog today.

The mistake that is made in omitting crucial evidence for a claim is not like ignoring evidence *against* the claim at issue; it is simply a failure to supply the relevant evidence necessary to make the case in its favor. It is the crucial but missing piece of the puzzle. Without it, the argument will not work.

Some of the most glaring cases of omitting the key evidence involve human relationships. Whether to pursue or maintain a romantic relationship involves a number of important factors. These factors might be such things as mutual love, attraction, compatibility, respect, maturity, and availability. Failure to consider any one of these in an argument dealing with the future of the relationship would be a case of omission of key evidence.

Example "Let's get married, Jessica. We like the same things, we both love your dog, we go to the same church, we share the same tastes in food and movies, and we can save money on living expenses. So, what do you say, huh?" What most people think are key issues to be considered in a marriage decision—whether they love each other and whether they want to spend the rest of their lives together—are completely omitted.

Example Suppose you wanted to nominate a professor for an award as "Teacher of the Year." The reasons that you might give for why Professor Mitchell should receive the award are many: She is bright, she is widely published, she is dedicated to her job, she is always willing to talk to students, she is always kind and caring toward students, she returns papers quickly, and she is excited about her discipline.

These are all very good reasons for giving her an award, but the list does not even mention what is surely the most important or key reason for such an award—her teaching ability. Do the students learn from her? Does Professor Mitchell generate enthusiasm for good writing? A successful case for giving her the award must include at least positive answers to these questions.

Example "I think we should buy that beautiful Tudor-style house in Emory Hills. It is big enough for our family, it is close to school, and it has a big yard for our dog, an attic for all our junk, and a huge eat-in size kitchen. It has the fireplace that we have always wanted. Indeed, it is the only house that everyone in our family has liked. It is just the ideal house to buy."

These may all be good reasons to buy the house, but a key premise in an argument for buying the house is whether the house is in the right price range. And that information is entirely missing.

Example "I propose that we add a new elective course in symbolic logic to our curriculum in philosophy. It is a standard part of most college offerings in philosophy. I am trained in the area and therefore qualified to teach it, there is room in my teaching load to take on an additional course, and it will require no additional budgetary allocations."

This just about covers everything but the issue of whether there is any student who is likely to take such a course, which is a crucial issue in the decision of whether to add a new course to a list of college course offerings.

Attacking the Fallacy The best way to address this fallacy is directly. Point out the evidence that you must have to be convinced of the conclusion. It is quite possible that the omission is simply the result of the arguer's carelessness and can be easily produced. In that case, the argument can quickly be made into a successful one.

It is possible, however, that the evidence was omitted for other reasons. The evidence may be not only missing from the argument, but missing altogether or at least yet to be found. Maybe the evidence is not as strong or as convincing as the arguer might wish it to be, and he or she is embarrassed by its feebleness. Moreover, the arguer may believe that mentioning these defects would make a weak argument even weaker. Finally, arguers may not even be aware of the crucial nature of certain kinds of evidence. In these cases, the glaring omission must be pointed out to those who are obviously not blinded by its glare.

If you are going to help correct the flaw in an argument with essential evidence missing, it is important to find out the specific reason for the omission and then to go about finding it. But for whatever reason the evidence is missing, it must be made clear that the argument, as it stands, is not a good one.

Exercises

In each of the following exercises (1) identify the type of fallacy of missing evidence illustrated; (2) explain what specific feature in the example causes it to be properly identified in that way; and (3) explain how the reasoning violates the criterion of sufficient grounds.

1. I know that my term paper is due today, Professor Raines, but would you please give me a two-week extension? You see, I have had a lot of work to do in my other classes, and I just haven't had time to start on the paper yet.

2. If you ever ate in our school cafeteria, you would see that institutional food is never very good.

3. How can you say that this cereal doesn't have any nutritional value? Just look at the box. See, it says, "Good tasting and good for you, too!"

4. Daughter: But, mother, I have given you several good reasons why you should let me go to Susan's party. Why won't you let me go?
   Mother: Just remember, dear, that "mother knows best."

5. This time-share deal looks like a good one. If I buy a time share at this resort, all I have to pay is an annual maintenance fee and I'll be guaranteed a vacation week every year at the same time at a place I and my family really like to go.

6. If I just hadn't dropped out of college, I'd be working now rather than standing in this unemployment line.

7. John Stuart Mill, a nineteenth-century English philosopher, was an extremely intelligent child who was taught most academic subjects at a very early age. If it had been possible to give him an IQ test, he would have had an IQ of at least 185.

8. The black people in this country must be happy with their situation now. There haven't been any protest marches or any loud voices of dissent for several years.

9. All three sex offenders arrested this month by municipal police had previous records for the same crime. It seems that once a sex offender, always a sex offender.

10. It is obvious that the speed limits on these curves are designed to ensure the safety of all persons on the road, but I am a very good driver. I can take these curves usually 15 miles an hour faster with no problem.

11. I'm sorry, Mr. Dunbar, but we cannot approve your loan application. We must assume that your credit is no good, because there is no record indicating that you have ever met any monthly installment payments.

12. If I had gone with him to the party, I could have kept him from making a fool of himself.

13. From a recent survey of a large number of representatively selected people in New York City, it has been discovered that less than 2 percent of Americans engage in hunting for sport.

14. One senatorial candidate says of the opposition candidate, "Ms. Bradford should come before the American people and make a complete financial statement as to her financial history, and if she doesn't, it will be an admission that she has something to hide."

15. Husband to wife at supermarket: "Why are you getting such a small box of laundry detergent? As much of this stuff as we use, we could surely save a lot of money if we bought this 'Giant Economy Size.'"

16. The FBI reports concerning the number of major crimes committed in the United States are quite deficient in at least one area—the number of rapes, because 70 percent of the victims of rape never report such crimes to the authorities.

17. Marsha: If that were a child of mine, I would have given him a good spanking rather than sitting down and talking with him about his behavior as you did.

    Bruce: Why do you think that your method is better?

    Marsha: I just think that "if you spare the rod, you spoil the child."

18. Hey, look at this ad, Ginger. They have a sale on selected paint at Emory Hardware at half-off the regular price. We said that we were going to paint our house this spring. Why don't we go get some of the paint while it lasts.

19. Melissa: John, you said that you wanted to be free to date other women. I don't understand how you can get angry when I date other guys.

    John: But every time I see you with someone else, it really hurts. Maybe it would be better if you didn't look like you were having such a good time. In fact, you look like you really like the guy. That can't be good for our relationship.

    Melissa: But *you* date other *women*.

    John: But you know that when I date other women, it's not serious. You know that you are the one I really care about.

20. A recent telephone survey of randomly selected people revealed that 75 percent of the American people watch at least one soap opera a day. Indeed, to ensure accuracy in the data, the way they conducted the study was to make the calls between 1 P.M. and 4 P.M. in the afternoon, and then ask what show the respondent was actually watching at the time.

CAUSAL FALLACIES

This section addresses faulty reasoning related to the causal relationships between events. Each of the fallacies treated is a different way of inferring causal explanations from premises that do not provide sufficient support for such explanations—a violation of the third criterion of a good argument.

Trying to understand the notion of *cause* has been an important and difficult philosophical problem for a long time, and this difficulty underlies a number of problems in reasoning. This section will distinguish as carefully as possible the different ways in which logical confusion has been exhibited in reasoning about causal relationships.

Causal analysis, more so than is the case with any other group of fallacies, requires that we draw from the entire reservoir of our knowledge and understanding. The more that we know about the nature of the complex causal relationships that exist in the world, the more likely we are to detect a faulty analysis.

Confusion of a Necessary with a Sufficient Condition

Definition   This fallacy consists in assuming that a necessary condition of an event is also a sufficient one.

A *necessary condition* of an event is a condition, or set of conditions, in the absence of which the event in question cannot occur. For example, if electrical power is necessary for the vacuum cleaner to work, the absence of electrical power guarantees the absence of a functioning vacuum cleaner. Even though a necessary condition of an event must be present in order for that event to occur, it alone, in most cases, is not sufficient to produce the event. Electrical power is necessary, but it alone is not sufficient for the event of a functioning vacuum cleaner.

The event in question will occur, however, when a sufficient condition is present. A *sufficient condition* of an event is a condition, or set of conditions, in the presence of which the event in question will occur. For example, a sufficient condition of a functioning vacuum cleaner is the presence of a set of conditions that might include a vacuum cleaner that is in good working order, a dirt bag or canister that is not completely full, a plug that is connected to the power source, and an available source of electrical power.

It is not uncommon, however, for many people to argue that an event will occur simply because its necessary condition is present. But such thinking mistakes a necessary condition for a sufficient one. A claim about the presence of the necessary condition of an event does not alone provide sufficient grounds for drawing any inference about the presence of the event in question.

Example   It is obviously necessary to water a plant in order to make it grow and stay healthy, but it would be fallacious to assume that watering a plant is a sufficient condition for the growth and health of the plant. A number of other conditions must be present also. Similarly, one must read a book in order to understand it, but reading it will not guarantee understanding it. Assuming that reading a book will guarantee an understanding of it is confusing a necessary condition with a sufficient one.

Example "You said that I would have to run the mile in less than six minutes to be on the track team, and I *did*. So why is it that I got cut from the team?"

The arguer has assumed that meeting the eligibility requirement of being able to run a mile in less than six minutes would be a sufficient condition of being on the track team. Meeting the requirement, however, was only a necessary condition. The sufficient condition for being on the track team would probably include the meeting of many other requirements.

Example Consider the common situation where a professor tells her students at the first of the term that, in order to pass the course, they will have to come to class regularly, read the daily assignments, participate in class discussions, take all tests and examinations, and submit a research paper. Some students have faithfully met such conditions and then have experienced genuine surprise when they failed to pass the course. Such puzzlement could possibly be eliminated if the students understood the difference between the necessary and the sufficient condition for passing the course. In the case in question, the professor mentioned the necessary but not the sufficient condition for passing the course. The sufficient condition would presumably include getting passing grades on the tests and the research paper.

Attacking the Fallacy Many people reason in a way that confuses a necessary condition with a sufficient condition because they do not understand exactly how the two differ. Hence, it might be helpful to clarify that distinction carefully when confronting such confusion. One of the most effective ways of doing this might be to use an example that would make the difference unmistakable. Suppose a young woman were to claim that she would become a great concert pianist because she had been practicing two hours a day for 15 years. It should be plain that, although practicing the piano regularly is a necessary condition of becoming a concert pianist, it alone is not a sufficient one. When that distinction becomes clear, your opponent should recognize the problematic character of his or her own argument, which exhibits the same form as the argument in the example.

Causal Oversimplification

Definition This fallacy consists in oversimplifying the relevant causal antecedents of an event by introducing factors insufficient to account for the event in question or by overemphasizing the role of one or more of those factors.

In causal explanations, it is a common practice to point to a very obvious antecedent of an event and to designate it as the cause. However, a careful analysis of the notion of cause would show that the *cause*, or sufficient condition, of an event in most cases includes a considerable number of antecedents that only *together* are sufficient to bring about the event. To point to only one of those factors in a particular causal explanation would most likely be an oversimplification. The argument cannot be a good one because an argument that fails to provide sufficient grounds for its conclusion does not satisfy the third condition of a good argument.

Example "Children spend an average of five hours per day watching television—time that used to be spent reading. That explains why Scholastic Aptitude Test (SAT) scores are dropping."

Even if the facts presented were true, it is unlikely that they are sufficient to account for the lower SAT scores. Increased viewing of television and reduction in the amount of reading may well be *one* of the causal antecedents, but to assign that weighty a role to such an event would seem to oversimplify a causally complex phenomenon.

Example "Corporal punishment is no longer allowed in public schools. This is why children have no self-discipline and are losing respect for authority."

The problems of self-discipline and loss of respect for authority are not new issues. The ancient Greeks used to wring their hands in anguish over such problems. But even if these were new problems, it is very unlikely that they could be causally traced directly to the doorstep of the abandonment of corporal punishment in the schools. These are very complex issues, and it is highly unlikely that they have a single cause.

Example A radio preacher recently argued in the following way: "Marriage would be greatly helped if husband and wife would read the Scriptures together and pray together every day. No wonder divorce has increased so much; family worship has dropped almost 90 percent in the last few years."

Apart from questions that might be raised about the reliability of the facts regarding the drop in the rate of family worship, it does not seem that the rise in the national divorce rate could be sufficiently accounted for by such data—even if the data were true. Because the reasons for the dissolution of a marriage are usually quite varied and complex, it seems inappropriate to reduce them to one principal factor.

Attacking the Fallacy It is almost always possible to question another's causal explanation, for the typical explanation of an event rarely includes all the literally hundreds of antecedent conditions that constitute the sufficient condition of that event. You should not, of course, expect a causal explanation to include every antecedent condition of an event in question. To do so would be virtually impossible; it would also be an inefficient use of time and energy. But a person must include enough of those factors to escape the charge of oversimplification.

If you suspect that a causal analysis is oversimplified because it seems insufficient to account for the event in question or because you think it overemphasizes the role of one or more particular factors, point out these problems to your opponent and request some further justification of the analysis. Remember that the burden of proof is on the one offering the explanation. You may help, of course, by suggesting additional factors that you think should be considered in the causal analysis and then ask your opponent for an evaluation of those suggestions.

Post Hoc Fallacy

Definition   This fallacy consists in assuming that a particular event, B, is caused by another event, A, simply because B follows A in time.

Establishing the temporal priority of one event over another is not a sufficient condition for inferring a causal relationship between those events. One cannot assume that *post hoc, ergo propter hoc*—that an event that occurs after another event therefore occurs *because* of that other event. A chronological relationship is only one of the indicators of a causal relationship. Other indicators might include a spatial connection or perhaps some history of regularity. If priority alone were sufficient to establish a causal relationship, then virtually any event that preceded another could be assumed to be the cause of it. This kind of thinking contributed to the creation of many of the superstitions in our culture. Something was often considered "bad luck" for no reason other than the fact that it preceded a misfortune. Such thinking mistakes a sheer coincidence for a causal relation.

If a person commits the *post hoc* fallacy, the question might arise as to why it would not be just as appropriate to charge him or her with the fallacy of causal oversimplification. The *post hoc* fallacy is not just a special case of causal oversimplification. Causal oversimplification usually occurs when particular causal antecedents are mistakenly regarded as constituting the sufficient condition of an event when they are not by themselves *adequate* to account for that event. In the case of the *post hoc* fallacy, there is no causal factor being oversimplified; indeed, the problem at issue is whether the events in question have any *causal* relationship at all.

One who commits the *post hoc* fallacy has clearly argued in a way that fails to comply with the conditions of a good argument. The primary flaw is that of using insufficient grounds for the conclusion drawn. What purports to be a causal argument has a premise that expresses no clear-cut causal factor—only a temporal priority is expressed. But the temporal priority of one event to another is not a sufficient reason to infer any causal connection between the two.

Example   "I can't help but think that you are the cause of this problem; we never had any problem with the furnace until you moved into the apartment." The manager of the apartment house, on no stated grounds other than the temporal priority of the new tenant's occupancy, has assumed that the tenant's presence has some causal relationship to the furnace's becoming faulty.

Example   "Ever since we quit going to church, business has been getting worse. If we want to keep from going completely bankrupt, we'd better start back to church." Again, the claim is that one event was brought about by another event simply because of the temporal relationship.

Example   "From the time of the Supreme Court decisions granting the accused more rights, the crime rate has steadily increased. It is the Supreme Court that brought about our increasing crime problem." It is conceivable that there is some causal relationship between the judicial situation created by the Supreme Court decisions and the increased crime rate, but it would have to be established by more evidence than that of the temporal priority of the Court decisions.

Attacking the Fallacy   It is difficult to believe that anybody really concludes that B is caused by A simply because B follows A in time. In most cases, there are probably additional factors that lie behind the causal claim. For example, in the illustrations above, the manager of the apartment house may have reason to believe that the tenant has tampered with the furnace, the operator of the business may have strong beliefs about divine punishment, and the critic of the Supreme Court may be able to present a convincing argument showing how the Court decisions have contributed to the increased crime rate. However, the claims themselves focus simply on the temporal character of the relationship of events. Insofar as other factors or assumptions are not specified or even mentioned, it is appropriate to point out the *post hoc* character of a claim and to indicate that you will regard such an explanation as adequate only if it is supplemented by other convincing evidence.

You should have no trouble finding absurd examples that could demonstrate the fallaciousness of *post hoc* thinking. Pick out any two temporally related events and claim that the prior one caused the succeeding one. For example, you might insist that the garbage truck must have caused the hall clock to stop, since it stopped right after the truck passed. It would be wise to select events that your opponent already knows to be temporally related but causally unrelated, so that he or she will be more likely to recognize the faulty analysis involved in your causal claim. If your opponent regards temporal priority as insufficient evidence for your causal claim, then perhaps he or she may be encouraged to abandon such grounds in his or her own argument.

Confusion of Cause and Effect

Definition   This fallacy consists in confusing the cause with the effect of an event or in failing to recognize that there may be a reciprocal causal relation between the two events in question.

When the Scarecrow asks the Wizard of Oz for a brain, the Wizard answers that he cannot give him a brain, but that he can give him a diploma from the University of Kansas. The Wizard has confused the brain with the effect of a brain, but nobody really cares, least of all the Scarecrow, because *The Wizard of Oz* is just an interesting story. In the real world, however, resolving such confusion can be very important, in that it can assist us in coming to an accurate understanding of our experiences and in anticipating the future.

An argument that confuses the effect with the cause of an event and then draws a conclusion about the causal relationship does not provide sufficient grounds for that conclusion. The grounds are not sufficient because the evidence, in this case, is the result of a faulty causal analysis.

There may, of course, be a reciprocal relation between the events that could account for the causal character of the relationship. But a failure to recognize or understand this reciprocity can also prompt one to draw a faulty causal inference. For example, even though some kind of reciprocal causal relationship may be understood as existing between pursuing a college degree and becoming educated, a failure to clearly understand this relationship could lead one to draw the unwarranted conclusion that getting a degree is a sufficient condition for being an educated person. Interestingly, this conclusion is not essentially different from the one drawn by the Wizard, namely, that getting a college diploma will *cause* one to have a developed brain.

Example   One prison inmate to another: "The governor appears to know when we're having a good meal. He always seems to time his annual inspection visit here on the one day of the year that we have sirloin steak."

Prison officials are no doubt given sufficient advance notice of the governor's visit to make culinary preparation for it. The inmate has it backward.

Example   "It's no wonder that Phillip makes such good grades and always does what the teacher asks. He's the teacher's pet."

It is more likely the case that Phillip is the teacher's pet because he makes good grades and cooperates with the teacher. Or perhaps there is a reciprocal causal relation between Phillip's being the teacher's pet and his admirable behavior—a possible explanation that the speaker also misses. The fact that Phillip is the teacher's pet would probably cause him to want to make even better grades and to be even more cooperative in his behavior.

Example   "This is the right thing to do, because God approves of it." This is one of two answers to the ancient Socratic question about the relationship between God and morality. Is a thing good because God approves of it, or does God approve of it because it is good? Socrates suggests that there may be a confusion of cause and effect here. While Socrates himself seems to take the position that it is more likely that "God approves a thing, because it is good" rather than the other way around, each view has serious moral and theological implications. It is therefore important to determine which is probably the confused causal analysis.

Attacking the Fallacy   Any confusion that obscures the truth should be avoided or challenged. For that reason, even if my small child were to say to me, "Look, Daddy, that tree moving over there is making the wind blow," I would consider it less an occasion for being amused than as an opportunity for giving the child a more accurate understanding of the nature of wind.

When the thinking of adults exhibits a confusion of cause and effect, then it is all the more dangerous, because adults are in a better position to have an effect on the thinking of others. Hence, any kind of causal explanation that represents what you believe to be a confusion of cause and effect should be challenged in a way that would be constructive in eliminating the confusion.

If an arguer draws a conclusion based on a confusion of cause and effect, the absurd example method may be the easiest way of exposing the error. If the Wizard of Oz example doesn't work, try the following somewhat more subtle example. One staff member to another at the unemployment office: "No wonder these people can't get jobs. Have you noticed how irritable they are?" If your opponent is able to recognize that reversing the cause and effect creates a more appropriate causal understanding of the factors in this situation—that the unemployed are irritable because they are unemployed—then maybe he or she will be able to do the same with regard to the faulty causal claim in question.

A confusion of cause and effect is sometimes not at all easy to detect. Even the absurd example method will not always ensure an acknowledgment by your opponent of a confusion in his or her own causal analysis. While your opponent may acknowledge that there is a clear confusion in the absurd example, he or she could still insist that no such confusion exists in the case at issue. In these cases, of course, it will be necessary to explain carefully why the reversal of the cause and effect makes more sense.

Neglect of a Common Cause

Definition   This fallacy consists in failing to recognize that two seemingly related events may not be causally related at all, but rather are effects of a common cause.

When two events are found together in what appears to be a causal relation, we tend to assume that one is the cause and one the effect. Such thinking, however, can obscure a proper understanding of the relationship. One should always be open to the possibility that both events may be effects of another event or common cause, which may not be immediately evident. To identify such a common cause often requires that one draw on a backlog of general knowledge or other information not provided in the situation.

An argument that causally connects two obvious events, while neglecting to consider the probability that a third less obvious factor or event may be the underlying cause of each of the other events, does not provide sufficient grounds for its causal claim. Neglecting what appears to be a common cause means that the arguer has failed to produce the best explanation of the event in question. Hence, the argument cannot qualify as a good one.

Example   If it were discovered that most elementary school teachers have children of their own, it might be concluded either that teaching stimulates an interest in parenthood or that being a parent stimulates increased interest in working with children. However, a more likely analysis of that situation is that another factor, the love of children, has caused many people to become both parents and elementary school teachers.

Example   Suppose that a young college student were both obese and depressed. A hasty, but typical, analysis of that situation might be that the obesity is causing the depression or that, because of the depression, the student tends to overeat. However, a more likely understanding of this case is that there is some underlying psychological or physical problem that is causing both effects.

Example   It is not infrequently heard that current movies and television are bringing about a "moral degeneration" in our country. In actuality, however, it is probably the case that there are a number of other factors at work in our culture that together are producing both the contemporary trend in films and our changing moral standards. Because these factors are obviously more difficult to detect or to isolate in a causal analysis, it is simpler, although simplistic, to blame the movie makers or the television programmers.

Attacking the Fallacy   Great care should be taken not to charge a person falsely with neglect of a common cause. In almost any causal relationship there will be peripheral factors common to the events in question, the neglect of which would constitute no fallacy. For example, if one's explanation of the allegedly causal relation between being a school teacher and being a parent failed to mention that being an adult was causally necessary to both effects, it would not be appropriate to charge him or her with neglecting a common cause. The common cause in this case is not a significant or importantly relevant one in the explanation. However, if one is attempting to explain or account for an allegedly causal situation between two things in terms of the two things themselves, and a more *adequate* account could be provided by appealing to an additional factor causally common to both, then it would indeed be fallacious to neglect that alternative explanation.

If you believe that the primary problem with a proposed explanation rests on its neglect of a common cause of the events in question, you should demonstrate just how attention to that feature could provide a more adequate explanation. Your opponent should then feel obligated to scrutinize your proposal and to show, if possible, why it is *not* a more adequate explanation.

Domino Fallacy

Definition   This fallacy consists in assuming, without appropriate evidence, that a particular action or event is just one, usually the first, in a series of steps that will lead inevitably to some specific consequence.

The name of the domino fallacy derives from the child's game of lining up dominoes on end about an inch apart and then pushing the first one over, causing a chain reaction of falling dominoes. The chain reaction works in the child's game, but not all events are arranged so that a falling-domino effect ensues. For each event in any so-called series of events, an independent argument must be presented. In no case should one assume that one event will lead to or cause another particular event or series of events without making a separate inquiry into the causal factors that might be involved in each of those events.

The domino fallacy has sometimes been referred to as the "fallacy of the slippery slope." As the name suggests, when we take one step over the edge of a slope, we often find ourselves slipping on down the slope, with no place to dig in and stop the sliding. While this image may be insightful for understanding the character of the fallacy, it represents a misunderstanding of the nature of the causal relations between events. Every causal claim requires a separate argument. Hence, any "slipping" to be found is only in the clumsy thinking of the arguer, who has failed to provide sufficient evidence that *one* causally explained event can serve as an explanation for *another* event or for a *series* of events.

Example "If we allow the government to limit the number of guns a person can buy each month, what's next? If they can limit guns they can limit how much liquor, how much food, or even how many cars you can buy. They already tell us how many deer we can shoot. Next thing you know, they will even be telling us how many kids we can have. They'll keep on until they totally control us."

There is no evidence here that any of these events are causally connected with one another. In fact it is difficult to imagine how such a connection might be made. While it is conceivable that good reasons might be given to put limits on any of these things, it is not because they are causally connected in any way to each other.

Example Examine the following hypothetical argument against allowing students to become members of faculty committees: "If you let students on the Academic Policies Committee, the next thing they will want is to be voting members of departments, and then members of the Board of Trustees. Before you know it, they will be hiring and firing the faculty."

The proposal to put students on certain faculty committees is one for which a number of very good reasons can be given. Whether it is wise to elect students as departmental members or to appoint students to the Board of Trustees would require separate arguments, because presumably different issues would be involved in each case. There is little reason to believe that students would not or could not distinguish between these issues and recognize that one event bears no logical or causal relationship to the other.

Example We have all heard arguments similar to the following one by a college professor to his students: "I do not permit questions in my class, because if I allow one student to ask a question, then everyone starts asking questions, and the first thing you know, there is not enough time for my lecture."

It seems doubtful that persuasive evidence could be presented to support such a claim. Indeed, a question in the mind of one student is usually independent of any question in the minds of others. At least, no causal relation between them could be justifiably assumed.

Attacking the Fallacy If you suspect a bit of "domino thinking," insist that the arguer give an independent causal explanation for each event about which a claim is made. Another strategy might be to counter with a claim about some obviously absurd causal series. For example, suggest that if you buy goods on credit, you will soon buy more than you can afford, you won't be able to pay your bills, the finance company will repossess your car, you'll lose your job because you'll have no way to get to work, and you'll be so unhappy you will kill yourself, all because you ran your credit cards to their limit. It should be obvious to your opponent that there is no reason to believe that such an event would bring about this series of events.

Likewise, it should become obvious that there is little reason to assume any causal relationship between the events in his or her series.

Gambler's Fallacy

Definition This fallacy consists in arguing that, because a chance event has had a certain run in the past, the probability of its occurrence in the future is significantly altered.

This is a fallacy that is typically committed by gamblers. They erroneously think that their chances of winning are better or significantly altered in their favor because of a certain run of events in the immediate past. Remember the loser who says, "I can't lose now, I'm hot," or the big loser who says, "My luck has got to change. I haven't had a single win all night. I'm betting everything on this one." Such people seem to be unaware that a chance event like the outcome of a coin toss or a roll of the dice is totally independent of all the tosses or rolls preceding it. To commit the gambler's fallacy, then, is to draw an inference principally on the assumption that the probability of a chance event's turning out in a particular way is affected by the series of similar chance events preceding it.

Even though this fallacy is common to the thinking of gamblers, it is not unique to them. Consider the parents who already have three sons and are quite satisfied with the size of their family. However, they both would really like to have a daughter. They commit the gambler's fallacy when they infer that their chances of having a girl are better, because they have already had three boys. They are wrong. The sex of the fourth child is causally unrelated to any preceding chance event or series of such events. Their chances of having a daughter are no better than 1 in 2, that is, fifty-fifty.

This fallacy, which seduces virtually every one of us from time to time, is nevertheless an argument that grossly violates one of the criteria of a good argument. One cannot infer anything about the probable occurrence of a single, genuinely chance event based on what has occurred with regard to similar events in the past. The grounds for such a claim are simply nonexistent. The fallacy confuses, among other things, a claim about statistical probability in a whole sequence of chance events with a predictive claim about a single chance event.

Example Reflection about our romantic concerns often involves use of the gambler's fallacy. Consider the college student who argues that since the last three blind dates worked out so badly, the chances of something more positive occurring on the next match are better. There is, however, no causal connection between the first three bad "matches" and the next one. The odds do not change with regard to any particular date. Each event stands alone.

Example "Every time I open my mail it seems I get an offer of chances to win a lot of money or other prizes in some kind of sweepstakes. I almost always mail back the entry form to see if I have won anything. Since I haven't won anything yet, I figure my time is coming." As long as this person is not sending in more than one entry for each contest, the chances of winning any particular contest do not improve as a result of past disappointments.

Example "It's been heads five times in a row. I'm sticking with tails." There is no more likelihood that the next toss of the coin will be tails than that it will be heads, in spite of the fact that most of us are inclined to believe that the odds would be in favor of its being tails.

Attacking the Fallacy An attack on this fallacy is peculiarly difficult. You could demonstrate repeatedly that in the case of a genuinely chance event, the chances of correctly predicting a single event are no better than 1 in X (whatever the number of theoretical options happens to be). But such a demonstration is not likely to be totally effective, primarily because your opponent is likely to *agree* with your criticism but still *hold* to the original claim. The intuition that one's chances alter with time and a repetition of chance events is so great that the arguer is not able to dismiss it easily, even if an analysis shows it to be totally without grounds. You may have to be content with simply reminding the gambler of the rightness of your analysis in the hope that in a particular instance you will be able to dissuade him or her from doing something foolish as a result of such thinking.

There is, however, one strategy that may work on some gamblers. You could try to show how such thinking could lead to contrary conclusions. Consider the once-a-month poker player who has had poor hands all evening. The longer this series of unfortunate events continues, the more such a player might be led to conclude that "this just isn't my night"; but one could just as well conclude that "surely my time is coming; I'm bound to get a good hand soon." Neither conclusion is warranted, because both derive from a misunderstanding of the character of chance events. Moreover, there is apparently no good reason why a person should draw one conclusion rather than its contrary. The choice appears to be almost wholly arbitrary. At best, it would depend on what one's mood happened to be.

Exercises

In each of the following exercises (1) identify the type of causal fallacy illustrated; (2) explain what specific feature in the example causes it to be properly identified in that way; and (3) explain how the reasoning violates the criterion of sufficient grounds.

1. The reason you caught such a cold is that you didn't wear a hat to the football game. I told you you'd be sick.

2. Senator Foster came out in favor of the budget bill just one week after he had a meeting with the president at the White House. The president must have really applied some pressure.

3. You said that if I'm going to make more friends, I will have to learn to control my temper. Well, I haven't lost my temper in over six months, and as far as I am able to tell, I haven't made a single friend.

4. Son, all it takes is *one* drink to start you on the road to alcoholism. The same is true with marijuana; it's that first smoke that is crucial. If you try it and like it, you'll want more, and the more you smoke, the more dependent you'll become. Then you'll try the harder stuff and finally end up completely "freaked out." Take my word for it; I've seen it happen time and time again.

5. We haven't shot a deer in three seasons. Surely we'll bag one this trip.

6. Recent studies show that most successful executives have very large vocabularies. I encourage you, then, to develop as large a vocabulary as possible if you wish to have a successful business career.

7. I think that the reason that Gina and Beverly have been so rude and irritable is that the customers have not been giving them many tips lately.

8. I was told that I had to have stable employment in order to get a loan at the bank, and I do. I've had this job I now have for three years. So I don't understand why I was turned down for the loan.

9. Medical records show that alcoholics tend to be undernourished. These data strongly suggest that a poor diet contributes to alcoholism.

10. Our study shows that 80 percent of the young people who are heavy users of hard drugs have serious difficulties in relating to their parents. Thus we can conclude that a stricter enforcement of our drug prohibitions could significantly reduce the domestic problems of these young people.

11. I don't understand why I'm always sick. I eat a well-balanced meal three times a day. I have always been especially careful about eating the right foods and in the proper amounts, but still I seem to have something wrong with me most of the time.

12. It was only three months after Harold got married that he started smoking pot. His wife must have got him started on the stuff.

13. If you speak softly but firmly to your children, they will not be boisterous or undisciplined. That is the way I have brought up my children, and they are very well behaved.

14. The food-stamp program *seems* innocent enough, but once we start providing people with free food, the next thing you know it will be free clothing, then free housing, and eventually probably a guaranteed annual income. Let's stop this madness while we still can. I say that we junk the food-stamp program now.

15. About the same time that I began drinking heavily, my grades began to go down. I guess that heavy drinking and good grades just don't mix.

16. We won't be here this weekend. We'll be up in the mountains enjoying the pleasures of fishing and hiking. Rain has caused us to postpone our camping trip for the past two weekends; this weekend is *bound* to be a pretty one.

17. No wonder children are joining gangs. When both parents work and spend so little time with their children, the children tend to look for some sort of family-like support.

18. Sally and Doug were the happiest couple I knew, until Sally started working outside the home. It just shows how the wife's abandonment of the traditional role can destroy a marriage.

19. No wonder Jane is such an extrovert. If I had as many friends as she has, I'd be outgoing, too.

20. I've never had an accident while driving drunk—so why should I find a designated driver for the party tonight?

Additional Exercises

In each of the following exercises (1) identify, from among all the fallacies we have studied, the fallacy illustrated; (2) explain what specific feature in the example causes it to be properly identified in that way; (3) indicate which criterion of a good argument is violated; and (4) explain how it violates that criterion.

1. Sampras and Agassi are both great tennis players. They would make an almost unbeatable doubles team.

2. The high rate of divorce can be directly traced to the feminist movement. It has encouraged women to be more independent and assertive in relationships.

3. The federal government never seems to be able to keep within the budget or at least never able to balance the budget. Just look at our huge deficit. Raising taxes would appear to be the only solution to the problem.

4. Trust me! If you vote for a Republican in this race, you are going to have to live with that burden the rest of your life. And you've been a part of the Democratic party long enough to know that that kind of betrayal is not easily forgiven.

5. Don't get those batteries, Teresa. Get these "heavy duty" batteries; they'll last a lot longer.

6. This country is like a machine. No matter who operates it, it will behave in essentially the same way. So it really doesn't make any difference who is elected president.

7. I dated a blond once, and you know, they really *are* dingbats.

8. I know why our club meetings are so boring; no one shows up for them.

9. Maybe you should switch from Kroger to Food Lion—that might save a little bit on your grocery bill. They sell basically the same brands, but Food Lion has "the lowest prices in town." Haven't you seen their ads?

10. Sharon: As treasurer of our sorority, you made the rest of us pay our dues weeks ago, but you have yet to pay your own dues. Why?
   Sandra: Well, I needed to pay some other bills at the time. Besides, as treasurer, I can pay anytime; I'm fully aware of who's paid and who hasn't.

11. Bar hostess: May I see your driver's license, please?
   Steve: I don't have one. I don't drive, but I have a student I.D. Do you want to see my I.D.?
   Bar hostess: I'm sorry, but you can't order any drinks. We have to see your *driver's* license.

12. Emory & Henry is the best college for me. It's the only school I ever had an interest in. If I get accepted, that's where I'm going.

13. Bill mowed his lawn for the first time with his new lawn mower yesterday.

14. People today eat way too much junk food. That's why the American population is so overweight.

15. I worked in Judge Thomas's office for over a year. Not one woman voiced a complaint of sexual harassment. Judge Thomas is not guilty of sexual harassment, because if he were guilty, someone would have said something about it.

16. President Clinton's presidency is the greatest in American history, because no administration has ever had such brilliant success.

17. Women have the ultimate weapon over men. A woman is the only one who knows who the real father of her children is. And she can always exploit her partner's doubts. Did you know that over 60 percent of the "fathers'" names listed on birth certificates are not the real fathers of those children?

18. Mother to children: "Everything will be better after we move to our new house in Memphis and get settled in."

19. Kay: I'm in real trouble, Genie. I'm pregnant and my parents will hit the ceiling. I don't want to get married, and I don't want to have to take care of a baby. Jeff wants us to get married and have the baby. What do you think I should do?

Genie: Well, "you've made your bed; now you must lie in it."

20. I didn't have a date with Karen last night. I just took her to dinner, and then we went to a movie.

21. If students don't stand up to the administration on this small issue, they will begin to take away more and more of our rights until we have none left.

22. Kathleen: Rob, you have been very irritable lately. Is there anything I can do to help things to be better for you?

Rob: So you think that you're *not* irritable!

23. Abortion is a very difficult issue. We ought to listen to both sides, the pro-life and the pro-death view, before we decide.

24. Those who major in philosophy and take the LSAT or the MCAT do statistically better than those from any other discipline. Therefore, if you want to do well on one of those exams, I suggest that you major in philosophy.

25. How can you say that you don't want to be dependent on me? We can't have a relationship without being able to depend on each other.

26. An overwhelming proportion of the members of Congress and state legislatures are lawyers. There must be something about law school or the practice of law that prompts people to run for office.

27. The best argument against the atheists is a simple one. According to a recent Gallup poll, over 98 percent of the American people believe in God. You can't get *that* many people to say that the earth is round. God *must* exist!

28. Why should I be arrested like a common criminal just because I had a few glasses of wine at the restaurant before I drove home? I am an upstanding citizen of this community.

29. Nobody keeps to the 55-mile-an-hour speed limit. Most everybody drives at least 60. The speed limit really ought to be raised 5 miles an hour.

30. It has been discovered from a survey of over 100,000 female college students that 1 in every 5 women in America has some kind of eating disorder.

31. I'm so mad that I couldn't get into the club last night. After all, I will turn 21 in two weeks. It seems to me that they could have gone on and let me in. It's not as if I were 16 or 17 years old.

32. It won't be long before Sue and Jim divorce. Jim went on a business trip last week, and Sue took right off for the beach. That's exactly the way it started with my brother and his wife before they divorced.

33. Don: A true friend would not date the ex-girlfriend of a friend—especially if she dumped him.

David: But Larry's friend Ed dated Larry's old girlfriend and they are still good friends.

Don: Are you sure? They don't spend time together anymore. Have you seen them together more than once in the last year?

34. Professor Purifoy said that if there had been TV in 1896, William Jennings Bryan would have won the presidential election.

35. When you asked my advice about what to do, don't you remember what I told you? I told you to just do the right thing, son. But obviously you didn't take my advice very seriously. I certainly didn't mean for you to sell the house and go with her to Texas.

36. Since the defendant did not take the stand to defend herself, she must have something to hide. She must be guilty.

37. No, I don't think you should invest your money in real estate or stocks. You know, "a bird in the hand is worth two in the bush."

38. I believe in God, and I also believe that He created the world, but the idea of evolution also makes a lot of sense. So, perhaps the best explanation is that God caused the first life to crawl from the primordial slime.

39. Right after I wrote the mayor about the property tax increase, she came out in favor of it. She must have been persuaded by my argument.

40. The National Rifle Association recently conducted a poll of its 18,000,000 members and discovered that Americans are overwhelmingly opposed to any further restrictions on gun buying in this country.

41. College president: "Professor Lewis, you have such great organizing ability, communication skills, and ability to work effectively with other faculty, administrators, students, and trustees. For those reasons, I would like very much for you to take the job as director of our institutional self-study. I was just telling the dean yesterday that you have always been willing, as long as I have known you, to accept any challenging task.

42. If we allow them to impose censorship on our school newspaper, they will soon censor the books and magazines in the library, our textbooks, and even the dictionaries and encyclopedias. Eventually, they will be telling the teachers what they can say and the students what they can think.

43. If only my parents hadn't divorced while I was in junior high school, I would be a happy, self-confident person today.

44. I can't believe that you are going to that school. Did you know that the land that college is on used to be a slave plantation? Sometimes I wonder if you even *have* a conscience!

45. No wonder she can run 5 miles so fast; she's in great shape.

46. I don't know why my car stopped; I have *plenty* of gas.

47. I have driven while drunk for many years and have never been caught, so I know that my luck is wearing thin. Somebody else better drive us home.

48. I really think that you ought to take my course in aesthetics, Ms. Culberson. In fact, if you don't take it, I think that I would have very serious reservations about writing you a strong recommendation for graduate school in philosophy.

49. Since The Who is a very successful rock group, I'm confident that any member of the group would be just as successful on his own.

50. We need to hire a full-time counselor at the high school. Over half of all teenage suicides could be prevented by appropriate intervention.

VII
Fallacies That Violate the Rebuttal Criterion

The fallacies in this chapter are ways of arguing that fail to provide an effective rebuttal to the strongest arguments on the other side of a controversial issue and to the criticisms of one's own argument and of the position that it supports. This rebuttal feature of good arguments is perhaps the most neglected aspect in the formulation and presentation of arguments. For that reason, we have given it a status and treatment in this text unlike that found in any other text on argument evaluation.

There are several distinct ways that arguments fail to meet this criterion. The most obvious ways might be called the fallacies of counterevidence. Here the arguer either refuses to hear or unfairly minimizes counterevidence or simply ignores or omits reference to the counterevidence or arguments on the other side.

A second group of rebuttal-failing fallacies are the *ad hominem* fallacies. In these fallacies the critic is attacked instead of his or her criticism or counterargument. This is done by attacking the person in a personal, abusive way; by claiming that the critic acts or thinks in a way similar to the way being criticized; or by claiming that the criticism is poisoned by the impure motives or questionable circumstances of the critic. Not only are these personal attacks ways of avoiding the obligation of providing an effective rebuttal to another's criticism or counterargument, but they also are considerations that are irrelevant to the truth or falsity of the issue under review—a clear violation of the relevance criterion as well.

A third way of failing to address counterevidence or criticism effectively is to use one of the fallacies of diversion. These are argumentative devices that help to maneuver one into a more advantageous or less embarrassing position by directing attention away from the actual point at issue. In this way, the arguer can avoid responding to the criticism or the counterargument presented. Some common diversionary tactics are distorting the criticism or counterevidence, attacking only trivial points of the criticism or counterevidence, trying to distract everyone to a side issue, or ridiculing or making a joke out of the criticism or counterevidence.

An argument is not a good one if it does not satisfy the rebuttal criterion. To meet that criterion, it must effectively address the best arguments on the other side of a controversial issue. Each of the nine fallacies treated in this chapter violates the rebuttal criterion of a good argument in a distinctive way and belongs in one of the following categories: (1) the fallacies of counterevidence, (2) the *ad hominem* fallacies, or (3) the fallacies of diversion.

FALLACIES OF COUNTEREVIDENCE

Denying the Counterevidence

Definition   This fallacy consists in refusing to acknowledge, or to consider seriously, evidence that counts against one's claim. The most radical form of this fallacy is to be unwilling to acknowledge even any *conceivable* evidence that might count against one's position.

Those who commit the fallacy of denying the counterevidence are saying, in effect, that counterevidence is not relevant to their claim. Yet if *counter*evidence is not relevant to the claim, it would seem to follow logically that *supportive* evidence would be just as irrelevant. Just as it would be absurd to take an opinion poll and record only the positive responses, it is similarly absurd to disregard evidence that tends to falsify or weaken a claim and to use only the evidence that supports it.

Normally, evidence is the basis for accepting or rejecting a particular claim. When an arguer denies the counterevidence, he or she turns this norm upside down. Rather than letting evidence decide what to believe, a strong belief in the truth of a claim is used as a basis for deciding what evidence to accept or reject. But any method of thinking that allows blind adherence to empirical claims or to assumptions from which such claims may be inferred, without proper attention to relevant evidence, is obstructive to the task of discovering the truth. Indeed, such a pattern of thinking violates a methodological postulate of scientific or empirical thinking, namely, that every nondefinitional claim has the inherent possibility of being false.

Rather than denying the counterevidence outright, the arguer will sometimes simply refuse to take it seriously or will attempt to unfairly minimize its strength. Since the arguer has to consider the possibility that such counterevidence might seem credible to one's audience, he or she has to find some way of "explaining it away." At this point, the arguer usually does some very creative rationalizing. The counterevidence, so it is argued, is not really evidence against the arguer's position; it only *appears* to be counterevidence, for which there is some simple explanation. But insofar as the arguer does not give relevant, acceptable, and sufficient evidence in support of that "explanation," he or she does not escape the charge of denying the counterevidence.

The most extreme version of denying the counterevidence is the claim that there is no evidence that could possibly count against one's view. When asked by an opponent what it would take to make the arguer reconsider or change his or her mind about the matter, the denial becomes even more outrageous. "There is not even any *conceivable* evidence that could change my mind," the arguer says.

Usually the critic's "What will it take?" question is asked in desperation, after the arguer has "explained away" all the offered counterevidence. The critic is here attempting to get the arguer to identify some possible counterevidence that will be accepted as damaging to his or her position. If the arguer will name that conceivable evidence, the critic at least knows what he or she has to do. For example, if the arguer will not accept any of the evidence presented against his or her claim that smoking is *not* hazardous to human health, one might ask, "What would it take to convince you?" or "What evidence, if I could find it, would convince you that you are wrong?" If the arguer claims that *no* conceivable evidence could convince him or her of being wrong, then it is clear that the argument is not being conducted on evidential grounds at all and that further discussion would be fruitless.

Example Suppose that a first-year college student is discussing with his mother the possible legalization of marijuana. As a part of the discussion, the student calls attention to a number of recent government studies concerning marijuana use. These reports conclude that there is no strong evidence to suggest that moderate use of marijuana is in any way harmful. The mother retorts, "I don't care what the conclusions of your so-called government studies or any other studies are. Marijuana is obviously harmful and should not be legalized under any circumstances."

There is apparently no evidence that she would accept as weakening her position. Indeed, if the student were to ask her directly if there were any evidence that she might accept, she would probably reply, "Nothing could convince me that I am wrong."

Example "I couldn't care less what is in your biology textbook. I know that I didn't come from some monkey or lower form of life or whatever you call it. The Bible says that God created man in his own image. And unlike the Bible, your textbook was written by a mere human being. What's in those textbooks is just somebody's opinion."

It is clear that there is no evidence that could convince such a person on the matter of biological evolution, because any evidence offered would have been marshaled by a "mere human being." Further discussion of the issue would seem to be a waste of mental energy.

Example "Homosexuality is a learned trait. You don't have to *be* a homosexual. Your so-called 'studies' that say it is something you're born with were fabricated by the radical left to try to force us to accept the gay lifestyle. I'll tell you one reason it's not true: God did not create any homosexuals. I know that!"

This arguer denies that there is any credible counterevidence to her claim, but she also takes the evidence that is offered and tries to explain it away for any who may be taken in by it. By saying that it is the work of leftist radicals, she has used a label that she thinks is odious enough to destroy its merit.

Attacking the Fallacy   To demonstrate whether your verbal opponent is genuinely open to counterevidence, you could ask what particular kind of evidence, if it could be produced, might seriously weaken the claim. If the claimant cannot or will not specify such evidence, then there is probably no possibility of altering his or her opinion, and it would be more productive and less frustrating to move the discussion to some other issue. If it makes *you* feel better, you might point out to your opponent the fruitlessness of discussing something with someone who will entertain no counterevidence nor admit to even the possibility of being wrong.

If you can get your opponent to listen to counterevidence, ask him or her to respond to it or to evaluate it. If he or she complies with your request, seriously and without rationalizing, the violation of the rebuttal criterion is no longer a problem, and the discussion will have moved to the substantive claim at issue.

Ignoring the Counterevidence

Definition   This fallacy consists in arguing in a way that ignores or omits any reference to important evidence unfavorable to one's position, giving the false impression that there is no significant evidence against it.

If one holds very strongly to some particular point of view or conclusion, it is tempting to ignore evidence that could possibly throw that judgment into question. However, this pattern of reasoning violates a standard methodological principle of inquiry that one is obligated to investigate all sides of an issue and to accept the position that is best supported by the evidence.

It should perhaps be pointed out that there are at least two instances in our culture where deliberate "slanting" or "one-sided assessment" of evidence seems to be acceptable. One is in our adversary method of judicial procedure when dealing with criminal cases. The arguments of both the defense and the prosecution are typically presented with a very deliberate neglect of counterevidence. However, it is not acceptable for the jury and the judge to neglect any evidence in coming to a fair judgment in a particular case.

The other situation in which slanting, unfortunately, seems to be acceptable is in debating clubs and tournaments on the high school and college level. In this context the issue is not primarily that of arriving at the best answer to the question on which the debate is focused; it is evaluating the relative forensic abilities of the opposing debaters. It should be noted, however, that in both judicial and debate procedures, the *opposition* is specifically charged with the responsibility of presenting contrary evidence. Hence, evidence from all sides will be heard in each of those contexts.

However, winning a court case or winning a debate tournament is not the principal concern of one who is interested in the truth. Indeed, as truth-seekers, we should welcome the presentation of any evidence that might point out weaknesses in our position. If that evidence can be shown not to be damaging in any way, we can be all the more assured of the truth of our position. On the other hand, if that counterevidence is significantly damaging to our position, we should be grateful; it may lead us closer to the truth by steering us away from an indefensible or highly questionable conclusion.

An argument that ignores relevant evidence fails to satisfy the rebuttal criterion of a good argument. It fails to address the downside of an argument effectively. "Stacking the deck" in this way renders the conclusion questionable, because important evidence has not been evaluated. It is based only on that part of the evidence that makes the conclusion seem more defensible. By looking only at one side of the issue, one is excluding considerations that might raise serious questions about the sufficiency of the grounds in support of the conclusion. For this reason, the argument not only fails the rebuttal criterion but also fails to meet the criterion of sufficient grounds.

Example "Swift capital punishment for those guilty of committing capital crimes would be a very good idea, because it would quickly rid society of undesirables, thereby reducing the fears of the citizenry; it would lower by an enormous amount the costs involved in maintaining them in our penal institutions; and it would be a considerable deterrent to would-be criminals. The whole issue seems clear-cut to me."

Anyone familiar with the capital punishment debate would be aware of the fact that this argument ignores a number of relevant considerations, not the least of which is the injustice that might be done by the "swift" killing of those convicted. An appeal procedure is a standard and defensible part of our legal system that helps to assure that justice is done.

Example "Motorcycles are dangerous; they are noisy; only two people can ride at once; you can't ride them in cold or rainy weather; in most states you are required to wear an uncomfortable helmet; and the grease from the motor can completely ruin your clothes. I can't see why anyone would want to buy one."

The arguer has neglected to consider many other factors relevant to the desirability of owning a motorcycle. For example, the motorcycle is a relatively inexpensive form of transportation; it is more maneuverable than a car; it is easier to find a place to park it; and many people simply find it more enjoyable than a car.

Example "I can't see why anyone would want to go to the movies rather than watch television. After all, with television you can sit in the privacy of your own home; you don't have to pay for the movies you see; you don't have to get dressed up; and you don't have to pay those exorbitant prices for food and drinks. Also, you don't have to fight the traffic or pay for gasoline and parking the car."

This kind of argument could possibly persuade a number of people to stay home and watch television, but for many others it ignores a number of important factors. Network television does not usually run movies until two or three years after they are first shown in theaters; many people find it very enjoyable to dress up and go out for an evening; and many of the films that are shown at theaters probably never will be shown on television. These factors ought at least to be considered when one is evaluating the relative merits of watching films on television and going to movie theaters.

Attacking the Fallacy   Do not be surprised if one who presents you with an argument fails to accompany it with all the evidence against its conclusion. It is quite possible, of course, that the arguer has considered such evidence and is of the opinion that it does no damage to the claim at issue and therefore deserves no mention. However, in view of our general tendency to ignore evidence damaging to our favorite opinions, such an assumption would probably not be warranted. Hence, it is legitimate to ask an arguer to give at least some indication that all relevant factors have been seriously evaluated.

Be careful not to be misled by some of the tactics of the deckstacker. One clever device used by some is that of acknowledging and then disposing of a very *weak* objection to his or her position before going on with a one-sided assessment of the evidence. This gives the impression of objectivity and can sometimes be very disarming to the victim of this fallacy.

No one of us wants to lose an argument, mainly because we think we are correct in what we are saying. However, most of us would not want to win an argument by "cheating," that is, by deliberately ignoring evidence that we knew was damaging to our case, just as we would not want to win a tennis game by cheating, for example, by calling a close, but "in," ball, "out." It is quite possible that we might think that we are really a better player than our opponent, but we could hardly justify cheating to prove it. In tennis, the best player is determined as the one who wins the game. In reasoning, the best judgment is the one that is best supported in view of *all* the evidence. I could not feel comfortable claiming that my opinion was correct if I could "prove" my case only by ignoring important counter considerations.

If your opponent has ignored important counterevidence, it would probably not be discreet to accuse him or her of cheating. But surely there is nothing inappropriate about calling that evidence to his or her attention. If the arguer continues to ignore such evidence, then you could only conclude that he or she is not really interested in the truth or in following standard procedures of inquiry.

Exercises

In each of the following exercises (1) identify the type of fallacy of counterevidence illustrated; (2) explain what specific feature in the example causes it to be properly identified in this way; and (3) explain how the reasoning violates the criterion of rebuttal.

1. I don't care *what* the report of the president's Commission on Obscenity and Pornography says. I know that the viewing of pornographic materials *does* encourage people to commit sex crimes. We must not allow the supporters of this report to give free rein to the pornographers.

2. Why would anyone want to climb Mount Everest? The slope is steep, treacherous, and barren; the temperature is unbelievably cold; and one takes considerable risk to one's life. Besides, what can you do after you get to the top—just turn around and come back down. The whole thing seems worthless to me.

3. Steve would never kill anyone. I *know* my boy. He was always polite and thoughtful. We raised him right. He went to church with us every Sunday. No matter what the evidence says, I *know* he didn't murder anybody.

4. I don't *want* to discuss my religious beliefs with you. There is nothing that you could say that might make me change my mind.

5. I don't see any good reason to stop smoking cigarettes. They help me to relax; I like the taste of them; they give me something to do with my hands; and they keep me from gaining weight, which is probably the best reason of all, because the less I smoke the more I eat.

6. I don't see any reasons for attending classes. They are too time consuming. There are many things that I would much rather do. I can use the time I save not going to class to do more reading and preparation for the tests. Besides, if I go to class I have to take a shower, get dressed, walk to class in the cold, and, when I get there, sit in an uncomfortable chair for an hour, forcing myself to laugh at the professor's stupid jokes.

7. Physicians who say that steroids are bad for you must be jealous. Do you ever see a physician who looks as great as I do? I have used steroids for five years, and they haven't hurt me at all. I'm bigger, stronger, and healthier than I have ever been in my life.

8. Why should the president set up a commission to find out the causes of poverty in the United States? They're not going to find anything other than what we already know. We *know* what causes it. It's just laziness! That's all it is!

9. Why would you buy a Ford rather than a BMW? A BMW is a much faster, safer, and more luxurious automobile. It handles better, lasts longer, and is clearly built with the driver in mind.

10. Horses are too expensive and too much trouble to own, Carrie. They have to be fed in the winter with some kind of grain, they need hay to eat and straw bedding the year around, and they have to have salt licks and a fresh water supply, not to mention the costs of fence maintenance, veterinarians, and blacksmiths. Why subject yourself to such a burden? If you want to ride a horse, go rent one for a few hours.

AD HOMINEM FALLACIES

Abusive *Ad Hominem*

Definition   This fallacy consists in attacking one's opponent in a personal and abusive way as a means of ignoring or discrediting his or her position or argument.

The abusive *ad hominem* is not just a case of using abusive language against another person. There is nothing fallacious about calling people names. The fallacy is committed when one engages in a personal attack as a means of ignoring, discrediting, or blunting the force of another's argument.

An *ad hominem* argument is an argument directed "toward the person." The personal attack often takes the form of calling attention to some distasteful personal characteristic of an opponent. What that might be in any particular situation would, of course, depend on what the arguer finds repugnant. A person can be abused for being messy, unshaven, fat, foreign, a failure, a pacifist, an atheist, a lawyer, a feminist, liberal, conservative, gay, lesbian, ugly, physically uncoordinated, a tobacco chewer, or any number of other things.

Although some faulty arguers may use those things about their opponents that they find distasteful to manipulate the responses of their audience, most abusers apparently believe that such characteristics actually provide good reasons for ignoring or discrediting the arguments of those who have them. Logically, of course, the fact that any of these descriptions or characteristics might fit an opponent provides no reason to ignore or discredit his or her arguments or criticisms.

It is very important, however, that a distinction be made between the *argument* and the *testimony* of a person. For example, if a known liar or psychotic is testifying or giving an opinion, the fact that he or she is a liar or psychotic is indeed relevant to the credibility of such opinions or testimonials. However, if the liar or psychotic formulates and presents an *argument*, that argument can and should be evaluated independently of its source. It makes no difference whether it comes from a demented mind, a convicted felon, or a Nazi; an argument can and must stand on its own. After all, even the most despicable of persons may be able to construct a good argument. We could conclude, then, that although there may be personal characteristics of a person, such as his or her bias, psychotic nature, or lack of truthfulness, that might rightly affect our assessment of his or her opinions or testimony, it should have nothing at all to do with our evaluation of the person's arguments.

The abusive *ad hominem* obviously fails to satisfy the fourth condition of a good argument, since it is primarily a device to avoid complying with the rebuttal requirement. But it is also a violation of the first or relevance criterion, because the personal characteristics of a critic have no bearing on the merit of his or her criticism or counterargument. Therefore, any argument that uses what the arguer finds personally distasteful about an opponent as a reason for ignoring or rejecting his or her idea cannot be a good one.

Example

Sara: Professor Elliott gave an excellent lecture last night on sculpture and the creative process. She suggested that one of the best ways for a sculptor to make a piece of stone or metal to come alive is to imagine himself or herself inside the piece being sculpted—trying to get out.

Phillip: I have no interest in Professor Elliott's opinions. I'd be surprised if any piece of her sculpture has ever even "placed" in an art show. Have you ever seen any of her junk?

The fact that Professor Elliott may not be a particularly good sculptor is not relevant to a judgment about her insights concerning the creative process, which Phillip simply ignores. An attack on her artistic ability is simply a means of ignoring her lecture.

Example "No wonder you think promiscuity is all right. You know you've never had a really good relationship with a woman. So it's not strange that you'd resort to recreational sex."

An opponent's argument about the moral appropriateness of multiple sex partners should be evaluated apart from any consideration of his or her own particular sexual behavior or experience. The speaker abuses his or her opponent as a means of avoiding dealing with the merits of the opponent's argument.

Example

Cynthia: The landlord asked us to clean up our apartment so that it will look decent when he shows it to a prospective tenant Saturday. He said that he lost the prospective tenant he showed it to last week, because we had it so messy in here—especially the kitchen. He reminded us that we had agreed in our contract to keep it clean for showing to prospective tenants, once we had given notice to vacate.

Denise: What does he know about "clean"? He doesn't even keep his own *clothes* clean. He's been wearing the same filthy clothes for the last two weeks.

Denise is responding not to the landlord's argument about keeping the apartment clean during the "show" period, but to the landlord's personal habits, which are hardly relevant to the merit of his argument. Denise is simply pointing to a personal characteristic as a device to avoid dealing with the substantive claim at issue.

Attacking the Fallacy Perhaps the best way to confront an abusive *ad hominem* argument is to concentrate on not becoming angered or at least on not expressing any anger. When we are abusively attacked, there is a great temptation to counterattack in the same abusive way. If we yield to that temptation, listeners will love it, but such a tactic will not help to advance the debate on the real issue. Indeed, it could slow it down considerably. In spite of the fact that we often feel helpless when abused or ridiculed, the most constructive thing to do is to point out to an opponent that he or she is being abusive and then politely ask for a response to the *argument*.

Find ways to encourage your opponent to separate a strong dislike of a person from the ability to carefully evaluate the merit of that person's ideas or arguments. All of us are likely to encounter many unlikable people in our lifetime, many of whom will have good ideas. If we cannot separate a person from his or her ideas, we will probably fail to benefit from a great number of those ideas. If possible, take the first step and acknowledge the merit of one of your abuser's ideas, or at least respond to the idea itself rather than to the abuser. Such behavior just might encourage similar behavior on his or her part.

Poisoning the Well

Definition   This fallacy consists in rejecting a claim defended by another because of that person's special circumstances or improper motives.

This fallacy is called "poisoning the well" because its intended effect is to discredit the source of a particular argument or point of view in such a way that it precludes any need to consider the merit of that position. In other words, it "damns the source" in such a way that nothing that comes from that source will be or can be regarded as worthy of serious consideration. In this way the arguer tries to avoid answering the criticism, counterevidence, or counterargument that may come from that source; this is a violation of the rebuttal criterion of a good argument.

This fallacy gains its persuasiveness from its similarity to the fallacy of an appeal to a questionable authority. That fallacy cautions us not to accept testimony from a questionable source, but the issue in poisoning the well has nothing at all to do with anybody's *testimony*. The question is whether one should refuse to consider an *argument* that comes from a questionable source. If an argument in opposition to the death penalty comes from a death-row inmate, should that make it any less worthy of our consideration?

A person's special circumstances of sex, age, race, religion, profession, economic status, or political persuasion might, in some cases, prevent him or her from being a credible *witness*, but it should not in any way interfere with our willingness to consider his or her *argument* on the matter at issue. For example, we should be willing to consider the serious argument of a child concerning a new program for senior citizens, even if the child is not in a position to be a credible witness about the experiences of older citizens.

Similar things can be said concerning the charge of improper motives. A person whose motives are suspect might not be a credible witness, but it should not prevent us from giving serious consideration to the merit of his or her argument. For example, the fact that a particular landowner stands to gain financially from a new highway going through her property does not make her argument in support of such a project unworthy of consideration.

A good argument must provide an effective rebuttal or response to the criticism of or counterevidence for the position it supports. Therefore, an argument that has the effect of preventing a counterargument or criticism from even being heard and evaluated, by inappropriately questioning its source, cannot be a good one.

Example   "You can't believe what Professor Roberts has to say about higher salaries for teachers. As a teacher herself, she would naturally be in favor of increasing teachers' pay."

The fact that Professor Roberts is in favor of higher salaries for teachers is of no concern to us. The issue is whether she has a good argument in support of her claim.

Example   "You're not a woman, so anything you might say about abortion is of no significance." The special circumstance of not being a woman should not preclude a male from presenting an argument on the question of abortion that is worthy of serious consideration.

Example   "Since you are not a member of a sorority or fraternity, you are in no position to tell us how our pledges should be treated."

The frequency with which this attempt to poison wells is used should not deter us from pointing out its fallacious character. An argument for any action or change of action stands on its own. If the argument is a bad one, we should be shown what makes it bad. But if it is a good one, it matters not that it comes from one who is not a member of a Greek society.

Attacking the Fallacy   It is sometimes quite difficult to attack the poisoning-the-well fallacy, especially if it is your well that has been poisoned, because even your attack on such reasoning supposedly comes from a contaminated source. Perhaps the most constructive thing to do in such cases would be to confront the issue directly: "Okay, you've tried to poison my well, so that anything I say is suspect. That is a very effective device, and there's not a whole lot that I can do about it. But I do not intend to be silenced so easily. One reason you might want to silence me is that you think that what I say might seriously damage your position. I think I *do* have something significant to say, and I'd be interested in your response to it." It is possible, of course, that such a forceful response will not be necessary, for you may find some way of convincing your opponent that there can be no real debate if there is only one speaker.

"You Do It, Too" Argument

Definition   This fallacy consists in responding to an attack on one's ideas or actions by accusing one's critic or others of thinking or acting in a similar way or in a way that is equally hard to defend.

This counterattack on the critic by accusing him or her of acting in a similar way functions as a way of avoiding the obligation to rebut his or her criticism or counterevidence; this is a violation of the rebuttal criterion. It also is a violation of the relevance criterion, for the fact that some other person engages in a questionable practice or thought process is irrelevant to whether such a practice merits our acceptance.

If there is one fallacy that, in ordinary experience, does not strike most of us as fallacious, it is this one. Almost all children feel entirely justified in antisocial behavior if they can respond to the scolding parent, "But he (or she) did it first." Moreover, most adults tend to feel absolved of any guilt for their behavior if they can say to a critic, "You do the same thing!"

The Latin name of this fallacy, *tu quoque,* translates as "You [do it] too," and the arguer who commits this fallacy is implicitly saying to the critic that "since you are guilty of doing the same thing or thinking the same way that you are criticizing me for, then your argument is no good." Even though most of us would agree that "two wrongs don't make a right," it almost always seems to make us feel better, when our own behavior is questioned, if we can point out that our critic, or some other person, acts in a similar way. But there is no logical way that another's fault can absolve our own guilt for the same fault, nor does the behavior of another person or group constitute any logical justification for us to behave in a similar manner.

Most users of the "you do it, too" argument, however, are not trying to absolve their guilt; they are using it as a means of abdicating their responsibility to address the substance of the critic's questions or counterargument. For that reason, their arguments cannot be good ones.

Those who use the "you do it, too" argument may indeed want us to "practice what we preach." They may even think we are hypocrites. But while hypocrisy may be a moral defect, it is not a logical one. The inconsistency between what we say and what we do is in no way relevant to the merit of our criticism of our opponent's claim or argument. Counterarguments and criticisms deserve to stand on their own merit. And if the argument being criticized is to qualify as a good one, it must effectively blunt the force of our criticisms.

Example

Father: Owen, I really don't think that you should be drinking. Alcohol tends to dull your senses, reduces your physical control, and may even become psychologically addicting.
Son: That's not a very convincing argument, Dad, when you're standing there with that bourbon in your hand.

Although it might be tempting for Owen to point out to his father the apparent inconsistency between what he is saying and what he is doing, the proper action is to respond to the merit of his argument. In this case, Owen could attack with relevant evidence the claim about the effects of alcohol consumption, or he could accept the claim, if it were supported by the evidence, and perhaps adjust his behavior accordingly.

Example

Thurman: At your age, you really shouldn't work so hard, Roy. You're going to completely exhaust yourself and end up in the hospital.
Roy: You work just as hard as I do, Thurman, and you are not one bit younger than I am.

Roy has not really responded to Thurman's claim that, if he continues to work at the same level, he might develop some serious physical problems. Instead, he has used the "you do it, too" argument as a way to draw attention away from himself and to avoid dealing with the issue. He is, in effect, saying:

Since you (Thurman) have made an argument against my way of acting,

and you act the same way that I do,

Therefore, your argument is a bad one.

No! Roy's argument is a bad one. It miserably fails to meet the requirement of the rebuttal criterion.

Example   Suppose that the golf pro tells you in your first golf lesson that the first and most important thing to do in learning to become an effective golfer is "to keep your head down and your eye on the ball." It would be fallacious to conclude that you are not being given sound advice, simply because the golf pro doesn't always keep *her* head down when she plays tournament golf.

Attacking the Fallacy   Perhaps the best way of preparing yourself for confronting the "you do it, too" argument is to resist the strong temptation to commit it yourself. Even if an arguer defends a particular principle in arguing against your position and then denies that principle in an argument supporting his or her own position, you could not legitimately accuse that person of committing a fallacy. An evaluation of any particular argument should be confined to that argument alone.

If an inconsistency between your criticism of another's behavior and your own behavior is discovered, do not be intimidated or silenced by such a charge. It would be best to simply admit the truth of the charge and go on with your argument, insisting that your verbal opponent evaluate its merits. Even if your opponent points out an inconsistency between what you argued for in another argument and what you are arguing for now, politely ask him or her to respond to the quality of your present argument.

When charged with "you do it, too" reasoning, the arguer will probably acknowledge its faulty character. Not many people would defend, in principle, the view that "two wrongs make a right" or that improper behavior by one person justifies similar behavior by another. However, because this kind of reasoning is usually more emotional than logical, it is usually not fully recognized until it is brought to one's attention.

And that, of course, is your job.

Exercises

In each of the following exercises (1) identify the type of *ad hominem* fallacy illustrated; (2) explain what specific feature in the example causes it to be properly identified in this way; and (3) explain how the reasoning violates the criterion of rebuttal.

1. Mike: Just stop yelling at me! The only way that we're ever going to solve any problem is to sit down and talk calmly about it. Screaming at me will not help in any way!
   Erin: Well, you don't yell! You just cry all the time! Do you think that's any better?

2. Parishioner to priest: "You've never been married, so why should I listen to your advice concerning my marital problems? How could you possibly know what you're talking about?"

3. I really can't take your arguments very seriously, son. A 16-year-old just hasn't lived long enough to know what life is all about.

4. **Sue**: You know, Beverly, with all this stuff about AIDS, you really should be more careful with whom you choose to have sex.

   Beverly: Me? Be careful? You've had at least a half dozen partners since Christmas!

5. **Ms. Phillips**: My political opponent, Representative Abbott, is not telling the truth when he says that he has never missed a single roll-call vote in the House of Representatives during his long tenure. According to the *Congressional Record*, Mr. Abbott missed eight roll-call votes during his first term.

   Mr. Abbott: Ms. Phillips, is the *Congressional Record* the only piece of reading material that they would allow you to read at the mental hospital in which you were a patient during my first term?

6. You've never lost a loved one, Andy, so don't presume to tell me about death and how I should deal with it.

7. Do you really expect me to *dignify* your comments against my proposal by responding to them? They simply confirm what I've always thought about you, anyway. Your thinking is shallow, naive, and uninformed. And I feel that you're wasting my time.

8. **Betty Lou**: The most practical reason for not smoking marijuana is simply that it's illegal.

   John: Don't talk to me about obeying the law! You rarely drive within the legal speed limit, and most of the time you have more than the legal limit of alcohol in your system.

9. Don't tell me how to raise my children! I don't care how much you've studied child psychology; if you don't have any children of your own, you can't possibly understand kids.

10. **Professor Letson**: I thought about this committee proposal a great deal, and I think it would be in the best interests of the students and the faculty to implement it as soon as possible.

    Professor Hopp: Have you had time to talk with Dean Johnson about this?

    Professor Letson: No. Why?

    Professor Hopp: Well, he may not *like* your idea. I've heard that you rarely express an opinion about college matters without checking with the dean first.

FALLACIES OF DIVERSION

Attacking a Straw Man

Definition This fallacy consists in misrepresenting an opponent's point of view or argument, usually for the purpose of making it easier to attack.

"Straw man" is a metaphor used to describe the caricature of the opponent's argument that the faulty arguer substitutes for the flesh-and-blood original version.

Since it obviously takes no strong intellectual muscles to knock down a straw-built substitute for the real argument, the attack on the argument could make it appear to be weak one. However, the discovery of a serious weakness in one's own misrepresentation of the position at issue does not mean there is a flaw in the actual position or the argument that supports it.

It is the straw man argument that is the flawed argument, because it violates the rebuttal criterion. According to that criterion, a good argument must effectively address the strongest arguments on the other side; but by attacking only a deliberately weakened version of that argument, the arguer has failed to do that.

There are several different ways in which one may misrepresent an opponent's argument or position. First, one may reconstruct it in a distorted form. Such a reconstruction could use only a part of it, paraphrase it in carefully chosen misleading words, or subtly include one's own evaluation or commentary in it.

Second, one may oversimplify it. An opponent's complex argument can be made to look absurd when it is stated in a simplified form that leaves out important qualifications or subtle distinctions.

Third, one may extend the argument beyond its original bounds. This can be done by drawing inferences from it that are clearly unwarranted or unintended.

The principle of charity obligates us to represent fairly the arguments of others. Indeed, we are obligated to give their arguments the best possible interpretation. Since a misrepresentation of another's argument hardly qualifies as a fair treatment of it, the attacking of a straw man should be regarded as a violation not only of the rebuttal criterion but of the principle of charity as well.

Example   Misrepresentation or deliberate distortion is a clever and typical technique of politicians. If a candidate for national office argues for a decrease in the national defense budget by suggesting that billions can be saved by cutting out much waste and mismanagement, his political opponent might respond, "My opponent wants to weaken our defense posture around the world by cutting our defense spending. A cut could only mean reduction of our forces in strategic defense positions in Europe and Asia. I say that America cannot become a second-rate military power and still keep her commitments abroad."

This example shows not only how a position may be misrepresented but also how it may be extended beyond it's original bounds. Cutting out waste in defense spending does not necessarily entail reductions of armed forces in Europe and Asia nor America's becoming a second-rate military power.

Example   A very clear case of distorting by drawing unwarranted inferences is seen in this short exchange between a proponent and an opponent of a plan to construct a new dam.

> **Proponent**: Unless we construct a power plant in this area within the next ten years, we will not be able to meet the significantly growing demand for electrical power.

Opponent: What you're saying is that you couldn't care less what happens to the plant life and wildlife in this area or even to human lives that might be dislocated by the building of this dam.

The opponent has drawn an inference from the proponent's argument that is clearly unwarranted. In no way could one conclude from the argument that the proponent was unconcerned about the possible environmental dangers and other disruptions created by the erecting of a power plant in a particular area. Indeed, it is possible that every precaution had been taken to ensure that very little harm to living things would occur.

Example

Debra: There is no logical, moral, or legal justification for discriminating against a person on the basis of gender. Yet there is still legally sanctioned sex discrimination going on against persons in many areas of our culture. So, yes, I think there still may be a need for something like an Equal Rights Amendment to the U.S. Constitution.

Joe: Look, if you want men and women to have to use the same public restrooms, you go right ahead and support it. The way I see it, you women just don't want to do housework anymore.

Joe's representation of Debra's argument is surely a perverted one. He has not only drawn an unwarranted inference from it, he has oversimplified it beyond recognition.

Attacking the Fallacy   It is not always possible to know if an opponent has deliberately distorted your argument or has simply failed to understand or interpret it in the way that was intended. For that reason, it might be helpful to recapitulate the basic outline of any lengthy argument you present or, better yet, ask your opponent to summarize it for you. If he or she is willing to do so, that will put you in a better position to correct any misinterpretation or misrepresentation and to add any important omission.

If you have the opportunity, you should insist that a fruitful or constructive debate is not possible unless every attempt has been made to understand what is being said on both sides. If your opponent insists on continuing to misrepresent your position, call attention to this and correct the distortion in each counterresponse. In no case should you debate the issue on the distorter's terms; that is, you should not allow yourself to be forced into defending a misrepresented form of your position.

Trivial Objections

Definition   This fallacy consists in attacking an opponent's position by focusing critical attention on some point less significant than the main point or basic thrust of the argument.

The most likely time for the appearance of trivial objections is when the basic argument is least vulnerable to attack. Indeed, one may take it as a good sign that one has a decent argument when trivial objections rear their heads.

There are many ways that one might engage in hurling trivial objections at an argument. It may be an attack against a premise that bears no significant weight in an argument—a support that can be easily knocked down without doing any serious damage to the argument. It might be an attack on a minor or insignificant detail that has no crucial relation to the main or basic point of the argument. It might even be a criticism of an illustration used. In such cases, the basic argument remains intact, because even if the objection is legitimate, it is trivial.

The fallacy of trivial objections is not an attack on a misrepresentation or a weak version of an opponent's argument; it is simply an attack on a minor flaw in it. But those who commit the fallacy of trivial objections treat this flaw as if it were a major one. These nitpickers seem to think that any flaw found in an argument is sufficient to destroy it.

But one who resorts to a trivial objections argument uses a flawed argument, for it is a violation of the rebuttal criterion. By trying to dismiss an opponent's argument on the basis of trivial objections, the arguer has failed to address the strongest evidence or arguments on the other side of the issue.

Example "Yes, I've examined the case for Christianity, but I just can't swallow that stuff about a man walking on water or turning water into wine. You and I both know that's empirically impossible."

The speaker is surely raising trivial objections, for these are clearly some of the least significant features of the Christian perspective—at least for most nonliteralists. Indeed, they would hardly even qualify as weak supports. A successful attack on these features, then, would have no significant negative effect on the argument for the Christian faith.

Example

Dr. Gable: Walking is one of the best kinds of exercise you can get. One should walk rather than ride whenever possible. For example, rather than drive over to the cafeteria to eat lunch, it would be more beneficial to your health to walk.
Dean Luce: But, Doctor, I don't eat at the cafeteria.

Dean Luce is here attacking an illustration that Dr. Gable used to make her point. The fact that the illustration does not fit in Dean Luce's case is irrelevant to the basic thrust of the argument about the benefits of walking.

Example
Ben: Professor Provost, I don't understand why you failed me in philosophy this term.
Professor Provost: I think I can explain that very well. As you know, you failed the first test I gave, you were caught cheating on the last test, and you neglected to turn in any of the written assignments I gave. Besides, I don't think you ever contributed *anything* to class discussion.

Ben: But Professor Provost, my physician had given me strict orders to keep my talking to an absolute minimum because of some growths on my vocal cords.

Professor Provost: Oh, I didn't know about that. I can see now why you didn't speak up in class, and under the circumstances you could not have been expected to. How is your throat now?

Ben: Fine. But the important point is that you have admitted that your evaluation of my performance in your course was based on a false understanding, so I should not have failed the course. Right?

Wrong! Ben has blunted only the weakest point in Professor Provost's argument for failing him—his contribution to class discussion.

Attacking the Fallacy   One way to effectively disarm an opponent is to make it clear which are your strongest and which are your weakest reasons in support of your claim. If the arguer then chooses to attack one of your weaker supports, you will have already acknowledged that it is a weak support, so damage to it does not significantly affect the quality of your argument. Point out to your critic that if he or she is to have any degree of success in effectively damaging an argument, he or she must attack the *strongest* supports for a claim.

If a critic points out a minor problem in your argument, you should probably acknowledge it. But do not hesitate to point out that your basic argument is still unscathed and that you would be interested in hearing a response to *it*. If the critic insists that the objections raised are not trivial and indeed do damage to the argument, ask for a demonstration of exactly how the trivial matters attacked have any significant bearing on the truth or falsity of the basic claim being examined.

Red Herring

Definition   This fallacy consists in attempting to hide the weakness of a position by drawing attention away from the real issue to a side issue.

The strange name of this fallacy comes from the sport of fox hunting, where a herring, cooked to a brownish-red color, is dragged across the fox's trail in order to pull the hunting dogs temporarily off the scent. In argument, it takes the form of consciously or unconsciously steering a debate away from one issue to a different, although perhaps related, issue in such a way as to make it appear that the related issue is relevant to the issue at hand, but primarily as a means of avoiding the obligation of addressing the main issue or criticism.

A very common form of red herring is "empty consolation," which seeks to draw attention away from a complaint or criticism by claiming that the complainant should be satisfied with an undesirable situation, simply because "things could be worse" or because the situation of some other person or group is worse. Although it is true that "things" could almost always be worse than they are, that is not the issue, and drawing attention to such a notion is a way to avoid dealing with the initial criticism or complaint.

An argument that attempts to divert attention to a side issue rather than to deal effectively with the main issue cannot be a good argument, because a good argument must fulfill the rebuttal requirement. Moreover, insofar as we allow others to use the red herring against us, we ourselves are party to the failure to resolve the question at issue.

Example   Many of us have had the experience of complaining about the low or unfair wages we receive for our labors, only to be told by one of our parents, "Well, you *could* be making $35 a week as I did when I was your age." Such "consolation" usually sidetracks our complaint in spite of its irrelevance.

Example

Senator Clark: Why are you not willing to support the antiabortion amendment? Don't you have any feelings at all for the unborn children whose lives are being indiscriminately blotted out?
Senator Rich: I just don't understand why you people who get so worked up about the lives being blotted out by abortion don't have the same feelings about the thousands of lives that are blotted out every year by an indiscriminate use of handguns. Is not the issue of the sanctity of human life involved in both issues? Why have you not supported us in our efforts at gun-control legislation?

Senator Rich's concern here is no doubt a very important one, but that concern is not related in any obvious way to the abortion issue or at least to the question of why she is not supporting the antiabortion amendment. The issue of gun control in this context is a red herring; that is, it inappropriately directs attention away from the primary issue at hand.

Example

Dot: I'm convinced that your proposal to adopt an honor code here at Mason College just won't work. We don't have a tradition for it. Even institutions like West Point that have had a long history with an honor code are finding it difficult to maintain. Public school teachers, I understand, even refuse to listen to so-called "tattletales." In fact, it is the tattletale who is now considered to be at fault if he or she informs the teacher about the behavior of another student.
Georgeanna: But don't you agree that the honor code has worked well in the past for those institutions that have used it? And you can't deny that those who have lived under such a code have a genuine respect for it. If we had such a code here at Mason, we would be numbered among some of the most elite institutions in this country.

The issue is not whether the honor code has worked well in the past in certain institutions or whether it would place Mason College among the most elite institutions in the country. Those are red herrings that are made to appear to be relevant considerations in the discussion of the real issue, which is whether the honor code should now be initiated by an institution that has no tradition for it.

Attacking the Fallacy To "hold the reins" on a heated argument or discussion is indeed not an easy task. Red herrings creep very subtly into the counterarguments of most all of us. Detecting when the focus of an argument has been maneuvered from the main issue to a side issue requires constant surveillance.

Moreover, a frequent reminder of "that's not the issue" may not always be understood by your opponent. Therefore, you should be prepared to explain *how* the issue has been sidetracked or *why* a certain issue is appropriately classified as a red herring.

Since red herrings are often not consciously, or at least not deliberately, dragged into a discussion, one perhaps should be cautious about accusing an opponent of engaging in fallacious reasoning. If the bit of irrelevance is innocent, you should perhaps treat it as such. You would do well to save the charge of "red herring" for those who use it as a deliberate diversionary device or for those who refuse to get back on track.

Resort to Humor or Ridicule

Definition This fallacy consists in intruding humor or ridicule into an argument in an effort to cover up an inability or unwillingness to respond appropriately to an opponent's position. Humor is thereby used as a substitute for relevant evidence.

Humor is one of the most effective diversionary tactics available, because a clever and well-delivered remark can blunt very quickly the force of an opponent's argumentative advantage in the minds of an audience, toward whom such humor is primarily directed. Moreover, it can quickly bring an audience over to one's own side, even though there is no logical justification for such a shift.

Appeal to humor can take a number of different forms. It might be a pun created from a remark in an opponent's proposal or argument, a not-so-serious response to a serious claim or question, a humorous anecdote, or just plain ridicule of an opponent's position or remarks.

Ridicule of another person, of course, is an effective device only if it is not overly cruel; that is, it must be good-humored enough to elicit some spontaneous laughter. If it is too sharp, it might tend to weaken the position of the one who uses it by creating sympathy for the target.

Most arguers who use this tactic are very much aware of its diversionary effect. They are, in effect, using a joke, pun, or bit of ridicule as a means of ignoring or discrediting the criticism or argument. By doing so, they violate the criterion of rebuttal, which requires that the criticism or argument be directly rebutted with the best argument possible. Making fun of or ridiculing the argument is clearly not a way of meeting the fourth criterion of a good argument.

Example   During the 1984 presidential race, President Reagan's age was an issue of concern to many people. During one of the presidential debates on television with the younger, former vice-president Walter Mondale, Reagan was asked by a reporter whether he might not be too old to handle a nuclear war. "Not at all," replied Reagan, and then added that he did not want to make age an issue in this campaign. "I am not," he said, "going to exploit my opponent's youth and inexperience." The resulting extended laughter from the panel of reporters and the television audience was sufficient not only to diffuse the "age" issue but to prevent any further questioning about it.

Example   When a philosophy student notices that his political science professor has used a highly questionable contrary-to-fact hypothesis in his analysis of a particular issue in class discussion, he confronts him with it. Rather than examining the charge to determine if it is justifiable, Professor Stewart tries to blunt the force of the charge by saying, "Well, class, *Socrates* must have slipped into our class while we were not noticing. Now what did you say I did? Used a contrary-to-*fact* hypothesis? I didn't think philosophers were concerned about *facts*." If this tactic were to amuse his audience, the professor might be able to avoid facing squarely the charge against the soundness of his reasoning.

Example   Imagine the following conversation between Ross Perot and a young reporter at a news conference:

> **Reporter**: It seems to me that, if you were elected president, the Congress with which you would have to work would not be very cooperative at all. How could you, as president, bring about any reform or help enact any beneficial legislation with a Congress that was almost totally opposed to your programs?
>
> **Ross Perot**: Well, if I were elected, about half of the members of Congress would drop dead of heart attacks, and half of my problem would be solved from the outset.

Perot is clearly attempting to dodge the reporter's question, although it seems to be one that deserves a serious response.

Attacking the Fallacy   If the humorous intrusion is a genuinely clever one, you could perhaps show appropriate appreciation of it, for sound arguments need not be totally cheerless. A response in kind might even be an effective countermove on your part in order to regain your argumentative advantage or at least whatever position you previously had. However, at the appropriate moment, you should reiterate the basic claim at issue and insist on a serious response.

Exercises

In each of the following exercises (1) identify the type of diversionary fallacy illustrated; (2) explain which specific feature in the example causes it to be properly identified in this way; and (3) explain how the reasoning violates the criterion of rebuttal.

1. **Student**: The opinions of the students are completely ignored in the process of determining both curricular changes and social programs. The students should have a much greater voice in campus governance. We have a very great stake in this institution, and we think that we have a positive contribution to make.

    Professor: The faculty are the ones who need a greater voice. Professors can be fired without explanation, and they have no control over who is promoted or given tenure. Their opinions about budgetary allotments are completely ignored. Why aren't you concerned about the injustice the faculty is experiencing?

2. **Toni**: Rick, I'm tired of staying home every day, washing dishes, cleaning house, chasing the kids, and fixing meals. I would like to do something different with my life. I'd like to feel I was making some significant contribution. As it is, I feel worthless. How would you like to have to stay home and do the things I do every day—day after day?

    Rick: Look, Toni, into everyone's *wife* a little pain must fall.

3. **Professor Lang**: It doesn't make much sense anymore to prepare oneself for a specific vocation in college. In a technological age, change takes place so rapidly that job training usually becomes obsolete within eight years. I suggest that we maintain a strong nonvocationally oriented, liberal arts curriculum. That way our students will be prepared to go in a number of different vocational directions.

    Professor Reid: I'm not so sure, John. I think there are a lot of technological jobs that last longer than eight years.

4. You shouldn't complain! You're lucky that women on this campus can stay out until 1 A.M. Women here used to have to be in by 10 P.M.

5. **Clyde**: The installment method of buying has several advantages. It allows people with moderate incomes to have what they want—things they would have to go without if cash were required. It considerably expands the economy and raises the standard of living for millions of people. It even provides employment for many who are needed just to maintain records of installment accounts.

    Juanita: So? Even the "Mafia" provides gainful employment. But does that make the "Mafia" a good *idea*?

6. **Daughter**: If two people really love each other and have committed themselves to each other, I don't see any reason why they shouldn't live together. Philip and I really do love each other, Mother. Someday we may get married, but right now we simply want to be close to each other.

    Mother: The way I see it is that you're just looking for an excuse to go to bed together. Your whole attitude about this thing makes sex something cheap!

7. I don't see why you are so concerned with the problem of alcoholism; the drug problem is in many respects no less an important national problem.

8. Two candidates for public office are debating in a public forum:

Challenger: If I am elected, I promise to do everything I can to make our streets safe enough that our wives can walk the streets at night.

Incumbent: What is it you want to do—make hookers out of our wives?

9. **Mother**: I think it would be a good idea for us to encourage the children to watch less television and to get more physical exercise.

Father: You think I've let the kids become a bunch of lazy, unhealthy television addicts, don't you?

10. **Professor**: I think the administration is entirely justified in dismissing Professor Melton. He's never prepared for his lectures, he makes off-color remarks to his female students, he grades arbitrarily, and he isn't even friendly toward his students.

Student: I disagree with you. He always says "hello" to me every time I see him.

Additional Exercises

In each of the following exercises (1) identify, from among all the fallacies we have studied, the fallacy illustrated; (2) explain what specific feature in the example causes it to be properly identified in that way; (3) indicate which criterion of a good argument is violated; and (4) explain how it violates that criterion.

1. A recent study shows that those who drive their cars fast suffer from a high degree of stress. It must be that their feelings of stress cause them to drive their cars faster than normal.

2. You *do* think this dress looks okay to wear tonight, don't you, Scott?

3. **Janice**: People would be a lot healthier if they used fish and poultry as their main sources of protein.

Laura: But some people are allergic to fish and poultry.

4. **Andrew**: I bet you can't guess what kind of magazine I saw your father looking at down at the news stand.

Carrie: What kind?

Andrew: Well ... maybe I'd better not say.

5. I think I'll trade in my Mazda 626 for a new one. I love the new colors for this year's model. And mine is almost a year old.

6. If I had a choice, Joan, I would take a nice apartment over a house anytime. House payments are much higher than apartment rents for about the same amount of living space. But even more important, you don't have to cut the grass, rake the leaves, or get out the old paintbrush when the paint begins to peel. If anything breaks, you just call "maintenance" to fix it. You don't have to buy and repair appliances; they usually come with the apartment. You don't have to pay taxes or insurance. And the best thing of all is that you don't have to deal with obnoxious vinyl siding or replacement windows salespeople. Why would you want to buy a house, Joan?

7. I don't know why John is going out for the basketball team; he wasn't any good in high school.

8. You can't get a realistic-looking tan with just one week at the beach. Why don't you use some of that Natural Look Tanning Oil while you are there?

9. I don't see why you want a raise. You know, don't you, that you already have the biggest, nicest office on this floor of the building.

10. A recent poll of over 2,000 adults conducted in the Southeast revealed that over 65 percent of Americans believe strongly in their religious faith and attend worship services weekly.

11. **Teresa**: Aren't you going to put on some sunblock before you go out on the beach? Recent articles in a number of prestigious medical journals say that the sun's rays, whether they burn or not, can cause cancer of the skin.

    Valerie: I don't care what the doctors say. The doctors can be wrong. Unblocked sun gives me a great tan, and anything that makes me look and feel this good has to be *good* for me.

12. Don't you want to support me in my new job and move to Kansas City with me?

13. **Jeff**: I believe that if we create a minority seat on the council, there would be equal representation and diversity of opinion expressed. The African-Americans do not feel adequately represented here as it is.

    Bill: Why did you come to a predominantly white school in the first place, when you knew how things were?

14. **Daughter**: Mom, Jack doesn't want to get married right now. He thinks we should live together for a while so that we are more certain of what we want. What do you think?

    Mother: I don't think you should move in together, Dawn.

    Daughter: Why not?

    Mother: "Why would he buy the cow, when the milk is free?"

15. **Dr. Gable**: You really shouldn't be smoking that much, Ms. Fox. Not only is it likely to cause you to have cancer, but since you smoke around others, it is damaging to the health of family and co-workers.

    Ms. Fox: I noticed that you put out your cigarette just as you were entering the examining room, Dr. Gable.

16. **Taylor**: Since we both use the car, we agreed that whoever empties the gas tank should have the responsibility to fill it up. The tank is empty, Mindy, and I haven't used the car for a week.

    Mindy: Yes, but why don't you fill it up, Taylor? I just hate to have the smell of gas on me all the rest of the day, after I use the pump.

17. I can't understand why I suddenly am having problems with my car. I never had a bit of trouble with it until I had it serviced by that new mechanic. He must have messed up something.

18. **Supervisor**: I'm going to have to let Joan go. She is almost always late for work, she makes frequent errors that turn out to be very costly, she

spends a lot of time making personal phone calls, and she never has dressed appropriately for our kind of business.

Fellow worker: I don't think that wearing blue jeans once in a while is reason enough to fire someone.

19. He's not so smart! When I asked him to help me with my math homework today, he said that he *couldn't*.

20. **Thelma**: I know that God exists.

Joe: How do you know?

Thelma: It says so in the Bible.

Joe: What makes the Bible an authority?

Thelma: Because it's the Word of God.

21. **Mother**: Have a good time, son, and don't forget to put your bicycle helmet on.

Son: Why should I? You ride with me sometimes, and you don't even *own* a helmet.

22. If you have some money to invest, I suggest that you put it in bank certificates of deposit. That way your money is safe. CDs are insured by the federal government.

23. If we allow gay and lesbian marriages, next there will be some who want group marriages, and soon no one will even bother to get married.

24. **Father**: Do you think we should have our baby circumcised if it is a boy?

Mother: Of course!

Father: Why? We're not Jewish, and according to everything that we have read in the medical journals, there is no good health reason for doing so.

Mother: Well, it is something that is always done for male children. We've been doing it for over 3,000 years. I would feel sort of odd if we didn't. Wouldn't you?

25. Well, naturally you beat us. What do you expect? Your team had the tallest player on the basketball court.

26. It must be Terry who has been stealing from the petty cash fund. Almost everyone on the office staff thinks he's the one.

27. **Student**: I don't understand why I have to give you my parents' name and address just to get a phone line put into my apartment.

Telephone representative: You're a student, aren't you? We have to have parental information on all students. That's company policy.

Student: But I'm a 43-year-old graduate student.

Telephone representative: A rule is a rule.

28. The phone keeps ringing and ringing. Leo must not be home.

29. The army certainly doesn't seem like an attractive option to *me*, Jerry. You have to be up at the crack of dawn, and you are under someone's direct command 24 hours a day. Rarely are you allowed to think for yourself; most things are already decided for you. Besides, the physical demands can be awful. Have you thought about that?

30. Raising taxes on the rich will have little effect on them. The rise to 36 percent brings in a lot of revenue, but probably won't even be noticed in the paychecks of the rich. We could probably raise it to 38 percent without any problem.

31. This flashlight should work; I just bought new batteries for it.

32. **Father:** I think Grandma might be better cared for in a nice nursing home.
    Son: What you're saying is that you are tired of taking care of her—that she's a burden to you.

33. Professor Kellogg didn't say how many classes we could miss, so I guess that means we can miss as many as we want.

34. Your next car should be a Ford. Did you know that six out of the eight last winners in the Nascar circuit were driving Fords? And we export more Fords than any other American car.

35. You could put all of your savings in government bonds or you could invest all of it in the stock market, but it would be best to avoid either extreme by investing half of it in government bonds and the other half in the stock market.

36. No one dislikes me enough to slice my tires. I'm sure of it. It must have been an act of random violence or a case of mistaken identity.

37. The lieutenant governor's plan for reform of the procedures for dealing with victims in rape trials cannot be taken seriously. You know that his wife was raped last fall, don't you?

38. I'm not going to play the lottery anymore. I won $5,000 last week. I've had my share of luck; there's no way I would win again for a long time.

39. **Jessica:** Your position about birth control is just not realistic. We need to talk seriously to our children about birth control and about alternative contraceptives.
    Karen: Well, it seems to me that if you were a little shorter and had an accent, you would be a regular Dr. Ruth.

40. There's got to be a good movie on HBO tonight, because there hasn't been one on for weeks.

41. **Prosecution witness:** It is my considered opinion, as a practicing psychiatrist, that the defendant is as sane as any member of the jury.
    Defense attorney: How many of these insanity defense trials do you do a year, Dr. Chesterfield? How much do you get paid for each gig? How many days a year are you on the road traveling around the state from courtroom to courtroom? When do you have time to practice your profession, Doctor? Aren't you getting a little rusty? No more questions, your honor.

42. You know why you never got married? You have just become *too* self-reliant!

43. Whatever happened to southern hospitality? The people in Atlanta are not friendly at all. I got lost while I was visiting there last weekend and had to stop several times to ask people for directions. And they were not the least bit friendly.

44. You have never been in the military service, so how can your argument about gays in the military be taken seriously?

45. People who buy stocks are no different from people who bet on horseracing. They both risk their money with little chance of making a big profit.

46. Jim has two daughters. His oldest daughter, Annette, is very bright.

47. Surely you're not supporting this war. What if your own sons were going off to die for a little country like this—a country we never heard of—filled with people who aren't even Christian?

48. Bob: But all studies and every expert says that you cannot get the AIDS virus from casual contact.

Mark: I don't care what the studies say. I'm not going to touch anyone who has AIDS. I don't intend to die because of what some study says.

49. Just as you can know that the wind exists because you can feel it, even though you cannot see it, God exists, because even though you cannot see Him, you can feel His presence.

50. If only I had made my husband see a physician, he would still be with us. It's all my fault.

51. Doug's three mares are so unpredictable and unpleasant for riding. One minute they are as stubborn as mules. Then they turn around and are obedient as they can be. I can assure you that when I buy a horse, it certainly won't be a mare.

52. Scott: The laws against sodomy should stay just as they are in this state. Sodomy is against the laws of nature. Sodomy never produced a single human life.

Paul: Oh yeah? Then where do you think lawyers came from?

53. If we're going to save American jobs and keep down health care costs, we need to stop the flow of the 785,000 illegal aliens that sneak into this country every year.

54. Because philosophy has never been taught on the high school level before, I see no reason to begin now. If philosophy were suitable for a high school curriculum, it would have been introduced long ago.

55. I'm not homophobic. I just want homosexuals to stay away from me.

56. Senator Taylor: I think that to impose these standards on the automotive industry by next year would put the American auto industry at a disadvantage in the world automobile market.

Mr. Wilkins: It's not surprising that you would side with the automakers in their fight against tougher environmental standards. You've never really cared about the environment, anyway. You only pretended that you were concerned about the environment to get elected. You couldn't care less, could you?

57. I never really wanted to join a sorority anyway. It's lucky that I didn't get a bid. I just went through rush because my friends wanted me to. I'd really rather stay independent. That way I can hang out with whomever I want.

58. Rachel: I've thought about this for a long time, and I've come to the conclusion that *sane* people do not commit suicide.

Cynthia: What about your friend Shelby, who surprised you and everyone when he committed suicide?

      Rachel: Well, he certainly *seemed* sane, but I guess we didn't know the real story.

59. **Rebecca**: After listening to both candidates, I think that Ms. Lowman is better qualified for the job.

      Robert: In other words, you're voting for her because she's a woman.

60. Professor, you clearly said that an argument has to be understood to qualify as a good argument. You admitted that my argument is perfectly understandable. So why isn't it a good argument?

VIII
A Code of Conduct for Effective Rational Discussion

The primary focus of this book has been on the construction of good or fallacy-free arguments. More specifically, it has focused on the description and treatment of the numerous ways that arguments can go wrong. Throughout the text we have tried to demonstrate how these argumentative wrong turns or fallacies are best understood as one or more violations of the criteria of a good argument.

In this last chapter, we will spell out some basic rules of intellectual behavior that a rationally mature person would be expected to follow when participating in a discussion of disputed issues. The alert reader, however, will notice that these rules are actually a kind of summary of the criteria of a good argument and other elements of effective argumentation that have been addressed throughout the text. Compressing these features of the book into an economically stated list of principles should provide a kind of code of conduct for participants in rational discussion.

This code of rational conduct can be construed as an important standard of behavior in two different senses. First, it represents a kind of standard of effectiveness, because it describes the kind of intellectual behavior that is most often successful in resolving the issues that divide us. Moreover, the kind of discussion that actually helps to confirm or revise beliefs is usually conducted in accordance with principles like these. The code, then, is simply a formalizing of those ways of dealing with issues that work.

Rules similar to the ones we suggest have recently been formulated by some researchers in speech communication theory. They have discovered empirically that discussions that follow certain procedural ground rules are more successful in settling issues than those that do not. My own experiences as an unreluctant arguer and my experimentation with these principles in my college classes over the last several years have yielded the same gratifying results.

Second, the code represents an important ethical standard. While it may seem a bit odd to suggest that failure to carry on a discussion in accordance with the principles outlined here is *immoral*, it is surely *not* strange to suggest that one *ought* to argue fairly. Insofar as a spirit of fair-mindedness demands of all participants in rational discussion a commitment to the same minimal standards of intellectual behavior, these rules clearly take on an ethical dimension. Consider how often we find ourselves in situations in which our verbal opponent refuses to abide by what we regard as the rules of the game. This not only shuts down the discussion, but more important, it prevents the issue at stake from being decided or at least further explored. In such situations we frequently become indignant toward our opponent, and our demand for compliance is more than a mild irritation; it has decidedly *moral* overtones. We clearly expect fair play on the part of others, and we obviously should expect no less of ourselves.

The following principles exhibit these two important standards, but they also serve as a review of virtually all the matters covered in the text. Making them a part of your intellectual style should help you to avoid committing the most common errors in reasoning, to construct the strongest possible arguments for your views, to escape any charge of unfairness, and most important, to do your part in resolving those conflicts concerning issues that matter to us.[1]

THE FALLIBILITY PRINCIPLE

When alternative positions on any disputed issue are under review, each participant in the discussion should acknowledge that possibly none of the positions presented is deserving of acceptance and that, at best, only one of them is true or the most defensible position. Therefore, it is possible that thorough examination of the issue will reveal that one's own initial position is a false or indefensible one.

The fallibility principle is generally regarded as a standard principle of serious inquiry. To employ it in discussion is consciously to accept the fact that you are fallible, that is, that you may very well be wrong in your view, or at least not in possession of the most defensible view on the matter in dispute.

If you refuse to accept your own fallibility, you are, in effect, saying that you are not willing to change your mind, no matter what—even if you hear a better

[1]For a practical application of the principles governing good argumentation summarized in this chapter and addressed throughout the book, see the detailed critique of several popular points of view, including those of Shirley Maclaine and Ronald Reagan, in Lawrence L. Habermehl's *The Counterfeit Wisdom of Shallow Minds: A Critique of Some of the Leading Offenders of the 1980's* (New York: Peter Lang Publishing, Inc., 1994).

argument. This is also strong evidence that you do not intend to play fairly. Consequently, there is no real point in pursuing the discussion any further, for there is little likelihood that any significant progress will be made. A confession of fallibility, however, is a positive sign that you are sincerely interested in the kind of honest inquiry that may lead to a fair resolution of the issue.

The assumption of mutual fallibility is the crucial first step for discussants to take. Unfortunately, this move is rarely made in discussions of religion and politics, which is probably the reason that so little progress is made in those important areas of dispute. It *is*, however, the standard principle of inquiry among scientists, philosophers, and most other academics. Indeed, these truth-seekers would probably argue that it is a necessary condition of intellectual progress.

If there is any doubt about the appropriateness of accepting the fallibility principle, take any issue about which there are a number of alternative and conflicting opinions held. For example, consider the area of religion. Since each of the hundreds of conflicting theological or ecclesiastical positions is different in some respect from all the others, we know before we begin any examination of those positions that only one of them has the possibility of being true—and even that one may be seriously flawed. So it turns out that not only is it *possible* that our own religious position is false or indefensible, it may even be *probable* that it is.

It is quite possible, of course, that our own position is more defensible than *many* of the others—especially if we have spent time developing and refining it in accordance with the available evidence and the tools of reason. Nevertheless, it is unlikely that out of all of the conflicting religious positions currently held, many of which are vigorously defended by good minds, it will be only our position that will be the correct one. Although we may *believe* that our own view is the most defensible one, we must keep in mind that others believe the same thing about *their* views—and only one of us, at best, can be right.

Several years ago at a conference on critical thinking, a panelist defined a critical thinker as "a person who by force of argument had changed his or her mind about an important issue at least once during the last year." He went on to say that it is highly unlikely that any person would just *happen* to be correct on every position held on important matters. On the contrary, given the great number of issues that divide us and the large number of different positions on each of those issues, it is more likely that a person would turn out to be wrong on more issues than he or she would be right.

The most convincing evidence of the fallibility of human opinions comes from the history of science. We are told by some of science's historians that virtually every knowledge claim in the history of science has been shown by subsequent inquiry to be either false or at least seriously flawed. And if this is true of the past, it may be true as well of present and future claims of science, even in spite of the more sophisticated techniques of inquiry used by modern science. Moreover, if such observations can be made about an area of inquiry with fairly standard evidential requirements, it seems reasonable to assume that nonscience claims would suffer an even worse fate. In the face of such findings, we should at least be intellectually humbled enough to be less than certain about our claims to truth.

The important point here is that a confession of fallibility is a clear indication that we are consciously prepared to listen to the arguments of another person. Although it is not easy to admit honestly that a firmly held position may not be true, it is a discussion starter unlike any other. It not only calms the emotional waters surrounding the treatment of issues about which we feel deeply, but it has the potential for opening our ears to different and better arguments. We may even become critical thinkers, that is, persons who change our minds by the force of those arguments.

If you are skeptical about how effectively this tactic works, be the first to confess your own fallibility. At least make it clear that you are willing to change your mind. Your opponents will surely enter the confessional right behind you, if only to escape intellectual embarrassment. If they refuse to do so, you will at least know the futility of any further conversation about the matter at issue.

THE TRUTH-SEEKING PRINCIPLE

Each participant should be committed to the task of earnestly searching for the truth or at least the most defensible position on the issue at stake. Therefore, one should be willing to examine alternative positions seriously, look for insights in the positions of others, and allow other participants to present arguments for or raise objections to any position held with regard to any disputed issue.

The truth-seeking principle is also a standard principle of inquiry. It has gone hand in hand with the fallibility principle since the time of Socrates, who taught that we come to true knowledge only by first recognizing our own ignorance or lack of knowledge. The search for truth then becomes a life-long endeavor, which principally takes the form of discussion, wherein we systematically entertain the ideas and arguments of fellow seekers after truth, while at the same time we thoughtfully consider criticisms of our own views.

Since, as we have seen, it is not likely that the truth is now in our custody, all of our intellectual energies expended in discussion should be directed toward finding it or *at least finding the most defensible position possible for the present time*. That position, of course, is the position that is supported by the strongest or best argument encountered.

If the truth were already held, there would obviously be no use in any further discussion. To those who might claim that a discussion could at least be used to convince others of what we already know to be the truth, it should be pointed out that the "others" are probably making the same assumptions about the views that they now hold. Hence, it is unlikely that any truth will be changing hands. If we really are interested in finding the truth, it is imperative not only that we assume that we may not now have the truth, but that we listen to the defenses of alternative positions and encourage criticism of our own arguments.

There are some issues, of course, about which we have already done the hard work of investigation. We have thoroughly examined the issue, have listened to and found seriously wanting the arguments on the other side, and have entertained and found weak and nondamaging the criticisms of our position. In such a situation, we should not give the impression that we have an open mind about the issue and carry on a pseudodiscussion. We have two other alternatives. If we really are tired of the issue and anticipate little or no possible evidence that might change our mind, we should admit that to our opponent and perhaps skip the discussion. But if we genuinely believe that we might have missed something that could cause us to alter our position, then, by all means, we should enter the debate as an honest seeker. The outcome may be that we convince our opponent of *our* position, but we should enter the debate only if we ourselves are willing to be turned around by the force of a better argument.

In our better moments we probably all want to hold only those opinions that really are true, but the satisfaction of that interest comes at a price—a willingness to look at all available options and the arguments in support of them. Otherwise, we might miss the truth completely. The problem, of course, is that most of us want the truth to be what we now *hold* to be the truth. We want to win, even if we have to cheat to do it. For example, we obviously *want* our newborn child to be the most adorable child in the hospital nursery, but to declare our child the contest winner, before objectively examining the features of every other child, is simply dishonest.

Real truth-seekers do not try to win by ignoring or denying the counterevidence against their positions. Real winning is finding the position that results from playing the game in accordance with the rules. To declare yourself the winner before playing the game or by refusing to play by the rules fails to advance the search for truth and is in the end self-defeating.

THE BURDEN OF PROOF PRINCIPLE

The burden of proof for any position usually rests on the participant who sets forth the position. If and when an opponent asks, the proponent should provide an argument for that position.

A good discussion is not simply a verbal contest in which opinions are traded between opposing parties. A good discussion will include arguments in support of any opinion found by one of the participants to be questionable. Many opinions, of course, are shared by the parties involved and thus require no defense in a particular context. However, the central claims at issue in a dispute will almost always require some support. Therefore, if asked, the one who makes a controversial claim has the burden of proof, that is, the responsibility to provide an appropriate argument in support of it.

To ask others to accept your claim without any support or to shift the burden of proof to them by suggesting that your position is true unless they can prove otherwise is to commit the fallacy of arguing from ignorance. For you are, in this way, making a claim based on no evidence at all. Indeed, you are basing the claim on the absence of evidence, that is, on *ignorance*. You can see the absurdity of such a move by taking any highly questionable claim and arguing that it is true in the absence of any counterevidence. For example, you could argue that it is true that your great-grandfather died of AIDS unless someone can prove otherwise, or that it is true that pornography causes sex crimes, unless someone can prove that it doesn't. In this way you fail to take responsibility for your own claims and even attempt to get your opponents to do your work for you. Moreover, since negative claims are notoriously difficult to establish, you are attempting to set yourself up for a "win" by default. But in this game, there are no wins by default; the merit of any position can be only as good as the argument given in support of it.

We do not want to give the impression, of course, that a good discussion must be carried on with the formal style of the courtroom. When the mutual interest of the parties is in finding the truth or the best solution, participants often assume an informal burden of evaluating any claim presented, sometimes without waiting to hear the initial argument in its behalf. This approach is sometimes a good one, because it is more natural and often saves time, but no one should be led into believing that the burden of proof thereby no longer rests on the shoulders of those who make controversial claims, nor that it can be shifted without blame to others.

It should perhaps be pointed out that "proof," in the context in which it is being used here, does not mean absolute, knock-down proof. It does not even mean, for example, "beyond a reasonable doubt," as required of the prosecutor in a criminal trial. To provide proof for one's position is to present what appears to be a good, that is, fallacy-free, argument in its behalf. Just recently a tobacco industry representative argued that "they have not yet proved any connection between the smoking of cigarettes and health problems." It is not entirely clear what he meant by *proved*, but it was obvious that he was going to defend the tobacco interests, even at the risk of appearing foolish. I presume that he was using the term with a meaning that is close to that kind of absolute proof associated with mathematical or geometric theorems. Such proof, however, is not likely to be found for any claim typically encountered in informal discussion; nor would it be reasonable to expect it.

THE PRINCIPLE OF CHARITY

The argument presented for any position should be one that is capable of being reconstructed into a commonly accepted or standard argument form. If a participant's argument is reformulated by an opponent, it should be expressed in the strongest possible version that is consistent with the original intention of the arguer. If there is any question about that intention or about implicit parts of the argument, the arguer should be given the benefit of doubt in the reformulation.

If we expect our discussions to be effective ones, the arguments we present must actually *look* like arguments. They must be capable of being reconstructed either by us or by our opponents into some commonly accepted or standard argument form, so that the quality of the argument may be properly evaluated. An argument may be either deductive or inductive; it may be, for example, a statistical, analogical, or causal argument. But if it is an argument, it must exhibit the necessary or standard features of an argument. It must make either an explicit or implicit claim that is accompanied by at least one other explicit or implicit statement or piece of information that is thought to be supportive of the truth of the claim.

It is usually helpful to reconstruct an opponent's argument into a recognizable argument form, so that there will be no misunderstanding or confusion about what is being evaluated. Once formulated, one should also allow the arguer to refine the argument further, so that it will be the best possible version of the argument that is under scrutiny.

If you are the one who is reconstructing your opponent's argument, you should make every effort to be as fair as possible in formulating the argument that you think he or she actually intended to make. While you don't need to turn it into a different or better argument than it is, you should give the arguer the benefit of any doubt that you may have about his or her intention. This means that you should be willing to supply any unstated or implicit parts of the argument and maybe even use words that are more precise or clear than those used in the original argument. The arguer's complementary act of fairness is not to wrongly accuse an opponent of distorting his or her argument, simply because the opponent's reformulation of the argument exposes its weaknesses.

It should be clear by now that good discussion in general and argumentation in particular clearly impose an ethical requirement on us. But there is also a good practical reason for being fair with one another's arguments. If we create a straw man to attack, we not only will waste time and risk losing our intellectual integrity, we also will quite possibly fail to achieve the very goals the discussion was designed to serve. If we are really interested in the truth or the best answer to a problem, then we will want to evaluate the best version of any argument set forth in support of one of the options. Hence, if we don't deal with the best version now, we will eventually have to do so, once an uncharitable version has been corrected or improved on by its author or others. We would do well simply to be fair with it in the first place. Moreover, an honest treatment of our opponents' arguments creates less stress for all the players and is especially disarming to our strongest critics.

THE CLARITY PRINCIPLE

The formulations of all positions, defenses, and attacks should be free of any kind of linguistic confusion and clearly separated from other positions and issues.

Any successful discussion of an issue must be carried on in language that is understood by all the parties involved. Even if what we have to say is perfectly clear to us or maybe even to those in our linguistic circle, others may not be able to understand us. Consequently, they will not be able to respond to us in any helpful way. A necessary condition of an effective exchange is that all parties understand what is being said. A position or a criticism of it that is expressed in vague, ambiguous, equivocal, or contradictory language will fail to reach and may even mislead those toward whom it is directed. But, most important, if clear language is not used, there will be little progress in resolving the issue at hand.

Moreover, if every participant makes the effort to keep the discussion on target, it will also be a less time-consuming and even less stressful one. Every position or criticism that is expressed in confused language not only delays the potential resolution of the issue but often creates an unhealthy frustration among the participants.

Perhaps the most difficult problem in achieving clarity is that of being able to concentrate clearly on the main issue at stake. In informal discussion it is not easy to keep focused on the central issue. Controversial issues usually have many related features, and all of them may be important to deal with. To be successful, however, we must usually deal with issues one feature at a time. Each party to the dispute must therefore exercise great care in trying to keep other interesting yet distracting issues from clouding the discussion.

Finally, there is a special hell prepared for those who attempt to end a discussion by smugly suggesting that "our disagreement is just a matter of semantics." Such people are more villainous than benign, because they thereby contribute to the failure to resolve what is probably an important matter. Linguistic confusion is not the place to stop a discussion; it is usually the starting place from which we need to escape. We must not let the potential resolution of an issue that matters to us falter on the rock of verbal confusion.

THE RELEVANCE PRINCIPLE

One who presents an argument for or attacks a position should set forth only reasons or questions that are directly related to the merit of the position at issue.

The reasons given in support of a position should always be relevant ones. Relevant reasons are those the acceptance of which provides some reason to believe, counts in favor of, or makes a difference to the truth or falsity of the conclusion. Relevance is the criterion of a good argument that is applied first, because if a reason given is not relevant to the truth of the conclusion, then there is no use in even considering whether it merits our acceptance. It can be safely ignored.

There are a number of typical ways that arguments fail to conform to the relevance principle. Some arguers try to use reasons that are simply emotional appeals, such as the fallacies of appeal to pity and to fear. Other irrelevant appeals are to common opinion and to inappropriate authorities.

Other fallacies that violate the relevance criterion are the so-called *ad hominem* fallacies—those that attack the person presenting the argument, rather than the argument itself. These fallacies are primarily ways of violating the rebuttal criterion, for they are most typically used as a means to avoid addressing the strong points of an opponent's argument. But since personal attacks have no role to play in determining the truth or falsity of any position under review, they are also irrelevant features of any argument.

The very first step in the reconstruction of another's argument is to check it for any obvious irrelevancies. In the context of informal discussion, we usually encounter quite a number of colorful yet irrelevant pieces of material. Most of these features, however, are not viciously irrelevant or even intended as a crucial part of the argument and therefore do not rise to the level of being called fallacies. For that reason they can simply be excluded from the reconstruction.

Many arguments, however, contain irrelevant reasons or premises that the arguer clearly regards as relevant. Indeed, that is why they were included as a part of his or her argument. These premises should therefore be included in the reconstruction of an opponent's argument, even if subsequent evaluation may show them to be irrelevant. It is entirely possible, of course, that what *appears* to be irrelevant may be shown to be quite relevant after further reflection on the matter.

Finally, we should all examine the relevance of our own premises as closely as possible. It is a waste of time for our conversational partners to expend energy evaluating premises that probably shouldn't have been included in the first place.

THE ACCEPTABILITY PRINCIPLE

One who presents an argument for or attacks a position should attempt to use premises or reasons that are mutually acceptable to the participants or that at least meet standard criteria of acceptability.

The principal test by which we determine the quality of an argument is whether the reasons set forth in support of the conclusion are acceptable. A reason is acceptable if it is the kind of claim that would be accepted by a rational person in the face of all the relevant evidence presented or at least available in its defense. This criterion is similar to the instructions that judges give jurors in a criminal trial. They are asked to find the defendant guilty if the key evidence presented by the prosecutor and evaluated by the defense attorney is evidence that a reasonable person would accept as true or would treat as beyond reasonable doubt. Absolute truth is too difficult a criterion to meet. The most that we can legitimately expect is what a reasonable person would *accept* as true.

What seems rational to some people, of course, does not always seem rational to others. For that reason we have listed a number of specific guidelines in the text that should be helpful in bringing us to more agreement on the question of what is or is not an acceptable claim. For example, it would probably be reasonable to accept the testimony of an uncontroverted expert or an uncontroverted eyewitness. At the same time, it would probably *not* be rational to accept a claim that contradicts a well-established claim or contradicts testimony from what appears to be a credible source.

In real life, of course, we already use the notion of acceptability in place of the notion of truth. When we swear to tell the truth, the whole truth, and nothing but the truth in a court of law, we are obviously telling what we *accept* as true, not what *is* true. The reason we know this is that contradictory claims are the rule rather than the exception in the courtroom, so at least one of the claimants is telling only what is accepted as true. If the criterion of absolute truth were employed, we would hear little or no courtroom testimony, and few disputes would ever be resolved.

Hence the pragmatic criterion of acceptability. But we should always keep in mind that this criterion does not mean that a reason or premise is acceptable simply because someone accepts it or because we can get someone to accept it. We know too well how easy this is, especially if one is preaching to the saved, to the immature, or to the easily tricked. A claim is acceptable only if it would be the kind of claim accepted by a rationally mature person using generally agreed-on standards of acceptability.

There are several types of fallacies that violate the acceptability criterion. A claim that is expressed in language that is confusing is not acceptable simply because of that confusion; we obviously cannot accept a claim that we do not understand. Other violations are the begging-the-question fallacies. These fallacies violate the acceptability criterion because the argument uses a premise that is as questionable as the claim it allegedly supports—mainly because the supporting claim, in effect, *is* the claim it supports. Finally, a common way of violating the acceptability criterion is found in the so-called unwarranted assumption fallacies, wherein reasons that are based on highly questionable implicit assumptions are used to support other claims.

THE SUFFICIENT GROUNDS PRINCIPLE

One who presents an argument for or attacks a position should attempt to provide reasons that are sufficient in number, kind, and weight to support the acceptance of the conclusion.

Once one has examined an argument for the relevance and the acceptability of the premises, there is still plenty of work to do. Relevant and acceptable premises do not necessarily a good argument make. An argument must also meet the demands of the sufficient grounds criterion. There must be a sufficient *number* of relevant and acceptable premises of the appropriate *kind* and *weight* in order for an argument to be good enough for us to accept its conclusion.

Some sciences have well-developed sufficiency criteria in place. Statisticians, for example, have determined what constitutes a proper sample from which to draw defensible conclusions. Witness the accuracy of most election predictions. But in informal discussion, it is sometimes very difficult to determine what constitutes sufficient grounds. The application of the criterion in practical areas of discussion, such as morality, politics, and religion, leaves much to be desired. Each area of inquiry seems to have its own standard of sufficiency. Not only the amount of evidence but also the kind and weight of evidence required seem peculiar to each context.

The feature of the sufficiency criterion that is the most difficult to apply has to do with the assignment of weight to each of the pieces of supporting evidence. Indeed, it is probably the disagreement over this issue that causes the most problems in informal discussions. What one participant regards as the most important piece of evidence, another may regard as trivial by comparison with other considerations. It is not likely that we will come to cloture in our disputes until we come to some kind of agreement about what weight to give to critical kinds of relevant and acceptable evidence used in support of our conclusions.

There are two fundamental ways in which arguments fail to satisfy the sufficiency requirement. First, there are what might be called the fallacies of missing evidence. These are cases where the kind of evidence needed to support a conclusion is simply not there. Some examples of these fallacies are too small a sample, unrepresentative data, and special pleading. Other fallacies violating the sufficient grounds criterion are the causal fallacies. Each of these fallacies is a different way of inferring causal explanations from premises that simply do not provide adequate support for such explanations. Some examples of these fallacies are causal oversimplification, the domino fallacy, and the gambler's fallacy.

THE REBUTTAL PRINCIPLE

One who presents an argument for or attacks a position should attempt to provide effective responses to all serious challenges or rebuttals to the argument or position at issue.

Meeting the demands of the criterion of rebuttal is perhaps the most difficult of all argumentative tasks. It is, at least, the weakest part of my own arguments and of the arguments of my students, children, wife, friends, relatives, and colleagues. But an argument is not a good one if it does not or cannot successfully blunt the force of not only the counterarguments to the position being defended but also the arguments mustered in behalf of alternate positions.

Any argument can be made to look good if it does not engage the principal challenges to its strength. For example, virtually every jury in a criminal trial is impressed by the quality of the prosecutor's argument. If that were the only argument heard, nearly all juries would convict the accused. It is the defense attorney's rebuttal and the prosecutor's response to that rebuttal that give the jury the whole picture and the proper basis for decision.

The honest seeker not only will allow the questioning of his or her position, but will encourage such challenges. In most cases, of course, there is the assumption that one will be able to render any challenge impotent, but the underlying reason for the invitation to challenge should be to enlist help in exposing a possibly faulty position.

The rebuttal should be the primary driving force behind the formation of every argument. In this way one will have a constant reminder that an argument is not finished until one has finished off the counterarguments. If you look at most controversial issues and the arguments in their behalf, you will notice in many cases that both of the opposing arguments have relevant, acceptable, and seemingly sufficient support. But at least one of the arguments cannot be a good one, because it is not possible for both of the conflicting positions to be true. The solution to this dilemma of "double truth" is most often to be found in the manner in which one of the arguments can effectively meet the most serious challenges to its own position or can damage the strongest arguments for the other position.

What is a serious challenge? It is one that reasonable persons, following all the guidelines suggested in this code and text, would regard as looking forceful enough on the surface to require some answer. Even if the arguer thinks that there is an effective response to the criticism, he or she should treat it as a serious challenge, if for no other reason than to ultimately convince its holder and others of its weakness. Indeed, the arguer would do well to anticipate the most obvious challenges as part of his or her original argument. It not only shows that one has done one's homework, but it disarms the critic in advance. The alleged "big guns" are rendered ineffective before they are fired.

What is an effective response? It is one that a reasonable person, following all the guidelines suggested in this code and text, would accept as seriously damaging or destroying the force of the criticism or counterargument. In other words, an effective response to a serious challenge is one that should cause a reasonable person to no longer regard the challenge as a serious one.

There are several ways that arguments can fail to meet this criterion. The fallacies of diversion call attention to several diversionary tactics commonly used by those wishing to avoid the responsibility of rebuttal. For example, arguments that respond to a serious challenge by misrepresenting the criticism, by bringing up trivial objections or a side issue, or by resorting to humor or ridicule are using devices that clearly fail to make effective responses. The same can be said of those arguments that ignore or deny the counterevidence against one's position. Finally, those arguments that try to avoid responding to an argument by attacking the arguer instead of the argument are among the most morally questionable ways of violating the obligation to respond honestly to the arguments of our verbal opponents.

THE RESOLUTION PRINCIPLE

An issue should be considered resolved if the proponent for one of the alternative positions successfully defends that position by presenting an argument that uses relevant and acceptable premises that provide sufficient grounds to support the acceptance of the premises and the acceptance of the conclusion and provides an effective rebuttal to all serious challenges to the argument or position at issue. Unless one can demonstrate that these conditions have not been met, one should accept the conclusion of the successful argument and consider the issue, for all practical purposes, to be settled. In the absence of a successful argument for any of the alternative positions, one is obligated to accept the position that is supported by the best of the good arguments presented.

If the purpose of rational discussion is ultimately to decide what to do or believe, then coming to cloture should happen more often than it does. There are many good arguments out there, and if what we have suggested as appropriate procedures for discussion really have merit, then we should be resolving issues much more frequently than we do.

Issues such as the effect of cigarette smoking on health, the creationism \evolution debate, and questions of gender and race bias should be settled. The arguments have been made, and they are good ones, but the debates go on. How much more discussion is needed, just because some refuse to recognize the presence of a successful argument?

Unfortunately, very few controversial issues ever come to rational resolution. If you have doubts about this, then ask yourself when was the last time you allowed the force of argument to change your mind about an important issue—even though changing one's mind in the face of a successful argument should not be a difficult thing to do for a genuine truth-seeker.

So why does it not happen? Why are issues not resolved? Probably there are a number of reasons. It could be that one of the parties to the dispute has a blind spot; that is, he or she simply can't be objective about the particular issue at hand. Or maybe he or she has been rationally but not psychologically convinced by the discussion. Another possible explanation is that one or all of the parties have been rationally careless or at least guilty of not thinking as clearly as they may think they have. It is even possible that one of the parties has a hidden agenda—an issue to defend other than the stated one. Or maybe the parties involved are simply not being honest with themselves, for they may want to win the argument more than they want to find a solution to the problem. Finally, perhaps the parties are in what might be called "deep disagreement"; that is, they are divided on the issue because of fundamental underlying assumptions that have yet to be explored.

Unfortunately, none of these explanations is a justification for not resolving our disputes. Indeed, each causal explanation rests on identifiable features of uncritical thinking or violations of the code of intellectual conduct, which we are allegedly committed to try to avoid.

It is possible, of course, that some matters are left unresolved for more respectable reasons. Perhaps the evidence available is regarded as presently too skimpy to lead to a conclusion on the matter, or perhaps one of the parties is still looking for an effective counterargument that he or she thinks is out there to be found. There may even remain serious disagreement over whether an argument presented has indeed been successful—especially with regard to the sufficiency requirement.

These are all reasons that may make one less confident in adopting the conclusion of one of the arguments presented, but since few arguments are ever found to be totally successful, one is obligated to accept the position that is supported by the *best* of the good or near-successful arguments presented. Otherwise, since one can always claim that there has been no *absolute* proof presented, one could leave unresolved forever virtually every issue discussed. Besides, we have tried to show that there are objective criteria available to determine the quality of an argument.

Judges and juries do it routinely, and there is no reason why the rest of us cannot do it as well. We are not saying that there is one monolithic logic to which all discussion participants must bow down; we are simply saying that there are more objective ways of evaluating arguments than some are willing to admit.

THE SUSPENSION OF JUDGMENT PRINCIPLE

If no position comes close to being successfully defended, or if two or more positions seem to be defended with equal strength, one should, in most cases, suspend judgment about the issue. If practical considerations seem to require an immediate decision, one should weigh the relative risks of gain or loss connected with the consequences of suspending judgment and decide the issue on those grounds.

If the appropriate evidence is so lacking that one has no good basis for making a decision either way on an issue, it may be quite appropriate to suspend judgment on the matter and wait until there is more of a basis for decision. This alternative should not, however, be seen as a clever way to avoid the psychological fright of making a difficult decision or of moving into unfamiliar territory.

The same might be said of the second condition for suspending judgment—the equal strength of the arguments. This situation is likely to be a very rare phenomenon, for one argument is almost always better than the others if judged by the objective standards available. Equal strength, then, means that one really cannot decide between the two arguments at present.

Some issues, of course, do not allow such suspension. If the decision is a forced or momentous one, such as deciding whether to have an abortion, one has to decide on the grounds of the practical consequences of *not* making the decision.

THE RECONSIDERATION PRINCIPLE

If a successful or at least good argument for a position is subsequently found by any participant to be flawed in a way that raises new doubts about the merit of that position, one is obligated to reopen the issue for further consideration and resolution.

No argument may be regarded as permanently successful. There is always the possibility that new evidence will come to light that will raise new doubts about a position held on what were thought to be good grounds. Under these conditions, further examination is always appropriate. Pride in good or successful arguments past should not become an obstacle to reopening the issue in the present if conditions warrant it. The principles of fallibility and truth-seeking are as important at this point as they were in the original inquiry.

The new doubts, however, should not be the same old doubts in new clothing. Reopening the issue should come only from the impetus of uncovering new or reinterpreted evidence not considered in the earlier treatment of the issue. Otherwise, the re-examination of the issue is the worst form of the violation of the resolution principle—simply a device to continue to haggle over the same ground.

Glossary of Fallacies

Accent, Improper: This fallacy consists in directing an opponent toward an unwarranted conclusion by placing improper or unusual emphasis on a word, phrase, or particular aspect of an issue or claim. It is sometimes committed by lifting portions of a quotation out of context in a way that conveys a meaning not intended by the person quoted.   (p. 67)

Ad Hominem, **Abusive:**   This fallacy consists in attacking one's opponent in a personal and abusive way as a means of ignoring or discrediting his or her position or argument.   (p. 150)

Ambiguity: This fallacy consists in presenting a claim or argument that uses a word, phrase, or grammatical construction that can be interpreted in two or more distinctly different ways, without making clear which meaning is intended.   (p. 64)

Arguing in a Circle: This fallacy consists in either explicitly or implicitly asserting, in one of the premises of an argument, what is asserted in the conclusion of that argument. Moreover, it uses a premise that probably would not be regarded as true, unless the conclusion were already regarded as true.   (p. 77)

Attacking a Straw Man: This fallacy consists in misrepresenting an opponent's view or argument, usually for the purpose of making it easier to attack.   (p. 157)

Authority, Irrelevant or Questionable: This fallacy consists in attempting to support a claim by quoting the judgment of one who is not an authority in the field, the judgment of an unidentified authority, or the judgment of an authority who is likely to be biased in some way.   (p. 31)

Causal Oversimplification: This fallacy consists in oversimplifying the relevant causal antecedents of an event by introducing factors insufficient to account for the event in question or by overemphasizing the role of one or more of those factors.   (p. 129)

Cliché, Improper Use of a: This fallacy consists in using an aphorism or cliché in place of relevant evidence for a claim.   (p. 118)

Common Cause, Neglect of a: This fallacy consists in failing to recognize that two seemingly related events may not be causally related at all, but rather are effects of a common cause.   (p. 134)

Common Opinion, Appeal to: This fallacy consists in urging the acceptance of a position simply on the grounds that most, or at least great numbers of, people accept it, or in urging the rejection of a position on the grounds that very few people accept it.   (p. 34)

Composition, Fallacy of: This fallacy consists in assuming that what is true of the parts of some whole is therefore true of the whole.   (p. 90)

Confusion of Cause and Effect: This fallacy consists in confusing the cause with the effect of an event or in failing to recognize that there may be a reciprocal causal relation between the two events in question.   (p. 132)

Confusion of a Necessary with a Sufficient Condition: This fallacy consists in assuming that a necessary condition of an event is also a sufficient one.   (p. 128)

Continuum, Fallacy of the: This fallacy consists in assuming that small differences in a sequence of things are insignificant or that supposed contraries, connected by intermediate small differences, are really very much the same. Hence, there is the failure to recognize the importance or necessity of sometimes making what might appear to be arbitrary distinctions or cut-off points.   (p. 88)

Contrary-to-Fact Hypothesis: This fallacy consists in making a poorly supported claim about what would have happened in the past if other conditions had been present, or about an event that will occur in the future. This is done in such a way as to treat hypothetical claims as if they were statements of fact.   (p. 116)

Counterevidence, Denying the: This fallacy consists in refusing to acknowledge, or to consider seriously, evidence that counts against one's claim. The most radical form of this fallacy is to be unwilling to acknowledge even any *conceivable* evidence that might count against the claim.   (p. 145)

Counterevidence, Ignoring the: This fallacy consists in arguing in a way that ignores or simply omits any reference to important evidence unfavorable to one's position, giving the false impression that there is no significant evidence against it.   (p. 147)

Distinction Without a Difference: This fallacy consists in attempting to defend an action or point of view as different from some other one, with which it is allegedly confused, by means of a very careful distinction of language. In reality, however, the action or position defended is no different in substance from the one from which it is linguistically distinguished.   (p. 74)

Division, Fallacy of: This fallacy consists in assuming that what is true of some whole is therefore true of each of the parts of that whole.   (p. 92)

Domino Fallacy: This fallacy consists in assuming, without appropriate evidence, that a particular action or event is just one, usually the first, in a series of steps that will lead inevitably to some specific consequence.   (p. 135)

Equivocation: This fallacy consists in directing an opponent toward an unwarranted conclusion by making a word or phrase, employed in two different senses in an argument, appear to have the same meaning throughout.   (p. 62)

Fake Precision, Fallacy of: This fallacy consists in making a claim with the kind of mathematical precision that is impossible to obtain.   (p. 120)

False Alternatives: This fallacy consists in assuming too few alternatives and, at the same time, assuming that one of the suggested alternatives must be true.   (p. 93)

Faulty Analogy: This fallacy consists in assuming that because two things are alike in one or more respects, they necessarily are alike in some other respect.   (p. 101)

Feelings and Attitudes, Exploitation of Strong: This fallacy consists in attempting to persuade others of one's point of view by exploiting their strong emotions or by manipulating their positive and negative attitudes toward certain groups or ideas, instead of presenting evidence for one's view.   (p. 51)

Flattery, Use of: This fallacy consists in attempting to persuade others of one's view by engaging in excessive praise of them, instead of presenting evidence for one's view.   (p. 53)

Force or Threat, Appeal to: This fallacy consists in attempting to persuade others of one's point of view by threatening them with some undesirable state of affairs instead of presenting evidence for one's view.   (p. 47)

Gambler's Fallacy: This fallacy consists in arguing that, because a chance event has had a certain run in the past, the probability of its occurrence in the future is significantly altered.   (p. 137)

Genetic Fallacy: This fallacy consists in evaluating a thing in terms of its earlier context and then carrying over that evaluation to the thing in the present.   (p. 36)

Golden Mean, Fallacy of the: This fallacy consists in assuming that the moderate or middle view between two extremes must be the best or right one simply because it is the middle view.   (p. 99)

Guilt by Association, Assigning: This fallacy consists in attempting to manipulate others into accepting one's view by pointing out that the opposing view is held by those with negative esteem, instead of presenting evidence for one's position.   (p. 54)

Humor or Ridicule, Resort to: This fallacy consists in intruding humor or ridicule into an argument in an effort to cover up an inability or unwillingness to respond appropriately to an opponent's position. Humor is thereby used as a substitute for relevant evidence.   (p. 163)

Ignorance, Arguing from: This fallacy consists in assuming that a claim is true because there is no evidence or proof that it is false or because of the inability or refusal of an opponent to present convincing evidence *against* it. Conversely, it consists in assuming that a claim is false because there is no evidence or proof that it is true or because of the refusal or inability of an opponent to present convincing evidence for it. (p. 113)

Illicit Contrast: This fallacy consists in a listener directly inferring from a speaker's claim some related but unstated *contrasting* claim by placing improper or unusual emphasis on the words or phrases in the statement. (p. 69)

Innuendo, Argument by: This fallacy consists in directing one's listeners to a particular, usually derogatory, conclusion, by a skillful choice of words or the careful arrangement of sentences, which implicitly *suggests* but does not *assert* that conclusion. The force of the fallacy lies in the impression created that some veiled claim is true, although no relevant evidence is presented to support such a view. (p. 70)

Insufficient Sample: This fallacy consists in drawing a conclusion or generalization from too small a sample of cases. (p. 109)

Is-Ought Fallacy: This fallacy consists in assuming that because something is now the practice, it *ought* to be the practice. Conversely, it consists in assuming that because something *is not* the practice, it *ought not* to be the practice. (p. 95)

Label, Inference from a: This fallacy consists in assuming that evaluative or identifying words or phrases attached to people or things constitute a sufficient reason for drawing conclusions about the objects to which such labels are attached. (p. 119)

Leading Question: This fallacy consists in "planting" a proposed answer to a question at issue by the manner in which the question is asked. (p. 83)

Loaded or Complex Question: This fallacy consists in formulating a question in a way that presupposes that a definite answer has already been given to some other *unasked* question, or in treating a series of questions as if it involved only one question. (p. 81)

Novelty, Fallacy of: This fallacy consists in assuming that a new idea, law, policy, or action is good simply because it is new. (p. 103)

Omission of Key Evidence: This fallacy consists in constructing an argument that fails to include some of the key or principal evidence that is critical to the support of the conclusion. (p. 124)

Personal Circumstances or Motives, Appeal to: This fallacy consists in urging an opponent to accept or reject a particular position by appealing solely to his or her personal circumstances or self-interest, usually when there is some more important issue at stake. (p. 50)

Pity, Appeal to: This fallacy consists in attempting to persuade others of one's point of view by appealing to their sympathy instead of relevant evidence, especially when some more important principle or issue is at stake. (p. 44)

Poisoning the Well: This fallacy consists in rejecting a claim defended by another because of that person's special circumstances or improper motives. (p. 153)

Post Hoc **Fallacy**: This fallacy consists in assuming that a particular event, B, is caused by another event, A, simply because B follows A in time. (p. 131)

Principle, Misuse of a General: This fallacy consists in assuming that a generalization or rule has no exceptions, thus misapplying it in a particular instance. Conversely, it consists in attempting to refute a generalization or rule by means of an exceptional case.   (p. 98)

Question-Begging Definition: This fallacy consists in attempting to establish an irrefutable position in an argument by means of a questionable definition. What appears to be a factual or empirical claim is often rendered impervious to counterevidence by being subtly, and sometimes unconsciously, interpreted by the claimant as a definitional statement. The claim at issue thereby becomes "true" by definition.   (p. 84)

Question-Begging Language: This fallacy consists in discussing an issue by means of language that assumes a position on the very question at issue, in such a way as to direct the listener to a particular conclusion about the issue. (p. 80)

Rationalization: This fallacy consists in using plausible-sounding but usually false reasons to justify a particular position that is held on other less respectable grounds.   (p. 37)

Red Herring: This fallacy consists in attempting to hide the weakness of a position by drawing attention away from the real issue to a side issue.   (p. 161)

Special Pleading: This fallacy consists in applying principles, rules, or criteria to another person, while failing or refusing to apply them to oneself or to a situation that is of special personal interest, without providing sufficient evidence to support such an exception.   (p. 122)

Tradition, Appeal to: This fallacy consists in attempting to persuade others of one's point of view by appealing to their feelings of reverence or respect for some tradition instead of evidence, especially when there is some more important principle or issue at risk.   (p. 48)

Trivial Objections: This fallacy consists in attacking an opponent's position by focusing critical attention on some point less significant than the main point or basic thrust of the argument.   (p. 159)

Unrepresentative Data: This fallacy consists in drawing a conclusion from exceptional cases, or from unrepresentative or biased data.   (p. 111)

Vague Expression, Misuse of a: This fallacy consists in attempting to establish a position by means of a vague expression or in drawing an unjustified conclusion as a result of assigning a very *precise* meaning to another's word, phrase, or statement that is quite *imprecise* in its meaning or range of application.   (p. 72)

Wishful Thinking: This fallacy consists in assuming that because one *wants* something to be true, it *is* or *will be* true. Conversely, it consists in assuming that because we do not want something to be true, then it *is not* or *will not* be true.   (p. 96)

Wrong Conclusion, Drawing the: This fallacy consists in drawing a conclusion other than the one supported by the evidence presented in the argument.   (p. 38)

Wrong Reasons, Using the: This fallacy consists in attempting to support a claim with reasons other than the reasons appropriate to the claim.   (p. 40)

"You Do It, Too" Argument: This fallacy consists in responding to an attack on one's ideas or actions by accusing one's critic or others of thinking or acting in a similar way or in a way that is equally hard to defend.   (p. 154)

Answers to Exercises

Chapter IV

Fallacies of Relevance (p. 43):   **1.** Using the wrong reasons. **2.** Drawing the wrong conclusion. **3.** Irrelevant or questionable authority. **4.** Appeal to common opinion. **5.** Rationalization. **6.** Appeal to common opinion. **7.** Rationalization. **8.** Drawing the wrong conclusion. **9.** Using the wrong reasons. **10.** Genetic fallacy. **11.** Using the wrong reasons. **12.** Genetic fallacy. **13.** Drawing the wrong conclusion. **14.** Genetic fallacy. **15.** Irrelevant or questionable authority. **16.** Irrelevant or questionable authority. **17.** Rationalization. **18.** Genetic fallacy. **19.** Appeal to common opinion. **20.** Irrelevant or questionable authority.

Irrelevant Emotional Appeals (p. 56):   **1.** Appeal to tradition. **2.** Exploitation of strong feelings and attitudes. **3.** Use of flattery. **4.** Appeal to force or threat. **5.** Appeal to pity. **6.** Appeal to personal circumstances or motives. **7.** Appeal to pity. **8.** Exploitation of strong feelings and attitudes. **9.** Assigning guilt by association. **10.** Appeal to tradition. **11.** Appeal to pity. **12.** Appeal to force or threat. **13.** Appeal to personal circumstances or motives. **14.** Appeal to force or threat. **15.** Appeal to tradition. **16.** Use of flattery. **17.** Assigning guilt by association. **18.** Appeal to personal circumstances or motives. **19.** Exploitation of strong feelings and attitudes. **20.** Assigning guilt by association.

Additional Exercises (p. 58):   **1.** Appeal to personal circumstances or motives. **2.** Rationalization. **3.** Appeal to force or threat. **4.** Using the wrong reasons. **5.** Appeal to pity. **6.** Irrelevant or questionable authority. **7.** Assigning guilt by association. **8.** Appeal to common opinion. **9.** Appeal to personal circumstances or motives.

10. Use of flattery. 11. Drawing the wrong conclusion. 12. Use of flattery. 13. Genetic fallacy. 14. Exploitation of strong feelings and attitudes. 15. Appeal to tradition. 16. Exploitation of strong feelings and attitudes. 17. Irrelevant or questionable authority. 18. Appeal to tradition. 19. Drawing the wrong conclusion. 20. Appeal to tradition. 21. Using the wrong reasons. 22. Assigning guilt by association. 23. Appeal to personal circumstances or motives. 24. Appeal to common opinion. 25. Appeal to pity. 26. Genetic fallacy. 27. Appeal to force or threat. 28. Drawing the wrong conclusion. 29. Using the wrong reasons. 30. Rationalization.

Chapter V

Fallacies of Linguistic Confusion (p. 76): 1. Misuse of a vague expression. 2. Illicit contrast. 3. Argument by innuendo. 4. Ambiguity. 5. Misuse of a vague expression. 6. Ambiguity. 7. Equivocation. 8. Illicit contrast. 9. Improper accent. 10. Equivocation. 11. Improper accent. 12. Distinction without a difference. 13. Ambiguity. 14. Argument by innuendo. 15. Equivocation. 16. Ambiguity. 17. Equivocation. 18. Distinction without a difference. 19. Illicit contrast. 20. Argument by innuendo.

Begging-the-Question Fallacies (p. 86): 1. Loaded or complex question. 2. Question-begging definition. 3. Leading question. 4. Arguing in a circle. 5. Loaded or complex question. 6. Question-begging language. 7. Arguing in a circle. 8. Question-begging language. 9. Question-begging definition. 10. Leading question. 11. Question-begging definition. 12. Leading question. 13. Loaded or complex question. 14. Arguing in a circle. 15. Question-begging definition. 16. Arguing in a circle. 17. Question-begging language. 18. Leading question. 19. Question-begging language. 20. Loaded or complex question.

Unwarranted Assumption Fallacies (p. 104): 1. Faulty analogy. 2. Misuse of a general principle. 3. Fallacy of novelty. 4. Fallacy of composition. 5. Fallacy of the continuum. 6. Fallacy of division. 7. False alternatives. 8. Is-ought fallacy. 9. Wishful thinking. 10. Fallacy of the golden mean. 11. Fallacy of composition. 12. Fallacy of the golden mean. 13. Fallacy of division. 14. Faulty analogy. 15. Fallacy of the continuum. 16. Fallacy of novelty. 17. False alternatives. 18. Is-ought fallacy. 19. Misuse of a general principle. 20. Wishful thinking.

Additional Exercises (p. 106): 1. Argument by innuendo. 2. Wishful thinking. 3. Irrelevant or questionable authority. 4. Equivocation. 5. Is-ought fallacy. 6. Question-begging definition. 7. Faulty analogy. 8. Argument by innuendo. 9. Ambiguity. 10. Use of flattery. 11. Fallacy of composition. 12. Fallacy of novelty. 13. Illicit contrast. 14. Appeal to personal circumstances or motives. 15. Fallacy of the golden mean. 16. Misuse of a general principle. 17. Leading question. 18. Fallacy of the continuum. 19. Arguing in a circle. 20. Appeal to force or threat. 21. Leading question. 22. Loaded or complex question. 23. Misuse of a vague expression. 24. Distinction without a difference. 25. Fallacy of division. 26. Fallacy of the golden mean. 27. Illicit contrast. 28. Fallacy of composition. 29. Loaded or complex question. 30. Fallacy of division. 31. Appeal to pity. 32. Question-begging definition. 33. Question-begging language. 34. Wishful thinking. 35. Fallacy of novelty. 36. Assigning guilt by association. **37.** Misuse of a vague expression. **38.** Improper accent. **39.** Question-begging language. **40.** False alternatives.

Chapter VI

Fallacies of Missing Evidence (p. 126): **1.** Special pleading. **2.** Insufficient sample. **3.** Inference from a label. **4.** Improper use of a cliché. **5.** Omission of key evidence. **6.** Contrary-to-fact hypothesis. **7.** Fallacy of fake precision. **8.** Arguing from ignorance. **9.** Insufficient sample. **10.** Special pleading. **11.** Arguing from ignorance. **12.** Contrary-to-fact hypothesis. **13.** Unrepresentative data. **14.** Arguing from ignorance. **15.** Inference from a label. **16.** Fallacy of fake precision. **17.** Improper use of a cliché. **18.** Omission of key evidence. **19.** Special pleading. **20.** Unrepresentative data.

Causal Fallacies (p. 138): **1.** Causal oversimplification. **2.** *Post hoc* fallacy. **3.** Confusion of a necessary with a sufficient condition. **4.** Domino fallacy. **5.** Gambler's fallacy. **6.** Neglect of a common cause. **7.** Confusion of cause and effect. **8.** Confusion of a necessary with a sufficient condition. **9.** Confusion of cause and effect. **10.** Neglect of a common cause. **11.** Confusion of a necessary with a sufficient condition. **12.** *Post hoc* fallacy. **13.** Causal oversimplification. **14.** Domino fallacy. **15.** Neglect of a common cause. **16.** Gambler's fallacy. **17.** Causal oversimplification. **18.** *Post hoc* fallacy. **19.** Confusion of cause and effect. **20.** Gambler's fallacy.

Additional Exercises (p. 140): **1.** Fallacy of composition. **2.** Causal oversimplification. **3.** Drawing the wrong conclusion. **4.** Exploitation of strong feelings and attitudes. **5.** Inference from a label. **6.** Faulty analogy. **7.** Insufficient sample. **8.** Confusion of cause and effect. **9.** Inference from a label. **10.** Special pleading. **11.** Misuse of a general principle. **12.** Omission of key evidence. **13.** Ambiguity. **14.** Causal oversimplification. **15.** Arguing from ignorance. **16.** Arguing in a circle. **17.** Fallacy of fake precision. **18.** Fallacy of novelty. **19.** Improper use of a cliché. **20.** Distinction without a difference. **21.** Domino fallacy. **22.** Illicit contrast. **23.** Question-begging language. **24.** Neglect of a common cause. **25.** Equivocation. **26.** Neglect of a common cause. **27.** Appeal to common opinion. **28.** Special pleading. **29.** Is-ought fallacy. **30.** Unrepresentative data. **31.** Fallacy of the continuum. **32.** Insufficient sample. **33.** Question-begging definition. **34.** Contrary-to-fact hypothesis. **35.** Misuse of a vague expression. **36.** Arguing from ignorance. **37.** Improper use of a cliché. **38.** Fallacy of the golden mean. **39.** *Post hoc* fallacy. **40.** Unrepresentative data. **41.** Use of flattery. **42.** Domino fallacy. **43.** Contrary-to-fact hypothesis. **44.** Genetic fallacy. **45.** Confusion of cause and effect. **46.** Confusion of a necessary with a sufficient condition. **47.** Gambler's fallacy. **48.** Appeal to force or threat. **49.** Fallacy of division. **50.** Fallacy of fake precision.

Chapter VII

Fallacies of Counterevidence (p. 149): **1.** Denying the counterevidence. **2.** Ignoring the counterevidence. **3.** Denying the counterevidence. **4.** Denying the counterevidence. **5.** Ignoring the counterevidence. **6.** Ignoring the counterevidence. **7.** Denying the counterevidence. **8.** Denying the counterevidence. **9.** Ignoring the counterevidence. **10.** Ignoring the counterevidence.

Ad Hominem **Fallacies (p. 156):** **1.** "You do it, too" argument. **2.** Poisoning the well. **3.** Poisoning the well. **4.** "You do it, too" argument. **5.** Abusive *ad hominem*. **6.** Poisoning the well. **7.** Abusive *ad hominem*. **8.** "You do it, too" argument. **9.** Poisoning the well. **10.** Abusive *ad hominem*.

Fallacies of Diversion (p. 164): **1.** Red herring. **2.** Resort to humor or ridicule. **3.** Trivial objections. **4.** Red herring. **5.** Trivial objections. **6.** Attacking a straw man. **7.** Red herring. **8.** Resort to humor or ridicule. **9.** Attacking a straw man. **10.** Trivial objections.

Additional Exercises (p. 166): **1.** Neglect of a common cause. **2.** Leading question. **3.** Trivial objections. **4.** Argument by innuendo. **5.** Omission of key evidence. **6.** Ignoring the counterevidence. **7.** Genetic fallacy. **8.** Inference from a label. **9.** Red herring. **10.** Unrepresentative data. **11.** Denying the counterevidence. **12.** Loaded or complex question. **13.** Red herring. **14.** Improper use of a cliché. **15.** "You do it, too" argument. **16.** Special pleading. **17.** *Post hoc* fallacy. **18.** Trivial objections. **19.** Ambiguity. **20.** Arguing in a circle. **21.** "You do it, too" argument. **22.** Omission of key evidence. **23.** Domino fallacy. **24.** Appeal to tradition. **25.** Causal oversimplification. **26.** Appeal to common opinion. **27.** Misuse of a general principle. **28.** False alternatives. **29.** Ignoring the counterevidence. **30.** Fallacy of the continuum. **31.** Confusion of a necessary with a sufficient condition. **32.** Attacking a straw man. **33.** Arguing from ignorance. **34.** Using the wrong reasons. **35.** Fallacy of the golden mean. **36.** Wishful thinking. **37.** Poisoning the well. **38.** Gambler's fallacy. **39.** Resort to humor or ridicule. **40.** Gambler's fallacy. **41.** Abusive *ad hominem*. **42.** Confusion of cause and effect. **43.** Insufficient sample. **44.** Poisoning the well. **45.** Faulty analogy. **46.** Improper accent. **47.** Exploitation of strong feeling and attitudes. **48.** Denying the counterevidence. **49.** Equivocation. **50.** Contrary-to-fact hypothesis. **51.** Insufficient sample. **52.** Resort to humor or ridicule. **53.** Fallacy of fake precision. **54.** Is-ought fallacy. **55.** Distinction without a difference. **56.** Abusive *ad hominem*. **57.** Rationalization. **58.** Question-begging definition. **59.** Attacking a straw man. **60.** Confusion of a necessary with a sufficient condition.

Index

Absurd example method, 27–29
Abusive *ad hominem*, 26, 150–152, 187
Accent, improper, 67–69, 187
Acceptability:
  conditions of, 14
  criterion, 13–15
  of premises, 12
  principle, 180–181
Accident, fallacy of (*See* Misuse of a general
    principle)
Ad hominem fallacies:
  abusive, 26, 150–151, 187
  poisoning the well, 153–154, 190
  "you do it, too" argument, 154–156, 192
Aesthetic argument, 9
"All," careless use of, 65
Ambiguity:
  false, 67
  semantical, 64–65, 187
  syntactical, 65, 187
Amphiboles, 65
Analogical argument (*See* Faulty analogy)
Anecdotal data, 16
Aphorism (*See* Improper use of a cliché)
Appeal to common opinion, 34–36, 95, 188
Appeal to the crowd (*See* Exploitation of
    strong feelings and attitudes)
Appeal to force or threat, 47–48, 189
Appeal to personal circumstances or motives,
    50–51, 190
Appeal to pity, 44–47, 190
Appeal to shame, 52
Appeal to tradition, 48–50, 95, 191
Arguing in a circle, 77–79, 187
Arguing from ignorance, 113–116, 189–190
Argument:
  criteria of good, 12–17
  deductive, 8, 13
  definition, 4
  inductive, 8–9, 13
  by innuendo, 70–72, 190
  moral, 9–11
  standard form of, 5–6, 18–21
  strength of, 8–9, 17
Argumentative leap, 31
Assessment, one-sided (*See* Ignoring the coun-
    terevidence)
Assigning:
  guilt by association, 54–56, 189
  irrelevant goals and functions, 41
Attack, personal (*See* Abusive *ad hominem*)
Attacking the fallacy, 7, 26–29
Attacking a straw man, 157–159, 187
Attitudes, exploitation of strong feelings and,
    51-53, 189
Authoritarianism, 47
Authority:
  biased, 32
  definition, 32

transfer of, 32
unidentified, 32–33

Bandwagon fallacy (*See* Appeal to common
    opinion)
Beard, fallacy of (See Continuum, fallacy of the)
Begging-the-question fallacies:
  arguing in a circle, 77–79, 187
  leading question, 83–84, 190
  loaded or complex question, 81–83, 190
  question-begging definition, 84–86, 191
  question-begging language, 80–81, 191
Belief, fallacy of (*See* Wishful thinking)
Black-and-white fallacy (*See* False alternatives)
Burden of proof, 7, 114
  shifting (*See* Arguing from ignorance)
  principle, 176–177

Camel's back fallacy (*See* Continuum, fallacy
    of the)
Causal fallacies:
  causal oversimplification, 129–130, 131, 188
  confusion of cause and effect, 132–134, 188
  confusion of a necessary with a sufficient
    condition, 128–129, 188
  domino fallacy, 135–137, 189
  gambler's fallacy, 137–138, 189
  neglect of a common cause, 134–135, 188
  post hoc fallacy, 26, 131–132, 190
Causal oversimplification, 129–130, 131, 188
Charity, principle of, 6–7, 19, 45, 158, 177–178
Circular argument (*See* Arguing in a circle)
Clarity principle, 178–179
Cliché, improper use of, 118–119, 188
Common cause, neglect of, 134–135, 188
Common opinion, appeal to, 34–36, 95, 188
Complex question (*See* Loaded question)
Composition, fallacy of, 90–92, 188
Compromise (*See* Golden mean, fallacy of the)
Conclusion:
  drawing the wrong, 38–40, 41, 191
  identifying the, 4
Conditions of acceptability, 14
Conditions of unacceptability, 15
Confusion of cause and effect, 132–134, 188
Confusion of a necessary with a sufficient
    condition, 128–129, 188
Consensus gentium (*See* Appeal to common
    opinion)
Constructing arguments, 22–23
Continuum, fallacy of, 28, 88–90, 188
Contradictories, 94
Contraries, 94
Contrary-to-fact hypothesis, 116–118, 188
Contrast, illicit, 69–70, 190
Counterevidence, fallacies of:
  denying the counterevidence, 145–147, 188
  ignoring the counterevidence, 147–149, 188
Counterexample, method of, 27

Credible witness, 14–15, 153
Criteria of a good argument:
    acceptable premises, 12, 13–15, 180–181
    effective rebuttal, 12, 16–17, 182–183
    relevant premises, 12–13, 179–180
    sufficient grounds, 12, 15–16, 181–182
Critical thinking, 1
Crowd, appeal to the (*See* Exploitation of
    strong feelings and attitudes)

Damning the source (*See* Poisoning the well)
Data:
    insufficient, 109–111
    unrepresentative, 111–113
Deductive argument, 8, 13
Definitional claim, 84
Denying the counterevidence, 145–147, 188
Dishonesty, 37
Distinction without a difference, 74–76, 188
Distortion (*See* Attacking a straw man)
Diversion, fallacies of:
    attacking a straw man, 157–159, 187
    red herring, 161–163, 191
    resort to humor or ridicule, 163–164, 189
    trivial objections, 159–161, 191
Dividing the question (*See* Loaded or com-
        plex question)
Division, fallacy of, 92–93, 189
Domino fallacy, 135–137, 189
Drawing unwarranted inferences (*See*
        Attacking a straw man)
Drawing the wrong conclusion, 38–40, 41, 191

Effective rebuttal (*See* Rebuttal criterion)
Either-or thinking (*See* False alternatives)
Elliptical construction, 65
Emotional appeals (*See* Irrelevant emotional
        appeals)
Empirical claim, 84
Empty consolation, 161
Equivocation, 62–64, 189
Evaluating arguments, 17–22
Exploitation of strong feelings and attitudes,
        51–53, 189

Fake precision, fallacy of, 120–122, 189
Fallacies:
    deceptive character of, 24–25
    naming of, 25
    organization of, 26
Fallacy, definition, 24
Fallacymonger, 29–30
Fallibility principle, 173–175
False alternatives, 93–95, 189
False ambiguity, 67
False cause (*See* Causal fallacies)
False precision (*See* Fake precision, fallacy of)
Faulty analogy, 101–103, 189
Feelings (*See* Exploitation of strong feelings
        and attitudes)

Flattery, use of, 53–54, 189
Force (*See* Appeal to force or threat)

Gallery, playing to the (*See* Exploitation of
        strong feelings and attitudes)
Gambler's fallacy, 137–138, 189
Generalization:
    exception to, 98
    hasty, 91, 110
    with insufficient sample, 109–111, 190
    one-instance, 111
    particular inference from, 92
    with unrepresentative data, 111–113, 191
Genetic fallacy, 36–37, 189
Goals and functions, assigning irrelevant, 41
Golden mean, fallacy of, 99–101, 189
Good argument:
    criteria of, 12–17
    importance of, 1–2
Grounds, sufficiency of, 15-16
Group loyalty, appeal to, 52
Guilt by association, assigning, 54–56, 189

Hasty generalization, 109
Humor (*See* Resort to humor or ridicule)
Hypocrisy, 155

Ignorance, arguing from, 113–116, 189–190
Ignoring the counterevidence, 147–149, 188
Illicit contrast, 69–70, 190
Illustration, attacking an (*See* Trivial objections)
Implicit:
    conclusion, 6
    moral premise, 11
    premise, 6
Improper accent, 67–69, 187
Improper or questionable motives (*See* Poi-
        soning the well)
Improper use of a cliché, 118–119, 188
Inconsistency, 16, 155–156
Indicator words, 6
Inductive argument, 8–9, 13
Ineffective rebuttal fallacies (*See* Rebuttal
        fallacies)
Inference from a label, 119–120, 190
Innuendo, argument by, 70–72, 190
Insufficient grounds, fallacies of:
    causal fallacies, 128–140
    fallacies of missing evidence, 109–127
Insufficient sample, 109–111, 190
Irrelevance, fallacies of:
    appeal to common opinion, 34–36, 95, 188
    drawing the wrong conclusion, 38–40, 191
    genetic fallacy, 36-37, 189
    irrelevant or questionable authority,
        31–34, 153, 187
    rationalization, 37–38, 191
    using the wrong reasons, 40–43, 191
Irrelevant conclusion (*See* Drawing the wrong
        conclusion)

Irrelevant emotional appeals:
    appeal to force or threat, 47–48, 189
    appeal to personal circumstances or mo-
        tives, 50–51, 190
    appeal to pity, 44–47, 190
    appeal to tradition, 48–50, 95, 191
    assigning guilt by association, 54–56, 189
    exploitation of strong feelings and atti-
        tudes, 51–53, 189
    use of flattery, 53–54, 189
Irrelevant evidence (See Wrong reasons,
    using the)
Irrelevant goals and functions, assigning, 41
Irrelevant or questionable authority, 31–34,
    153, 187
Irrelevant premise, fallacies of:
    fallacies of irrelevance, 31–44
    irrelevant emotional appeals, 44–60
Irrelevant reasons (See Using the wrong reasons)
Is-ought fallacy, 95–96, 190

Label, inference from, 119–120, 190
Language, question-begging, 80–81, 191
Leading question, 83–84, 190
Lifting out of context (See Improper accent)
Limited alternatives (See False alternatives)
Linguistic confusion, fallacies of:
    ambiguity, 64–67, 187
    argument by innuendo, 70–72, 190
    distinction without a difference, 74–76, 188
    equivocation, 62–64, 189
    illicit contrast, 69–70, 190
    improper accent, 67–69, 187
    misuse of a vague expression, 72–74, 191
Loaded language (See Question-begging lan-
    guage)
Loaded question, 81–83, 190
Lonely fact, fallacy of, 110
Loyalty, appeal to, 52

Manipulation of negative feelings, 54–56
Methods of attacking faulty reasoning:
    absurd example, 27–29
    counterexample, 27
    self-destruction, 7, 27
Minor point, attacking (See Trivial objections)
Misrepresenting an argument (See Attacking
    a straw man)
Missing evidence, fallacies of:
    arguing from ignorance, 113–116,
        189–190
    contrary-to-fact hypothesis, 116–118, 188
    fallacy of fake precision, 120–122, 189
    improper use of a cliché, 118–119, 188
    inference from a label, 119–120, 190
    insufficient sample, 109–111, 190
    omission of key evidence, 124–126, 190
    special pleading, 122–124, 191
    unrepresentative data, 111–113, 191

Missing the point (See Drawing the wrong
    conclusion or Using the wrong rea-
    sons)
Misuse of a general principle, 98–99, 191
Misuse of a vague expression, 72–74, 191
Moderation, fallacy of (See Golden mean,
    fallacy of the)
Monday-morning quarterbacking (See
    Contrary-to-fact hypothesis)
Moral argument, 9–11, 45–46
Moral premise, 10–11, 45–46
Motives:
    appeal to personal circumstances or, 50–
        51, 190
    improper (See Poisoning the well)

Necessary condition, 128
Negatives (See Contradictories)
Neglect of a common cause, 134–135, 188
Non sequitur, 31
Novelty, fallacy of, 27, 103–104, 190

Objections, trivial, 159–161, 191
Omission of key evidence, 124–126, 190
One-sided assessment (See Ignoring the coun-
    terevidence)
"Only, "careless use of, 65
Opinion:
    appeal to common, 34–36, 95, 188
    distinguished from argument, 5
Opposites, 94
Organization of the fallacies, 26
Oversimplification:
    of an argument (See Attacking a straw man)
    causal, 129–130, 188

Parentheses, use of, 19
Personal attacks (See Ad hominem fallacies)
Personal circumstances or motives, appeal to,
    50–51, 190
Pity, appeal to, 44–47, 190
Playing to the gallery (See Exploitation of
    strong feelings and attitudes)
Poisoning the well, 153–154, 190
Post hoc fallacy, 26, 131–132, 190
Practice, appeal to common (See Is-ought
    fallacy)
Premise:
    definition, 6
    implicit, 6
    irrelevant, 12–13
    unacceptable, 13–15
Principle, misuse of a general, 98–99, 191
Principle of charity, 6–7, 19, 45, 158, 177–178
Proof, burden of, 7, 114, 176–177
Purposes of book, 2–3

Question-begging definition, 84–86, 191
Question-begging language, 80–81, 191

Questionable authority (*See* Irrelevant or questionable authority)
Quietism, fallacy of, 115

Rationalization, 37–38, 191
Rebuttal:
    criterion of, 12, 16–17
    principle, 182–183
Rebuttal fallacies:
    ad hominem fallacies, 150–157
    fallacies of counterevidence, 144–150
    fallacies of diversion, 157–166
Reciprocal causal relations, 132
Reconsideration principle, 185–186
Reconstruction of arguments, 6–7, 18–21, 177–178
Red herring, 161–163, 191
Relevance:
    criterion, 12–13
    principle, 179–180
Resolution principle, 183–185
Resort to humor or ridicule, 163–164, 189
Ridicule (*See* Resort to humor or ridicule)
Rules of the game, 29–30

Sample, insufficient, 109–111, 190
Self-deceit, 37
Self-interest (*See* Appeal to personal circumstances or motives)
Semantical ambiguity, 64–65, 187
Shame, appeal to, 52
Shifting the burden of proof, fallacy of (*See* Arguing from ignorance)
Slanted language (*See* Question-begging language)
Slanting (*See* Ignoring the counterevidence)
Slippery slope (*See* Domino fallacy)
Special pleading, 122–124, 191
Stacking the Deck (*See* Ignoring the counterevidence)
Standard form of argument, 5–6, 18–21
Statistics:
    unknowable, 120–122, 189
    unrepresentative, 111–113, 191
Straw man, attacking a, 157–159, 187
Strength of arguments, 8–9, 17
Strengthening arguments, 17
Sufficient condition, 128
Sufficient grounds:
    criterion, 12, 15–16, 187
    principle, 181–182

Suspension of judgment principle, 185
Syntactical ambiguity, 65, 187

Taking out of context (*See* Improper accent)
Testimony, 14–15, 151, 153
Threat (*See* Appeal to force or threat)
Tradition, appeal to, 48–50, 95, 191
Trivial objections, 159–161, 191
True by definition (*See* Question-begging definition)
Truth, 13–14
Truth-seeking principle, 175–176
Tu quoque argument (*See* "You do it, too" argument)
Two wrongs make a right (*See* "You do it, too" argument)

Unacceptability, conditions of, 15
Unacceptable premise, fallacies of:
    begging-the-question fallacies, 77–87
    fallacies of linguistic confusion, 62–77
    unwarranted assumption fallacies, 88–105
Unclear modifier, 65
Unclear pronoun reference, 65
Unknowable statistics (See Fake precision, fallacy of)
Unrepresentative data, 111–113, 191
Unwarranted assumption fallacies:
    fallacy of composition, 90–92, 188
    fallacy of the continuum, 88–90, 188
    fallacy of division, 92–93, 189
    fallacy of the golden mean, 99–101, 189
    fallacy of novelty, 103–104, 190
    false alternatives, 93–95, 189
    faulty analogy, 101–103, 189
    is-ought fallacy, 95–96, 190
    misuse of a general principle, 98–99, 191
    wishful thinking, 96–98, 191
Use of flattery, 53–54, 189
Using the wrong reasons, 40–43, 191

Vague expression, misuse of a, 72–74, 191
Validity, 8, 13

Wishful thinking, 96–98, 191
Witness, credible, 14–15, 153
Wrong conclusion, drawing the, 38–40, 41, 191
Wrong reasons, using the, 40–43, 191

"You do it, too""argument, 154–155, 192